The course of German nationalism

In the 1770s the map of central Europe was a colourful patchwork of more than four hundred territorial entities, each of them sovereign states jealously guarding their rights as part of the Holy Roman Empire of the German nation. A hundred years on, Bismarck had created the German Empire in their place, a military and industrial concentration of power on a scale Europe had never known before. The way from the old Empire to the nation-state of Bismarck was neither straight nor predetermined: it was marked by sharp discontinuities, u-turns, revolutions and wars.

In *The course of German nationalism* Hagen Schulze argues that the birth of the German nation only occurred in the course of the late 18th and early 19th centuries, in the guise of a constant revolutionary process which at different times assumed different guises. The transformation of Germany under Napoleon and the levée en masse of the wars of independence inter-reacted with the economic upheaval caused by industrialisation. Together they produced the March revolution of 1848. Subsequently revolutionary pressure from below was combined with the shattering of the central European order, resulting in the Empire of 1871. This was, of course, only one of many possible courses that German history could have taken.

The course of German nationalism provides students with a concise and accessible account of these tumultuous decades, supported by a chronology of events and full English-language bibliography.

The course of German nationalism

From Frederick the Great to Bismarck, 1763–1867

Hagen Schulze

Professor of Modern History, Universität der Bundeswehr, Munich

translated by Sarah Hanbury-Tenison

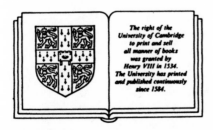

The right of the
University of Cambridge
to print and sell
all manner of books
was granted by
Henry VIII in 1534.
The University has printed
and published continuously
since 1584.

CAMBRIDGE UNIVERSITY PRESS
Cambridge
New York   Port Chester   Melbourne   Sydney

Published by the Press Syndicate of the University of Cambridge
The Pitt Building, Trumpington Street, Cambridge CB2 1RP
40 West 20th Street, New York, NY 10011, USA
10 Stamford Road, Oakleigh, Melbourne 3166, Australia

Originally published in German as *Der Weg zum Nationalstaat*
by Deutsche Taschenbuch Verlag 1985
and © 1985 Deutsche Taschenbuch Verlag
First published in English by Cambridge University Press 1991 as
*The course of German nationalism: from Frederick the Great to
Bismarck, 1763–1867*
English translation © Cambridge University Press 1991

British Library cataloguing in publication data

Schulze, Hagen
The course of German nationalism: from Frederick the Great
to Bismarck, 1763–1867.
1. Germany. Nationalism, history.
I. Title   II. Weg zum Nationalstaat. English.
320.540943

Library of Congress cataloguing in publication data

Schulze, Hagen.
[Weg zum Nationalstaat. English]
The course of German nationalism: from Frederick the
Great to Bismarck, 1763–1867 / Hagen Schulze: translated by Sara
Hanbury-Tenison.
        p.   cm.
Translation of: Der Weg zum Nationalstaat.
Includes bibliographical references.
ISBN 0 521 37379 4. ISBN 0 521 37759 5 (paperback)
1. Germany – History – 1848–1870. 2. Germany – History – 1789–1900.
3. Nationalism – Germany – History – 19th century.   I. Title.
DD204.S2413   1990
943—dc20   89–77388

ISBN 0 521 37379 4 hardback
ISBN 0 521 37759 5 paperback

Transferred to digital printing 2003

VN

Contents

Maps

Chronological table

1763 15 February: Peace of Hubertusburg: Consolidation of Prussia as a great power. The Austro-Prussian conflict dominates the German Question for the next hundred years.

1766 Friedrich Carl von Moser: *About the German National Spirit.*

1772 Johann Gottfried Herder: *Treatise on the Origin of Language.*

1789 Start of the French Revolution.

1803 Conversion of the Empire into a Confederation of sovereign rulers: through the Main Resolution of the Committee of the Imperial Diet (*Reichsdeputationshauptschluss*).

1806 Sixteen German princes secede from the Empire to form the Rhine Confederation (*Rheinbund*). Francis II abdicates the crown of the Holy Roman Empire of the German Nation, which marks the end of the Empire.

14 October: Prussian defeats at Jena and Auerstedt.

1807 7–9 July: Peace of Tilsit, Prussia is reduced to a middle-ranking power.

1807–11 State and administrative reforms in the (in part) newly-formed *Rheinbund* states following the French model.

1807–15 Prussian Reforms.

1807–8 Johann Gottlieb Fichte: *Lectures to the German Nation.*

1809 9 April–14 October: Franco-Austrian War.

28 April: Major von Schill begins his attempted rising.

31 May: Schill falls in a street fight in Stralsund.

1811 June: beginning of the Gymnastic movement Friedrich Ludwig Jahn erects the first gymnastics area on the Hasenheide in Berlin.

1812 24 June: the French invasion of Russia begins.

30 December: Convention of Tauroggen.

1813 17 March: Appeal *To my People* by Frederick William III.

16–17 October: 'Battle of the Nations' at Leipzig.

1814 Theodore Körner: *Leyer und Schwert* (*Lyre and Sword*).

30 May: Peace of Paris.

1814–15 Congress of Vienna.

1815 8 June: the German Federal Act is agreed.

12 June: foundation of the Jena *Burschenschaft.*

26 September: inauguration of the Holy Alliance.

18 October: Celebration of the battle of Leipzig.

1817 17–18 October: the Wartburg festival.

1818 18 October: Foundation of the General German *Burschenschaft*.

1819 Friedrich List founds the 'German Commercial and Manufacturing Society'.

23 March: von Kotzebue, poet and Russian state councillor, murdered by a *Burschenschaft* member called Georg Ludwig Sand.

20 September: the *Bundestag* confirms the Carlsbad decrees.

1820 15 May: last act for Vienna.

1822 the 'Association of German Naturalists and Doctors' is founded.

1825 the 'Exchange Association of German Book Dealers' is founded.

1828 Customs Unions are formed: Prussia with Hessen-Darmstadt; Bavaria with Württemberg; the Middle German Commercial Union.

1830–1 disturbances in several federal German states after the July Revolution in Paris.

1831 Paul Achatius Pfizer: *Correspondence between two Germans.*

1832 29 January: foundation of the 'German Press and Fatherland Society'.

27 May: Hambacher Festival.

1834 1 January: German Customs Union is established.

1835 7 December: opening of the first German railway-line, Nuremberg–Fürth.

1837 18 November: protest by the 'Göttinger Seven' against the lifting of the Hanoverian Constitution.

1840 Rhine Crisis.

18 September: Nikolaus Becker *Der deutsche Rhein* (*The German Rhine*)

1842 24 September: Cologne Cathedral Construction Festival.

1844 June: weavers' rising in Silesia.

1847 11 April–26 June: United Parliament in Berlin.

12 September: the south and west German Democrats' Offenburg Programme.

10 October: the south and west German Liberals' Heppenheim Programme.

1848 22–24 February: February revolution in Paris.

5 March: Heidelberg meeting of south German Liberals and Democrats: decision to call a pre-parliament.

12–13 March: revolution in Vienna: fall of Metternich.

18–19 March: barricade fighting in Berlin.

21 March: Friedrich Willhelm IV's proclamation: *To my Volk and to the German Nation!*

31 March–3 April: German Pre-parliament in Frankfurt; decision to call a German national assembly.

April: Republican rising in Baden.

18 May: opening of the Prussian constitution-making Assembly in Berlin.

26 August: cease-fire of Malmö.

18 September: leftist rebellion against the Frankfurt National Assembly; democratic risings in Baden, Hessen, Thuringia and the Pfalz.

19 October: start of constitutional discussions in the National Assembly.

27 November: Austria repudiates the Frankfurt draft for a constitution.

5 December: the king dissolves the Prussian National Assembly and grants a Prussian constitution.

18 December: Heinrich von Gagern, advocate of the little-Germany solution, becomes prime minister of the *Reich*.

1849 28 March: the German *Reichs* Constitution is completed: the National Assembly elects Friedrich Willhelm IV of Prussia emperor.

3 April: Friedrich Willhelm IV refuses the imperial crown.

31 May: After the withdrawal of most of the delegates, the Rump Parliament is shifted from Frankfurt to Stuttgart.

17 June: Dissolution of the Rump Parliament by the government of Württemburg.

1850 30 March–29 April: Union Parliament in Frankfurt.

29 November: the treaty of Ölmutz between Austria and Prussia: Prussia abandons its German-union policy.

1853 German Customs Union is renewed without Austria.

1853–6 Crimean War.

1854 Fiscal Union founded in 1834–5 (Hanover, Oldenburg, Schaumburg–Lippe) alongside the Customs Union.

1858 26 October: Prince William of Prussia assumes the regency: start of the 'New Era'.

1859 29 April–11 July: war between Austria and France/Piedmont in Italy.

15–16 September: foundation of the German National Society in Frankfurt.

10 November: celebrations on the occasion of Friedrich Schiller's centenary: Peace of Zurich; defeat of Austria in Italy.

1860 10 February: the Prussian Army conflict begins.

1861 6 June: foundation of the German Progressive Party.

1862 24 September: nomination of Bismarck as Prussian prime minister.

28–9 October: foundation of the 'great-Germany' German Reform Society.

1864 1 February: start of the Austro–Prussian war with Denmark.

30 October: Peace of Vienna between Austria, Prussia and Denmark.

1866 9 April: Prussia proposes a reform of the German Confederation and the exclusion of Austria.

13 May: last session of the committee of the German Reform Society, followed by its tacit dissolution.

15 June–26 July: Austria and the German Confederation at war with Prussia.

3 July: Battle of Koniggrätz.

26 July: preliminary Peace of Nikolsburg.

23 August: Prussia and Austria agree to Peace of Prague; dissolution of the German Confederation. Austria consents to formation of a North German Confederation under the leadership of Prussia.

3 September: acceptance of the indemnity proposal by the Prussian House of Representatives: end of the constitutional conflict in Prussia.

1867 12 February: election of the constitution-making North German *Reichstag* (Imperial diet).

12 June: the National Liberal Party is founded.

19 October: dissolution of the German National Society.

Map 1 The German Confederation 1815

1. County of Holstein
2. County of Lauenburg
3. Duchy of Mecklenburg-Schwerin
4. Duchy of Mecklenburg-Strelitz
5. Kingdom of Hanover
6. Duchy of Oldenburg
7. Principality of Schaumberg-Lippe
8. Principality of Lippe-Detmold
9. County of Braunschweig
10. County of Anhalt
11. Principality of Waldeck
12. Electorate of Hesse
13. Duchy of Hesse
14. County of Nassau
15. Landgravate of Hesse-Homburg
16. States of Thuringia
17. Kingdom of Saxony
18. Duchy of Luxemburg
19. Principality of Lichtenberg
20. Pfalz (Bavarian)
21. Duchy of Baden
22. Kingdom of Württemburg
23. Duchies of Hohenzollern

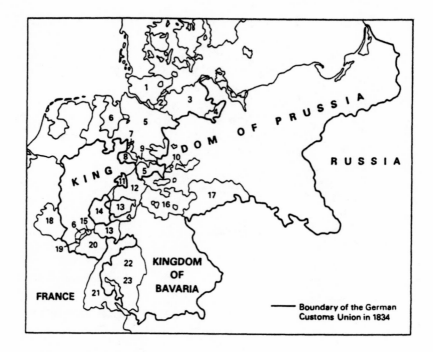

Map 2 The German Customs Union, 1834

1. County of Holstein
2. County of Lauenburg
3. Duchy of Mecklenburg-Schwerin
4. Duchy of Mecklenburg-Strelitz
5. Kingdom of Hanover
6. Duchy of Oldenburg
7. Principality of Schaumberg-Lippe
8. Principality of Lippe-Detmold
9. County of Braunschweig
10. County of Anhalt
11. Principality of Waldeck
12. Electorate of Hesse
13. Duchy of Hesse
14. County of Nassau
15. Landgravate of Hesse-Homburg
16. States of Thuringia
17. Kingdom of Saxony
18. Duchy of Luxemburg
19. Principality of Lichtenberg
20. Pfalz (Bavarian)
21. Duchy of Baden
22. Kingdom of Württemburg
23. Duchies of Hohenzollern

Introduction

Scarcely any phenomenon of recent German history has proved as many-sided and protean as the German nationalist movement, the social counterpart to the process of nation-formation in the nineteenth century. This theme has hitherto largely been avoided by historians, in spite of the unmistakable historical significance of the nationalist movement, on account of its vague and diffuse character – the result of the long-delayed unification of the central European area into one nation-state. Consequently, numerous contradictory projects and programmes, blueprints and Utopias aimed at the unification of Germany remained possible but unfulfilled for generations. Added to which, the one common denominator shared by all the many conflicting ideologies and parties of the age was the idea of nation. In an age of economic revolution, population explosion and permanent social change in Europe, when every value was overturned, the nationalist idea alone stood for legitimacy, community and a new order. The idea of nation as an organisation was not easy to pin down, being more of a mood than a programme, but it dominated the collective mentality of the two generations prior to the unification of the German *Reich* (Empire). It could almost be said to bear the marks of a new religion of the emergent industrial age. The nationalist movement was a religious movement – and this proved decisive in determining its success.

Our plan is to follow this movement's progress from its beginnings in small educated-middle-class circles at the end of the eighteenth century to the dawn of the unification of the German *Reich* when this idea, to borrow Karl-Marx's terminology, had long penetrated the masses, and had so become a material force. The history of the German nationalist movement is also the history of the social and political opposition to the powers of order of the age – firstly against the Napoleonic order, then against the German Confederation (*Deutsche Bund*). This is why our book does not end with the proclamation in 1871 of the Reich in the Hall of Mirrors at Versailles, but in 1866 with the Battle of Koniggrätz. Immediately thereafter the forces of the German nationalist movement made their peace with Bismarck and his little German (*kleindeutsch*) state-system, thereby promoting themselves to the status of an independent and social force of opposition: a finale at which new historical organisations also featured, with the emergence of the German

1

National Society (*Nationalverein*) and the foundation of the National Liberal Party in 1867, when the North German Parliament (*Norddeutsche Reichstag*) was formed. The argument of this book is that this finale did not signify the demise of the nationalist movement and that, contrary to the conventional interpretation, the creation of the German *Reich* was not just a 'revolution from above' but a revolution from two sides, Bismarck's and the nationalist movement's, and that the new *Reich* would never have come into being in this form had the German nationalist movement not put up such a determined fight.

I   Three weeks in March

1 Chronicle of the 1848 Berlin revolution

Early spring in Berlin, 1848. Never in human memory had the weather been so mild at this time of year. 'February was full of sunshine and March of the loveliest Spring air imaginable', as the writer Wilhelm Angerstein later recalled. 'The forces of reaction subsequently claimed that the Revolution could never have broken out in Berlin, or indeed anywhere, had not the spring been so lovely and come so early. This may perhaps be correct, I don't want to take issue with it – but it is certain that our Divine Father appeared to glory in what happened, since Heaven smiled steadily, dispensing the most splendid sunshine over sinful Earth.'[1]

There was in any case no question of revolution in Berlin at the end of February. Whereas in Italy, France and even Munich the first rumblings of the disturbances and popular uprisings of the coming revolutions could be heard, Berlin, the largest industrial city in Germany, already rivalling Vienna with her population of 400,000 citizens, was absolutely quiet – 204 policemen sufficed to keep the peace and maintain order. At the same time the warm weather was bringing crowds of people out into the streets, particularly into Berlin's splendid boulevard Unter den Linden – 'where the elegant dandy may be seen alongside the beggar, the officer and the student, the unemployed artisan and the pensioned councillor, where the respectable lady, the flashy whore, the nurserymaid or the country nanny are all engaged in the same pursuit, with the same purpose, namely that of strolling along, looking into the elegant shop windows or enjoying the first green shoots on the splendid old lime trees and chestnuts or, finally, listening out for the elusive tones of a march or a waltz being played just now by the military band by the *Wachparade* on the Konigswach.'[2]

Openness and sociability were the signs of the times – the upper middle classes met in salons or wine parlours, the less well-off patronised the coffee-houses by the city gates, and above all such *Konditoreien* (cake shops) as the one called 'josty', right in front of the Schloss, or 'Stehely', on the Gendarmenmarkt, where officials, journalists, army officers and political agents all met up to create a particular climate of slightly inhibited openness. The lower classes, on the other hand, the artisans, workers and servants, used to frequent tobacco shops, where smoking was allowed, a practice prohibited in public, and where the beer, now downgraded from national nutriment to a source of plebeian enjoyment, flowed profusely.

A distorted form of Biedermeier

This sort of Biedermeier cosiness was, however, already troubled. The 'Potato War' of April last year was in everyone's minds – when the inhabitants of the wretched eastern and northern proletarian suburbs had broken into the middle classes' elegant capital city in their thousands, driven by starvation and hatred of the potato dealers, who had driven the prices up by more than double within a year. The crowds had rampaged through the town, plundering it all day long until order was restored by General von Prittwitz's fusiliers. This event had shocked both the burghers and the government. The archetypal terror of revolution, which had gripped the courts of Europe since 1789, had suddenly coalesced into an immediate experience in the heartlands of Prussia, while simultaneously providing many a Liberal minded burgher with the exciting realisation that the Prussian *rocher de bronze* had been dented.

Besides, there was general disappointment in the king. Friedrich Wilhelm IV had ascended the throne in 1840 and seemed, unlike his father, to be an imaginative and idealistic leader whose mind was open to nationalistic thinking and who refrained from repressive measures. He nevertheless would have no truck with the middle classes' desire to participate in government, and his thinking was entirely along the lines of a romantic, backwards-looking sovereign lordship. He dreamt of unity between people and monarchy, modelled apparently on the feudal estates east of the Elbe, with the king as the highest landowner, whose duty as a Christian, order-loving and absolute ruler was to demonstrate paternal solicitude for his subjects and their well-being. At the beginning of April 1847, when Prussia's provincial parliaments merged into an United Parliament located in Berlin, there were high hopes that the King would finally recognise the signs of the times and carry out the promise his father made to allow Prussia national represent-ation and a (Liberal) constitution. But the King refused to recall Parliament at regular intervals in the future, pointing out at its opening, that he would 'once and never again allow a written paper to force itself between our Lord God in Heaven and this country . . . to rule us with its paragraphs'.[3] Thus the door to constitutional progress in the Liberal sense was slammed shut.

Scarcely any of those burghers strolling in the spring sunshine that February 1848 along Unter den Linden or discussing the newspaper reports from southern Germany and France in the Café Kranzler wished for the upheaval. However, nearly everyone was convinced that the prevailing conditions were untenable, feeling, like Jakob Grimm, who wrote to Gervinus after the King's Speech: 'how necessary to us, after all, are Freedom and a Fatherland in which we can take pride, without which we can have no security and no hope'.[4]

The revolution in Paris

On the morning of 28 February the rumour spread through the streets that Paris had proclaimed the Republic and had driven out Louis Philippe. This was indeed exciting news; everyone was aware of how the 1830 July Revolution in Paris had affected conditions in Germany too – in Braunschweig, Saxony, Kurhessen and Hanover it had led to barricades and fighting, which in their turn had resulted in Liberal constitutional demands being granted. Events in Paris were already four days old, but news still took a long time to cross Europe: the rail link between Berlin and Paris was yet to be completed, and telegraph messages were still at the experimental stage. Only that last summer artillery Lieutenant Werner von Siemens had tested the first lengthy underground experimental wire between Berlin and Grossbeeren – a distance of some twenty kilometers. Both the uncertainty of news communications and the censors of the press, who took every opportunity to suppress politically awkward announcements, fostered the wildest rumours. It was only on the next day, 29 February, when the Brussels and Cologne newspapers came in, that the Paris uprising was confirmed.

Public opinion immediately entered a stage familiar to the early history of all revolutions: that of widespread excitement and general exasperation, when opportunities for spontaneous outbursts are cultivated, without giving the police occasion for effective counter-attacks. 'The public places', wrote a contemporary observer, 'the reading-booths . . . presented an unusual appearance as overcrowded political meeting places; reading the newly arrived newspapers and reports out loud tirelessly and repeatedly was now not enough for the people's newly aroused political requirements, and the readings were accompanied by anti-police exclamations and followed by excited discussions, which were repeated day after day, throughout the week'.[5] The street scene was changing, with the stream of strolling and bustling pedestrians drying up and groups of debating and arguing people forming all over the place. The wildest rumours ran through the city and were believed: that French and Polish agents were actively promoting the revolutionary mood of the lower classes; that French money was circulating, that here and there posters exhorting the soldiery not to shoot on the people in the event of a fight had appeared on house walls; that a French revolutionary army had crossed the border and taken Saarlouis, massacring all its inhabitants. None of which was correct, but the myth of the foreign agents stirring up the decent populace helped the police to conceal their impotence and satisfied both the administration and the court, who were able to explain the unrest only in these terms.

The gathering in the Tiergarten

In any event, the Potsdam hussars and Uhlans, as well as one artillery division, were ordered to stand by ready to march. Meanwhile the king attempted a pacifying gesture: on 6 March he granted the United Parliament the regular sessions which he had refused it a year ago, as well as approving a regular assembly of the *Stände* Parliament. A year ago, this would have had an effect, but now this royal compliance left public opinion cold, and the drastic devaluation of the Prussian state credit notes at the Berlin stock exchange continued apace. A few days later the conjunction which the half-awakened revolutionary mood in the streets needed to focus on issues and come up with claims was found. Outside the city, in the Tiergarten halfway between the Brandenburg Gate and Schloss Bellevue, stood the '*Zelte*' (tents), a huddle of picturesque beer houses and coffee parlours, with a wooden podium in their midst, where public concerts were held in normal times. On the evening of 6 March a number of students and other young people, foremost among whom was a doctor of philology called Löwenberg, gathered in one of the beer houses to draw up the people's demands along the lines of other gatherings of burghers in Baden and Württemberg. They were unable to reach a conclusion which satisfied everyone, so the debate was continued on the following day. This being Shrove Tuesday, around 600 persons crowded into the pub and after lengthy and chaotic discussion, at about midnight, they all agreed on a text entitled an 'Address by the Youth', to be submitted to the king.

The wording of this address was moderate, even submissive. It made no demands, but expressed the wish to 'secure the accord between King and People, upon which alone the inner and outward strength of the nation rests'. Similar addresses had been submitted in Mannheim and Karlsruhe, Munich and Stuttgart, Hamburg and Bremen, and in all these places their respective governments had hastened to give way to the 'March demands': freedom of the press, of speech and of public assembly; amnesty for political prisoners; equal political rights for all citizens; independent judges; reduction of the standing army and the arming of the people; above all, however, more rights for the National Assembly and the convening of a German National Parliament. The Berlin authorities reacted as they had often enough before and were to subsequently, that is, sluggishly, half-heartedly and too late. On the following day, 8 March, while the Berlin Police President von Minutoli was engaged in a fatherly discussion with the spokesmen of the address movement, praising the orderly progress of yesterday's gathering and advising them to send their petition through the state postal system, because the King did not wish to receive a delegation, the newspapers reported a royal proclamation promising a 'thoroughgoing reform of the legislation regulating the press' but also insisting on 'guarantees, whereby the misuse of the freedom of the press may possibly be prevented'.

These reports had an aggravating effect on the public; on 9 March, from sunset on, the flow of people through the Brandenburg Gate towards the '*Zelte*' had increased, and was estimated by the police to be already more than 4000 people. To quote Angerstein again: 'These gatherings bore an individual character; they were half real popular Berlin festivities and half parliamentary proceedings. Women were pushing through the crowds with pickled gherkins, hot garlic sausages, brandy and buns, and boys were keeping up a constant '*Cigarro mit avec du feu*' (*sic*), as they peddled their tobacco-products, while on the bandstand, now transformed into a rostrum, the country and the future's weal and woes were being discussed.'[6] Today the matter under discussion was how to deliver the 'Address by the Youth' to the King. The outcome was lamentable: according to the *Mannheimer Abend-zeitung*, only three speakers were in favour of delivering the text directly to the King during an audience, while around thirty speakers competed with one another in 'abjuring the whole apparatus of cowardly fantasies; they referred to failed revolutions and riots, wild hordes and bayonets, barricades and rivers of blood, and finally a rigged vote (with the ayes allowed to remain in the open, where everybody was, and the nays obliged to walk into the dark and dank shrubbery) ended with the decision to allow their address to be delivered via the assembly of town councillors'.[7] However, since the civic parliament refused to play postman, they ended by sending their address through the post, as recommended by the Police President. What then happened to it is unknown.

Turmoil in the Town Hall

It was not that the town councillors, who met daily in the Cöllnische Rathaus on Gertraudenstrasse, had failed to read the signs of the times; however, the dignitaries who assembled at an extraordinary meeting on 11 March did not trust the street movement and they tried to find a middle way between popular discontent and statesmanlike restraint. This was no easy matter since their meeting was held in public, and the entrance-halls, landings and stairs were crowded with spectators hours before it started, with hundreds more milling about in the street, unable to squeeze in. For their benefit the meeting, room-doors were left wide open, allowing the public to take an energetic part in the events within, to such an extent that the chairman had several times to threaten to end the proceedings.

The first issue was that of their own address, to be directed to the King by the magistrates and town councillors. After lengthy debates and two votes against, they sent off a text which differed from that of the Tents resolution chiefly in its ornate and fawning style of composition. Nor did it mention 'freedom of the press', since the King's vague concessions in this quarter appeared sufficient to the majority of the assembly. The meeting grew livelier over the next point of order: the formation of a Civic Guard (*Schutzwachen*). During the Potato War of the previous year, various citizen volunteers had formed unarmed patrols to prevent looting and to intervene in altercations between the military and demonstrators. Nothing is known of their successes, if any, but Liberal faith in human reason and a convincing speech brought the institution of the 'protection commission' onto the agenda again.

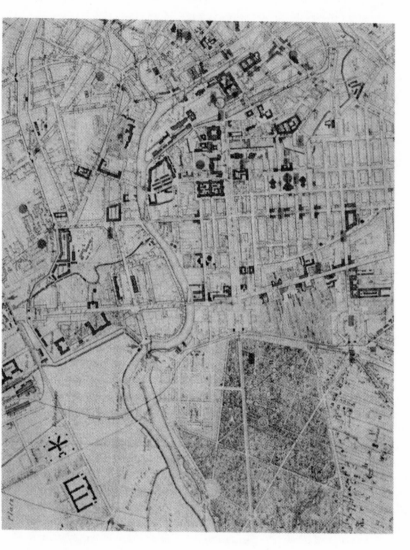

Map 3   Street plan of Berlin and immediate surroundings, 1850 (detail). Source: *Historischer Handatlas von Brandenburg und Berlin* (Veröffentlichung der Historischen Kommission zu Berlin), Walter de Gruyter, Berlin and New York 1962.

However, only one part of the assembly thought that the civic guards should be distinguished solely by their sticks and armbands, as they had been the year before; other town councillors argued in favour of arming the volunteers, even for a general arming of the populace to form a popular militia: 'the police', observed town councillor Nauwerk straightaway, 'are not dear to our hearts, there is a split between the civic and the administrative bodies; consequently he wished for police powers to return into the citizens' hands, this being a natural desire'.[8] The formation of unarmed 'protection commissions' was passed on a slim majority, upon which a tumultuous uproar broke out inside the hall and on the podium, with individual councillors standing up to address the public and advocating the immediate arming of the citizenry. When the chairman brought the meeting to a close, the audience refused to leave the room and, chanting vociferously, demanded a new vote.

Unemployment and mass poverty

The Liberal body of citizens now found itself in a fix. The March movement in the southern and central German states had shown that it was indeed possible to wrest concessions from a powerful and rigid authority (albeit one weak in legitimacy and insecure) by means of determined uprisings. However, nothing worked without the threat of street riots, involving an uncomfortable and unpredictable alliance with the 'mob'. Berlin was undergoing the throes of transition from a princely capital and administrative centre to an industrial metropolis – this was especially the case in the northern district beyond the city gates, where a new Berlin was growing apace, with around forty machine works, as many spinning shops and associated enterprises, thirty-five silk factories, twenty-two calico-printing works, ninety-five cloth factories and a considerable number of chemical, carpet and oilcloth factories as well as no fewer than thirty-one breweries. Around 40,000 factory workers, ten per cent of the population, lived in Berlin, of whom around 20,000 were apprenticed to various trades and who, given the general crisis in artisan trades and the transition to mechanical mass production, had only a miserable proletarian subsistence to look forward to. Finally, there was the army of servants, also around 20,000 strong, a poorly paid, harshly treated and dissatisfied class of population. Mass poverty was growing apace; during the 1840s the number of Berlin's inhabitants rose by 30 per cent, but the numbers receiving poor relief rose by more than 60 per cent. Almost half of the urban proletariat was already poverty-stricken; nearly a quarter of the capital's population lived below the officially defined poverty line, yet Berlin was still a magnet, drawing in the impoverished sub-peasantry from all over eastern Germany.

The city's social problems were further aggravated by the poor economic situation prevailing since the beginning of the previous year's recession. During those first days in March, for instance, Borsig, the biggest machine works in Prussia, sacked 400 workers in one go. The number of unemployed on the streets rose dramatically. On 9 March the newly established urban 'Employment Information Institute' opened its doors and that day 7000 people called in looking for work, but only a few of them could be provided with a job. The police reports were full of vague statements about communist agitation among the working classes (as happened in the French case) being spread by Frenchmen, Poles and South Germans using money and revolutionary texts. None of this can be proved; nevertheless, in recent years a few communist artisan apprentices had been up before the courts for having read Weitling's *Gospel of a Poor Sinner* and spread his message of the necessary revolutionary path to a just society of equal men. The judgements had been mild, and when Reinhart, the Württemberg ambassador, reported back to Stuttgart on 4 March that in Berlin 'the lower classes are less infected with socialist and communist doctrines than elsewhere', he was surely right.⁹

'A Ministry for Workers'

The 13 March was a Monday, the one free day of the week for trades apprentices; moreover, the weather was splendidly sunny, warm and springlike. The crowds in the Tiergarten and the '*Zelte*', on the Schlossplatz and Unter den Linden displayed a different character to that of the previous week: members of the artisan and working classes predominated. Recent news and rumours were going the rounds: the revolutionary government in Paris had appointed a workman as minister; the Prince of Prussia, the king's brother, had paid a visit to his barracks early in the morning and urged the troops to fight. At first the rumour ran that the troops were to move to the Rhine under the command of Prince Wilhelm, in order to meet the anticipated French attack, but now both prince and soldiers were staying in Berlin: were they getting ready to fight their own people? While this was in fact not the case, military preparations of a generally obvious nature were being taken, giving the rumours a new lease of life. The guards posted in front of the Schloss, the Zeughaus (arsenal) and the Seehandlung (merchant shipping house) were increased, cannons were set up in some spots, and dispatch riders and adjutants scurried tirelessly through the streets.

The debates, which had been conducted on a daily basis in the '*Zelte*' for the last week, on this day assumed a new tone. For the first time, workers and artisans made the speeches, from the bandstand or standing on chairs. The proceedings soon turned chaotic, with a carpenter praising the social achievements of the Paris Revolution from the podium being shouted down by the artisan next to him speechifying about the German fleet; national, Liberal and social demands were voiced, and in one corner a number of workers even gathered together to draw up their own address to the king: 'The state only blooms and flourishes there where the people can satisfy its basic needs through work and can realise its aspirations as a sentient human being' it stated. 'For we are oppressed by capitalists and usurers; the laws as they stand at present are not capable of protecting us from them.

Consequently, we dare most humbly to propose that Your Majesty appoint a ministry, a MINISTRY FOR WORKERS, to consist solely of employers and workers . . .' In spite of its humble tone, this constituted a Manifesto for social revolution, a distant precursor of the ideas of Ferdinand Lassalle, who was to attempt an alliance between the Prussian state and the workers against the exploitation of the propertied class. The extent to which these workers trusted the state was apparent in another corner of the gathering. Police President von Minutoli turned up at the '*Zelte*' in full uniform and on horseback, in order to assess the situation. A worker went up to him and complained that he had seven children, but had had no work for days. The President promised them all that they would be looked after, if they continued to conduct themselves peacefully, at which the crowd raised a cheer for him.

Prior to this expedition, Minutoli had made an announcement of quite a different nature to the Government: troops were to stand by to occupy the Schloss, the guards at the Stadtvogtei (city jail), the Brandenburg Gate and the Moabit State Prison were to be strengthened and, at 7 p.m., cavalry units were to proceed through the streets and the Tiergarten in order to impress the assembled populace 'or to drive it away or in the event of arrests, to surround it'. The Police President gave as his reason for such proceedings, that nothing had as yet occurred 'to rebutt his conclusion that today would result in a serious confrontation with the workers, since the attitude of this class seemed to be even more determined and insolent . . .'[10]

The Guard steps in

It can only be assumed that the Police President had lost his head over the imbalance between his 204 policemen and the daily increasing mass of debating and politically active persons in the streets. He had assumed his post in April last year, following the Potato War, and he was now anxious lest he should make the same mistake as his predecessor von Puttkamer by summoning military assistance too late. That evening, the army appeared punctually at the Brandenburg Gate in the form of two squadrons of Kurassier guards, which split up the crowd in the Tiergarten. Around 20,000 burghers streamed back into town through the gate's narrow entrance, hemmed in by the soldiers, who rode recklessly among the crowd and did not allow anyone to leave the procession. The crowd hissed, whistled and jeered at the soldiers, thus confirming them in their expectation of confronting a mob ready for any excess. 'The picture turned more and more dangerously warlike and hostile', as an eye witness later recalled, 'without the people actually providing any grounds for this, either by provocations or by unseemly behaviour. The number of confrontations increased in the Schlossplatz and the press assumed a frightening character.'[11] In the Stechbahn, between the Schlossplatz and Bruderstrasse, the cuirassiers lashed at the crowd with drawn sabres: women were wounded, others fell beneath the horses' hooves, and a young man was stabbed. The furious crowd counter-attacked; stones flew, people tried to storm the armouries and in Grünstrasse some artisans raised the first barricade using cobbles. However, sensible burghers who were also present urged restraint and discouraged violence. 'The king will surely give in', so it went. 'We don't need a revolution!' 'But the soldiers must go away', others shouted; '"Go away!" the crowd repeated in a menacing tone, redolent of their hostility and firm resolve.'[12]

Relations between the garrison and the townsmen had been uneasy for some time now. The generation of reformers, who had tried to reconcile soldiers and burghers after the events at Jena and Auerstedt, even wanting to unite them, had long since given up. The last of their kind was Hermann von Boyen; in 1841, when in his sixties, he had been appointed War Minister but he could no longer prevail against the new generation of solidly conservative army officers, and so resigned, retiring in 1847. The Army had long ago reacted in its own way to the dissolution of the pre-revolutionary feudal social order, to the politicisation of the public and to the emergence of the 'social question' in Prussia and Germany, by closing ranks against everything that seemed part of the '*Zeitgeist*'. The Prussian officer corps felt itself to be a wholly royal guard, not merely along the lines of Frederick the Great's officer corps with its aristocratic sense of superiority, but also in a consciously political and ideological sense: on the one side monarchical legitimacy and feudal order, on the other democratic and socialist revolution. The enemy dwelt within: the 'Revolutionary Party' was seen to be at work in 1844 in the Silesian regions of Langenbielau and Peterswalde when the starving weavers revolted in 1846, during the Martinmas Fair riot in Cologne, and in 1847 in the capital during the Potato War. The military thrust was directed in the first instance, not towards war, but against revolution.

Potsdam was quite a different world to Berlin, where the conflict between the military and the civil element was constantly in evidence, leading to recurrent clashes. Should, for instance, a lieutenant arrest a reservist for not saluting him, it could result in a riot lasting two hours and, conversely, should a group of brewery workers with lighted pipes in their mouths (smoking in public was prohibited) walk past the guard at the Hamburg Gate, they would sing mocking songs, blowing smoke in the soldiers' faces and throwing stones at them. The officers considered Berlin a trouble spot and they concealed their insecurity under a forced and self-conscious manner, which could also be provocative and arrogant. '*Das Volk*', or 'the people', which at the time of the War of Liberation was still an emphatic and positive term embracing the concepts of both 'nation' and 'state', now meant 'the mob' to the army – a senseless rabble easily roused by foreign agents, against which firm and unrelenting preventive measures were required. A saying by one of the higher-ranking officers was going around the streets of Berlin, according to which he was supposed to have replied to the question of whether the army would shoot on the people as follows: 'If the King gives the order, we will shoot, and gladly.'[13] It cannot be proven whether this was really said, but it could have been and was anyway believed to have been.

The King was, however, not prepared to give the order to fire and this pained some officers, to whom the king appeared to be surrounded by false and weak counsellors. 'They tried to appease', as a lieutenant of the Guard put it retrospectively, 'they hoped to achieve something through complaisance. Soldiers and officers, who had done their duty, behaving exactly according to the rule-book, were left in the lurch and where possible even accused of rough behaviour and of inciting the '*Volk*'. The term '*Volk*' was vague and never properly defined. Several people allowed themselves to be intimidated by such slurs, who should not have allowed themselves to be intimidated by a rabble of 10,000 . . . But a quibble soon arose. Officers who had acted precisely according to the regulations were being accused. What was to be done then?'[14] The insecurity extended to the highest ranks of the army; on the one hand there was General von Pfuel, the governor and commander-in-chief of the garrison, a sensible man keen on keeping the army out of sight as much as possible and who shrank from assuming police duties. On the other hand, there was General von Pritwitz, who commanded the corps of Guards; he rated as a blinkered military-minded martinet and enjoyed Prince William's particular confidence. He had advocated right from the start a determined intervention by the troops, subsequently acquiring the nickname of 'Cartridge Prince' from the Berliners. The military leadership's insecurity led in any case to large units of troops being disposed around the town, to meet any eventualities. While certain operational orders had not been given, the amassment of uniforms was viewed by the populace as a sign that the army wanted to attack, and following the events of 13 March, the irritation and bitterness of all those involved, both citizens and soldiers, mounted steadily.

What did the king want?

What did the King want? Even Frederick William IV was unsure. On 14 March, at around midday, he received a deputation from the town council, which read out selected speeches from the town councillors' meeting three days ago. The king praised them and spoke with great assurance and conviction: a free people and a free ruler was his solution; the United Parliament was to be summoned on 27 April, and all further developments would then be its concern; people should behave 'boldly and prudently'; the good old German order should not be disregarded; the feudal distinctions were also German, and anyone who strove against them was exposing himself to perils. Where Germany was concerned, her fate did not lie in his hands, but he would readily and earnestly devote all his powers to ensuring that even this time of crisis would result in German unity, strength and greatness.

The royal address was as fluent as it was unclear; the only clear part was that the Parliament (*Landtag*) would not be summoned immediately, as demanded by all sides, but only in one and a half months' time. The king did not tell them that he had already given instructions for drawing up a constitution which would divide the legislative and fiscal powers between the crown and the estates and would establish a ministry answerable to both sides equally. Nor did he reveal that Ambassador von Radowitz had been sent to Vienna to urge that a conference of German rulers be called to 'pave the way for the reorganisation and consolidation of Germany'.[15] Frederick William's words struck the public as being weak, fearful and evasive; nobody knew what he actually wanted. This was the peculiar feature of those weeks; a diffuse mixture of excitement and fear dominated the scene, constantly fed by news and rumours from other parts of the Kingdom, from Germany and Europe. Governments everywhere were giving way under public pressure. Even the Federal Parliament (*Bundestag*) in Frankfurt had lifted censorship of printed matter and had allowed the ancient German imperial eagle to be used as the Confederation's coat-of-arms, and the black, red and gold colours of the Liberal nationalist movement as the German Confederation's standard. On 13 March Vienna also had risen; radical and democratic students formed the spearhead of a broad popular movement, which demanded Metternich's retirement; meanwhile, a workers' revolt was rageing in the suburbs of Vienna. In Berlin, however, the people had no clear aims towards which to direct their energy and determination. The King's vacillations allowed them to hope for a peaceful transition to parliamentary and constitutional conditions; on the other hand, his hesitations and the massing of troops in the town contributed to the continuing unrest. The situation thus remained in the balance.

The first outbreaks

That day's performance was repeated in the evening of the next day, 14 March, only more vehemently and fiercely. Once again, crowds of people piled onto the streets and before the gates; once again the mounted patrols turned out in strength. This time, however, they were greeted by whistles and jeers from all sides. The level of disturbance rose, with the soldiers, for their part, growing increasingly irritated and exasperated, identifying those shouting insults as agents of the revolutionary party, who only avoided arrest because, in the army's general opinion, the police were too slack and because the hostile crowds were concealing them. Several elderly burghers deemed it sensible to go home and were just turning out of the Schlossplatz into Brüderstrasse when a squadron of Kurassiers burst out from the other end of the street, galloping wildly towards them and shrieking as if demented, spurring on their horses so savagely that some fell over, striking the front doors with their swords and finally slashing at the people coming towards them. Two heavily and eight slightly wounded burghers were left lying in the street, all of them respected, elderly and inoffensive men. Similar excesses were perpetrated in other streets. The next morning delegations of burghers from those parts of the town where clashes had occurred paid visits to the Minister of the Interior von Bodelschwingh, to the Town Commander General von Ditfurth, and to the Mayor, to lodge their complaints about the army's behaviour. They secured a promise that the soldiers would only appear again when their intervention was absolutely necessary. Police President von Minutoli even declared that he was highly offended by the army's intervention, when it had not been summoned by him; that very same day, however, he announced to the Government that 'the attitude of the masses is no longer in doubt, it is now only a matter of when the outbreak will come'. In any case, he recommended leaving the palace guard concealed within the inner courtyards, so as not to provoke the people. 'I beg you to leave the attack to the public; all good burghers will keep out of it and the rabble will disperse or be destroyed.'[16]

The scenes of the previous day were repeated on the evening of 15 March; once again the soldiers – this time the palace guard – were provoked by whistling and shouting civilians; they were placed under marching orders and the infantry issued out and drove the people from the Schlossplatz, wielding their bayonets and gun butts. Barricades of cobbles were immediately thrown up in the neighbouring streets to prevent the soldiers from advancing any further. In Breitenstrasse some determined artisans were trying to break into a gun-shop. They were driven back by a burst of gunfire; the soldiers also let off their guns as they stormed the barricades. One dead man and fifteen with bullet wounds were handed over to the palace guard at midnight.

On the following day, 16 March, the citizen 'protection commissions', the subject of the city officials' debates on 11 March, were finally set up. The burghers of each of the 102 town districts were to assemble under the direction of local government officials, wearing white armbands printed with the word '*Schutzbeamter*' (protection officials), and equipped with a white staff – the model for all this being the London police force. Notices were put up at various street corners: anyone resisting a protection official's instructions was liable to the same penalty as that for resisting a serving soldier or a police officer. In the event of disturbance, the army would only be able to intervene when the appropriate 'protection commission' admitted that it was no longer effective; only then could the Riot Law of 1835 be read out and three warning signals be given by drum or trumpet.

The Prince of Prussia wants to shoot

The protection officials' first opportunity to act as mediators between the people and the army arose that very afternoon. A crowd of people, consisting mostly of students, had collected in the Opernplatz between the University and the Zeughaus. A rumour was going around that the corpse of a supposedly shot student was about to be brought there. Officers of the watch, wearing the insignia of their office, tried to persuade the people to leave the square, but their pompously officious behaviour only aroused the derision of the crowd, which nicknamed them 'pallbearers with ball-bats'. Their pent-up aggression found a few outlets; some protection officials were actually attacked, causing them to run off and hide among the New Guard. A pack of pursuers was yelling at the guard, when the leader of an infantry company (which was just then marching past) allowed his men to make an about turn, beat their drums and finally, to fire. This resulted in two dead and several wounded. Rioting broke out again in front of the palace, and the guards standing before the gateway opposite Breitenstrasse were insulted by the crowd swaying to and fro, and stones were thrown. The 'protection commission' was ridiculed and nobody paid any attention to the drums warning them to disperse. Once again, bloodshed seemed inevitable, when General von Pfuel stepped through the gate and stood between the crowd and the soldiers. When the company captain warned him of the danger, he replied: 'I am old enough and willingly risk my life if I can avoid shedding citizens' blood.'[17] He managed to quieten the crowd and the Schlossplatz could then be emptied without further incident. The Prince of Prussia, who happened to be in the palace at the time, bitterly upbraided the General in the presence of witnesses in the palace courtyard for his patience, explaining 'in a lively manner and rather too loudly' that one ought to shoot at the people.[18] Pfuel complained to the king and asked to be relieved of his post. Friedrich Wilhelm reprimanded his brother and told him to apologise to the general.

This angry exchange of views in the palace courtyard revealed the tension prevailing among the king's entourage. On the one hand, there was the military party led by Prince William, whose remedy, in the words of Leopold von Gerlach, the royal adjutant general, ran as follows: 'the only way of withstanding the revolution was to avoid every concession and, instead of a parliament, to assemble an army . . .'[19] Berlin was consequently flooded with troops: on 16 March a further two battalions of the 1st Regiment of the Guard were moved from Potsdam, to be followed on the 17th by three batalions from Frankfurt on the Oder and Halle as well as two from Stettin, which were bivouacked on the town squares and outside the gates, giving the impression that a state of war prevailed. There was also a conciliation party at the court, which strove against the military policy of peace and order at all costs, with the Minister of the Interior Ernst von Bodelschwingh at its forefront. He told the King on 15 March that almost every German ruler had already been forced 'to change their ministers and to cast themselves into the arms of radicalism or ultra-radicalism; God preserve us from the same course of events! This can and will only be prevented if Your Royal Majesty undertakes the necessary reforms in this respect, while there is yet time.'[20]

Friedrich Wilhelm's plans
The King was impressed; the more so, given that news of uprisings and even of separatist attempts was arriving in Berlin from other parts of the state, especially from the Rhineland, and because the victorious revolution in

Vienna as well as Count Metternich's fall showed only too clearly how political obduracy was punished. The events in Vienna also brought down the foundations supporting the Holy Alliance, upon which Prussian policy had been based since the Congress of Vienna. 'The fall of Metternich', as the Hesse chargé d'affaires in Berlin reported back, 'was a kind of liberation for the Prussian government as well. Prussia now wants to pursue this new course openly and energetically – everything with Germany and everything for Germany!'[21] Friedrich Wilhelm had hitherto kept his romantic German ambitions under tight rein, since in his eyes the Habsburg Ferdinand I had the more ancient claim to the Imperial throne of a renewed German *Reich*. However, Austria was apparently finished. Prussia, on the other hand, was in a position to achieve the feat of seizing control of the German unification movement while defusing the revolution by applying cautious reforms. This was the line plotted in the ministerial council of 16 March, at the very same time as shots were being fired at the New Guard. The following day Bodelschwingh drafted a proclamation on behalf of the king and his state ministry: Germany must change from being a federation of states to a federal state, with a federal representative body, a federal constitution and a common military organisation under one federal commander; 'general right of German nationality and full freedom of movement within the whole body of German fatherlands'. Prussia was also to get a constitution and the United Parliament was summoned for the early date of 2 April. At the same time, legislation was passed removing censorship of the press in Prussia. A week ago, all these measures would have enthused the crowds in the streets and massed them behind the king. Even on that day, 17 March, the announcement might have taken the head of steam out of the revolution, but the proclamation was delayed on account of Prince Wilhelm's obstructive opposition. Furthermore, Bodelschwingh thought that the wave of revolution in the capital was already ebbing, since, unlike on previous days, Berlin had remained quiet.

The calm before the storm

It was the calm before the storm. The only reason why rioting and shooting did not occur on 17 March was that, for the first time since the beginning of the unrest, prospects for a decisive and organised action by the citizens were opening up. Since early morning, burghers, mostly members of the 'protection commission', had been meeting at various places in the town to discuss what could be done to prevent a repetition of the previous days' excesses. They were all brooding over the way the crowd had mocked them as staff-carrying 'pallbearers', the more so in that they had been unable to protect anyone from the soldiers' fire and had even frequently been obliged to run to the soldiers for their own protection. One theme predominated: the soldiers would have to leave Berlin and their duties be assumed by a guard of armed citizens. The most important meeting took place in a pub called 'Kemperhof' which stood in the Tiergarten. There it was decided to make a 'very forceful proposition' to the king, the details of which were to be discussed at a larger meeting to take place at midday the next day. Symptomatic of the mood change was the manner with which a plain-clothes police commissioner was treated when he turned up and urged the gathering to disperse. He was told in a friendly manner that they had no intention of so doing, but that he was welcome to stay and take part in the discussion, which indeed he did.

That afternoon they all met up in a pub in Köpenickerstrasse, their numbers swollen by a great many more protection officials. The speaker this time was the editor of the liberal newspaper *Der Staat*, a university doctor and lawyer called August Theodor Woeniger. Like many such figures which appear at the incubation phase of a Revolution, he was soon to fade from the scene. Such men have the gift of the gab and, enthused by the fiery speeches and the audience's applause, are easily incited to go far further than they would in cold blood. Such figures unleash avalanches which can easily bury them. So too with Dr Woeniger; he advocated nothing less than a 'peaceful demonstration of the people's wishes', and, in order to force the government's consent, all Berlin protection officials, bearing the insignia of their office, were to march on the palace in their thousands so as to endow their resolution with the necessary credibility when it was handed in to the king. Their demands, couched by Woeniger in ringing words, can be summarised as follows: the withdrawal of the army from Berlin, the organisation of an armed civil guard, the concession of 'the freedom of the press, which has been unconditionally guaranteed us for a generation now', and the summoning the United Parliament . . . Nobody outside the castle walls knew that the government had already agreed to the last two points.

Somewhat later on Woeniger, apparently intoxicated by his idea and success, turned up in the Cöllnische Rathaus where a crowd of town councillors and protection officials was waiting for him. 'He climbed onto a rostrum and depicted in glowing terms the significance of the moment to the assembly, pointing to Prussia's shame, should she allow Austria to prevail, and insisting that the protection officials should not be satisfied with curbing street disturbances, but that they too should exhort the government to do its duty. He ended by reading out the Address and encouraging the meeting to join the procession to the palace on the following day. 'A few, less excited, town councillors pointed out that this could have incalculable results and that one did not have to ape foreign countries in everything. At this, Woeniger surpassed himself: 'Gentlemen', he explained 'it is too late; our demands are coursing through the town, let every man ask of his own conscience what he owes the fatherland; if you reject the demonstration, you will reap the revolution.'[22]

Time had moved on more quickly than the speaker was aware; in fact, it was his initiative which created an acute revolutionary situation. All sorts of expectations were now concentrated on the demonstration of the following day; the word went round: 'Tomorrow's the day, tomorrow will be decisive.' It reached the artisans and workers in the suburbs too, and it reached the ear of Police President von Minutoli, who was already convinced that 18 March would be Revolution day. The police, whose main task had hitherto been that of arresting people for smoking in the streets, now received the order to arrest all political suspects; they searched for Woeniger, but he kept away from home and was not to be found.

18 March

On the morning of 18 March Berlin was bathed in spring sunshine, and the mood in the town hall was at its happiest: the cabinet's decision to summon Parliament and to allow freedom of the press was conveyed to them via a messenger and was greeted with enthusiastic applause. The town councillors and burghers hanging around the Cöllnische Rathaus embraced one another, 'intoxicated with delight', and they planned to light up the whole town that evening. The king had granted more than the boldest optimists had hoped for, and they were all united in their efforts to stop the planned demonstration in front of the palace, which, in the light of the new information, now seemed superfluous and to some even perilous. Police President von Minutoli in particular was prophesying dreadful things and the Foreign Minister, Freiherr von Canitz, was already claiming to have uncovered a conspiracy: the demonstrators were to occupy the palace in an apparently peaceful manner in order to force the king to grant further concessions.

But what had been planned could not now be prevented; since midday the masses had been pouring into the Schlossplatz, including most of the Berlin protection officials, lined up in their ranks and files, waiting impatiently for something to happen. There was no evidence of the angry revolutionary mood which had been felt on the streets over the last few days. In the meantime a notice appeared on the authority of the town council announcing new legislation for freedom of the press and the summoning of Parliament, and the crowd was jubilant. General von Pfuel went unconcernedly back to his lodgings and called up von Manteuffel, subsequently his aide-de-camp; 'Let's go now and be greeted by those Hurrahs!'[23] The grateful burghers wanted to see their King; the monarch appeared on the balcony to be greeted by jubilant 'Long lives' and von Bodelschwingh told them in ringing tones that 'the king wants freedom of the press to rule, the king wants the Parliament to be summoned immediately, the king wants a constitution that will embrace all German states on the most liberal basis; the king wants a German national flag to wave; the king wants every customs post to fall; the king wants Prussia to head the movement'.[24] The enthusiasm in the palace square now knew no bounds; the king had to show himself a second time, Bodelschwingh made a further speech which ended by voicing the king's desire that the gathering should now please disperse.

The whole sequence of events had by now assumed the nature of a ritual, one which was played out in nearly every German capital; the burghers' procession to the palace, the ruler's speech granting various liberal measures, resulting in an enthusiastic crowd and its peaceful withdrawal. Today, however, the sequence of events was not completed: the mass of people on the Schlossplatz was so enormous and the noise so deafening that only the people at the front could make out the balcony speeches. In consequence, the crowd did not disperse at all; on the contrary, more and more people were streaming in from the side streets, crowding the square unbearably, with the front rows being pushed forward so that they could look through the entrances and see the soldiers standing in the palace courtyards.

Their mood changed immediately to one of anger and many people snapped out of their royalist enthusiasm and remembered that there had as yet been no mention of an important demand. 'Soldiers – out!' they shouted, and the cry was finally taken up and chanted by the entire swaying mass of people. A new surge of anger was aroused when a Prussian black-and-white flag was unfurled from the balcony of a house opposite the palace. The crowd took this for a provocative gesture and they raised the cry for the black, red and gold standard.

Within the palace there was general consternation. The constant racket was making the king increasingly edgy and the Prince of Prussia's supporters, whose theory about a band of conspirators directing the crowd by means of invisible strings appeared to be substantiated, seized their opportunity; they persuaded the king to transfer the supreme command from General von Pfuel, who was hated by the court clique and rated as weak, and anyway was not just then present, to General von Prittwitz. Furthermore, they prevailed on the king to order the square to be emptied. General von Prittwitz was to clear the Schlossplatz with his cavalry and, as the king expressed it, to put an end to the scandal prevailing there.

Von Prittwitz, riding at the head of his squadron of dragoons, came out of the North gate and swerved into the Stechbahn. The General was forced apart from the other riders by a furious crowd, an action observed by Major von Falkenstein of the Kaiser Franz Regiment, who, believing his superior to be in mortal danger, disregarded his orders and instructed two infantry companies to make a sortie. In a moment, the Schlossplatz was swept clear, apart from a crowd of yelling people waving sticks, which still stood between Breitenstrasse and Langenbrücke. The Major sent a platoon against them, and as the soldiers marched, guns cocked, towards the bridge, two shots issued from their ranks.

The two shots
No event of those March days in Berlin has so stirred the imagination of later observers as these two shots, which unleashed the subsequent horror. First: given that the two shots undoubtedly provoked the outbreak of street fighting – could this provocation have possibly been planned? The conservative myth

of an unknown band of conspirators was now rivalled by the legend of a military clique consciously promoting battle.

There is not the slightest shadow of proof for either of these theories. Both non-commissioned-officer Hettgen's statement that a civilian had struck his rifle with a stick, thus setting it off, and that of grenadier Kuhn, that he had, contrary to orders, primed his rifle for attack and that it had gone off, has so far never been disproved. The latter statement is indeed truly questionable; there is much to be said for Veit Valentin's theory, according to which grenadier Kuhn had taken the first shot for the signal to fire and had then deliberately fired his own gun, albeit at random. Even Valentin, however, found no evidence for any command which could have led to these shots being fired.[25]

Far more interesting than the conspiracy theory is the discussion whether these chance shots had actually rendered revolution inevitable. Max Weber has employed this classic instance to elaborate his theory of adequate causation: an event is only historically relevant when it cannot be extracted mentally from its causal sequence, without the consequences necessarily being altered.[26] Anyone taking a look at the wider context of those March days will be inclined to attribute no significance to the shots; viewed from this perspective, the revolutionary mood of the Berlin population resembled a head of steam, which was building up and would sooner or later have to burst out of its container. But is this picture correct? Had the royal patents not released so much pressure that a happier sequence of events would have allowed constitutional conditions to be reached along a peaceful road, as in almost all the other German states? Everything hung in the balance on that afternoon of 18 March, and the slightest pressure would decide the direction events would take. It is indeed possible that those two shots provided that pressure.

The battle begins

Within an instant the scene changed. People were fleeing headlong into the sidestreets; the cry of 'Treachery! they're shooting at us' rang out from all sides and spread like wildfire through the whole town. In the minds of the burghers, artisans and workers who had just been cheering the king, the dim but compelling notion was now forming of a military trap, into which the citizens, by demonstrating on the Schlossplatz, had run. Revulsion overwhelmed even the most honest and loyal burghers, such as the apothecary, who called out on returning from the Schlossplatz: 'Yes, Gentlemen, such a thing has never happened before; this is arrant mockery, to promise everything and then to let them shoot, and on whom? On US, on wholly reputable persons, who raise their hats and wave when a princess drives by, and who pay their taxes promptly!'[27] It was no particular programme, not the thought of Liberal or national aims or any clearly defined desire for freedom, which turned burghers into barricade fighters, but an elementary mass psychosis, which elicited an automatic mass reaction. 'Crowds are fleeing along Königstrasse', an eyewitness recounted, 'burgers are coming, roused to wild fury, grinding their teeth, pale and breathless. They shout out that they have just been shot at in the Schlossplatz. Shrieks of rage and revenge erupt along Königstrasse and through the whole town. The town seethes like an earthquake: cobbles are ripped up, arms shops are plundered, houses are stormed, hatchets and axes are fetched out. In an instant twelve barricades rise up in Königstrasse made of *droschkas*, omnibuses, woolsacks, beams and of demolished pump-houses – excellent, exemplarily built barricades. Roofs are stripped, house by house. High up on their giddy edges stand the people, waiting for the soldiers, their tiles at the ready. The threatened sword-cutlers throw their weapons out at the door; everyone is armed, with pitchforks, swords, lances, pistols, with planks; the boys burst into houses to carry baskets of big stones onto the roofs . . .'[28]

Nothing had been prepared, there was no plan and no leader. Barricades grew up out of the ground, in places where there were enough willing hands to raise them from the available materials. The first barricade to be completed stood at the corner of Oberwallstrasse and Jägerstrasse, and consisted of two *droschkas*, a coach, the bank guard's sentry-box, the gutter-grating and a few barrels; the barricade at Friedrichstrasse was set up with the help of Mother Schmidecke's fruit-stall, which, as every Berliner knew, lay opposite the Polish Apothecary's, after the embattled burghers had helped her to at least stash her apples away safely; at the Königsstädtische Theatre they built street obstructions with the props, the general effect being more picturesque than defensive. In some streets several barricades rose up close behind the other, whereas strategically important sites, such as the corner between Friedrich-strasse and Behrenstrasse were provided with no obstructions at all. The distribution of weapons was similarly impetuous and spur-of-the-moment. The arms shops were plundered, with the promise that the weapons would be returned after the battle, as was in fact mostly the case. People equipped themselves with boards, cudgels, pitchforks, hammers, even clearing out the theatre's stock. Firearms of all sizes and epochs were brought along, the apothecaries provided powder, with marbles and coins serving for shot. The only properly armed people were the members of the Berlin civil guards; the soldiers found themselves very hard pressed by their fire from the housetops around Alexanderplatz and at the Cöllnische Rathaus. As this instance demonstrated, contrary to later claims by the government and historians, the street-fighters were not made up solely of 'young people, students, apprent-ices and factory workers',[29] but embraced the whole spectrum, including the class known in pre-March terminology as 'honourable burghers'.

Some people were still trying to prevent bloodshed. Bodelschwingh had a notice hastily printed, in which he explained as an eye-witness, that 'only two guns let off accidentally had given rise to the horrible rumour that peaceful burghers had been shot at'. Three gentlemen walked across the Schlossplatz and along the connecting streets, pursued by the crowd's taunts and insults and carrying a large banner on the king's behalf, which read 'A Misunderstanding! The King wants the Best [for you]!'. Town councillor Nobiling hurried from barricade to barricade reading out the royal patents about freedom of the press and summoning the Parliament (*Landtag*), only to encounter exasperated rejection. A solemn deputation of robed rectors and deacons issued out of the university to petition the king in the palace to recall the army; they were joined by Krausnick, the Mayor of Berlin, and several town councillors. Friedrich Wilhelm IV received them amicably, but unyieldingly; it was not he who had betrayed the people but the people who had betrayed him, by turning into a rebellious rabble which must now be treated accordingly. Town councillor Schauss contradicted him and the king reacted with such fury that Schauss fainted and had to be brought round by the Princess of Prussia with her smelling-salts. Nevertheless, Bishop Neander got the king to agree to delay storming the barricades near the Cöllnische Rathaus, so as to give the burghers the opportunity to pull them down themselves. This news did not, however, reach the soldiers or the burghers behind their defences. At 5 p.m. the army began storming them; the thunder of their gunfire appalled the king, now incapable of further thought. He buried his head in his hands and remained seated where he was, apathetic and occasionally sobbing.

On the barricades

The army concentrated on clearing the streets systematically, one after the other. They attacked the barricades from the front, thus exposing the cavalry's complete uselessness. The infantry was well equipped, being protected against stone projectiles by their helmets, back-packs and leather clothing, as well as being backed up by thirty-six cannon. For their part, the defenders had only three small cannon, known as 'marble beasts' since they were loaded with marbles. But they also had an army of helpers, as well as a better knowledge of the locality and above all, the better mood; anger and enthusiasm. This was a night for heroic deeds, which would later become an inseparable part of the revolutionary legend: take, for instance, Ernst Zinna, the sixteen-year-old apprentice locksmith, who defended the barricade on Jägerstrasse entirely on his own, armed only with a rusty sabre, until he was shot down. Or the unnamed workman who struck up the general march on a drum while standing on the steps of the d'Heurische Konditorei near the Cöllnische Rathaus and who remained miraculously unscathed when the building behind him collapsed. Or Gustav Hesse, a journeyman turner, who fetched a wounded man off the barricade in Alexanderplatz under a hail of bullets from the attacking soldiers; his comrades crowned him with oak leaves. Or the barricade in Taubenstrasse, where a student stood, sabre in one hand and the black, red and gold standard in the other, for the duration of the battle 'as steadily as if no bullet could hit him. His courage aroused so much admiration and enthusiasm that ladies braved the danger to wave their scarves from the windows at the youth.'[30] Since this was Prussia, however, other scenes were taking place as well; for instance, First Lieutenant von Krawell heard the shooting from his lodgings, mounted his horse and rode to his barracks. His way was barred by a barricade, with guns levelled against him. He said quietly: 'You must be mad if you don't realise that I have to go to report for duty?' At which, a gap in the barricade was willingly cleared for him and when he complained that the space was too narrow for his horse, it was duly widened and he passed through the barricade, which was closed up again behind him and defended. What's more, this barricade remained undefeated, since it was never attacked.'[31]

The desire to perform heroic deeds was weak on the part of the military. The troops were poorly prepared, both tactically and psychologically, for street fighting against a revolutionary opponent. 'The hoarse shouts of the fighters, the unbroken rumble of infantry gunfire, as well as the thunderous bass of the cannon, whose blasts reduced the windows of neighbouring houses to dust . . ., the continuous alarm-ringing of all the bells in every church situated in the insurgents' area, the darkness, illuminated by great flares of fire, all rendered the evening quite horrifying', artillery lieutenant Prince Kraft zu Hohenlohe remembered. 'Although the noise of battle is far greater . . ., the danger of death is far greater, street fighting in one's own country, in the midst of peace, has something indescribably horrible about it, like a raging earthquake. One cannot tell who or where the enemy is. The rioters' stratagems and murderous behaviour is horribly repellent and arouses one to fury and inhumanity.'[32] The soldiers were weary, angry and disorientated; no one understood what was actually happening. Added to which the enemy wore no uniform, fought in an irregular manner and the usual clear marks distinguishing between combatants and civilians were absent. On the whole the officers tried to distinguish between armed opponents and non-participants, but the distinction was a difficult one, with half-grown boys throwing stones from rooftops and women milling around with heavy iron bars. On top of which, night was falling and the officers could no longer hold their men on a firm leash. This led to encroachments and excesses; when the Cöllnische Rathaus was finally stormed by the soldiers of the 1st Guards Regiment, after long-drawn-out return fire from its defendants, the revolutionaries, who had long ago surrendered, were summarily executed. Prisoners were frequently handled with unbridled roughness; even Prittwitz admitted that 'the soldiers' excitement and bitterness reached an excessively high degree, almost beyond restraint'.[33]

Nevertheless, the commander-in-chief must soon have realised that his forces were not sufficient to take and hold the whole town. Towards midnight he reported to the king that the inner city between the Spree, the Neue Friedrichstrasse, the Spittalmarkt and Leipzigerstrasse had been taken, but that more could not be achieved. His proposal was that, instead of the troops being deployed to engage in street fighting, they be withdrawn from the inner city to surround Berlin and shoot down the pockets of resistance from outside. The king did not adopt the general's proposal; he gave orders for the fighting to cease and the positions simply to be held, and dismissed Prittwitz with an 'exceptionally gracious "good night and sleep well"'.

Battle is called off

In the meantime the king had pulled himself together. Late that evening, he had received Georg von Vincke, the Leader of the Opposition in the United Parliament, who explained two things: first, that the troops were not capable of sustaining a civil war, and secondly, that the situation should not be assessed from the purely military point of view. The bond between monarchy and citizens should not be cut, which meant that everything now depended on laying down arms in a conciliatory manner. This was thoroughly in accordance with Friedrich Wilhelm's own thoughts. During the last few days he had formulated an increasingly firm plan to use the popular movement in Germany to form a renewed *Reich* under Prussian leadership. The struggle against the popular movement now taking place in Berlin was threatening to upset the whole scheme and furthermore involved the dangers of growing separatism in the Rhineland and of Russian intervention. Added to which this Christian and patriarchal monarch felt that to fight against his own people was a sin; accordingly everything now depended on extending the hand of reconciliation.

General von Prittwitz had scarcely left him when the king sat down at his desk to draft a proclamation 'To my beloved Berliners'. Everything, he wrote, had been a crazy mistake, caused by 'a gang of rabble-rousers, mostly from foreign lands'. The people needed only to leave the barricades and send delegates to the palace 'filled with the true old Berlin spirit, with words such as are due to your King', and he gave his royal word that Berlin would immediately be cleared of troops, and that only the palace and the Zeughaus would retain their military guards for a short while. Both Berlin and the king would forget what had happened 'for the sake of our greater future, which will dawn under God's blessing of peace for Prussia and through Prussia for Teutschland'.[34] Bodelschwingh immediately arranged for this appeal to be printed and by dawn on 19 March town-criers were proceeding through the whole city, bringing the royal offer of peace to the people.

It was ineffectual. The criers met only with taunts and bitter rejection, and someone soon trimmed the heading 'To my beloved Berliners' neatly off the proclamation and pinned it above an undetonated grenade stuck in a wooden pump-house in Breitenstrasse, with 'Frederick William' pinned beneath it. In the palace, meanwhile, a deputation of other criers was just knocking at the door; the king, who had not slept and was depressed, scarcely heard them, waiting as he was only for a sign from the town that his message had succeeded. Mayor Naunyn next appeared to report that the people were tearing down the barricade in Königstrasse. The king did not enquire further, otherwise Naunyn would have had to admit that this was the only such instance in all Berlin and that the street fighters elsewhere were determined to resume the fight. Instead of which Minister Bodelschwingh appeared and called out, that since the barricades were being torn down, it was now time to withdraw the troops according to the royal promise. This led to a dramatic encounter between the minister and the Prince of Prussia, with the latter vainly insisting that there was as yet no question of barricades being cleared, and that consequently the Schlossplatz and Lustgarten must remain cut off by troops. However, the king and his minister were sick and tired of military arguments, and the order went out to the troops to vacate their positions.

The military withdraw

This procedure bore all the signs of defeat. As the companies withdrew, they were mocked by those manning the barricades and bombarded with stones. The troops then assembled between the palace and the arsenal before leaving the town 'with ringing music and in an orderly fashion, but in a horribly derouted condition'.[35] The shame of this retreat was never to be forgotten by the officer corps; their most deeply wounding realisation, that the king appeared to pursue the interests of absolute monarchy less singlemindedly than did the army, led to that increasingly political and ideological self-isolation of the Prussian military which was to have such far-reaching consequences for the history of Germany. An as yet unknown major of the guard, called Albrecht von Roon, that evening wrote these psychologically revealing sentences: 'My God, my God, why hast thou foresaken us? . . . The best that can now happen, that is still possible, is that very corruptible representative constitution, against which every impartial mind has hitherto had the right and the motive to struggle . . .'[36]

It emerged only later that, in all the hectic activity of that day and the muddle of criss-crossing commands and orders, the supreme command had somehow lost control over the withdrawal. Contrary to what was stated in the royal proclamation, no guard at all had been left in the arsenal and the palace was now guarded by no more than two battalions – far too small a force, given the size of the building, to ensure that the king was properly protected. The king's entourage was demoralised and obsessed by fears of the guillotine: officers were trying to conceal their uniforms under civilian clothing, and the aide-de-camp, First Lieutenant von Brauchitsch even sacrificed his moustache in order to render himself unrecognisable. After protracted dithering, the king gave way to his advisors, who were imploring him to follow the troops to Potsdam, but it was too late: the streets were blocked by the crowds of people milling around the palace.

The barricade fighters brought with them the bodies of those who had fallen in the night, laid out on rack-waggons and biers, covered with flowers, branches and laurels, their wounds exposed to view. The officer on guard allowed the procession into the palace courtyard: General von Prittwitz ordered his soldiers to remove their helmets, and the crowd demanded to see the king. Friedrich Wilhelm appeared, accompanied by the queen, both of them pale as death and close to collapse. Corpse after corpse was placed before the royal couple, their bearers telling them: 'Fifteen years old, my only son'; 'Slaughtered unmercifully, after he had surrendered'; 'The father of five small children . . .' The crowd's excitement mounted as the cry went up: 'Hat off!'; the king removed his military cap and tried to speak, but was prevented by the noise. The people started up the hymn 'In Jesus is my trust' (*Jesus ist meine Zuversicht*) and Friedrich Wilhelm heard it through to the end, bare-headed with Queen Elizabeth murmuring: 'All that's missing now is the guillotine.' Then the king led his weeping consort back into the palace; never before or since had a German monarch been so profoundly humiliated.

Smoking is permitted

The crowd remained in the palace courtyard, with more people pushing in, and they were close to forcing their way into the palace when young Count Lichnowsky sprang to the rescue. He climbed onto a table and, speaking loudly and clearly, said that the king had put an end to the fighting, had sent the soldiers out of town and had entrusted himself to the burghers' protection. Since all their demands had been granted, they should now go home quietly. 'When someone asked whether really everything had been granted, he answered "Yes, everything, gentlemen!"; "Smoking too?" rang out another voice; "Yes, smoking too", came the reply; "In de Dierjarten too?" the questioner persisted; "Yes, Gentlemen, smoking is allowed in the Tiergarten too." This did the trick.'[37] Besides getting rid of the law against smoking in public, which had clearly symbolised the police state from the pre-March period onwards, the most important issue was arming the people, which the king agreed to. The mood in the Schlossplatz swung around, the king was cheered, and in an instant, revolutionaries were transformed back into loyal burghers, who hurried home to look out their citizenship papers: everyone able to prove that he was a citizen of Berlin was immediately issued with a rifle from the arsenal.

At 5 p.m. the civil guard, dressed in splendid uniforms, feathers waving in their hats, marched up to the palace and took over the guard. The crowd cheered them, the women waved their scarves and shots were fired in celebration. 'This is the first ray of sunshine in these days of horror', wrote the correspondent of the *Breslauer Zeitung* enthusiastically, 'the first ray of sunshine! May it be sustained! Today the King's protectors are not cartridges, cannon and bayonets; the rulers' only defence lies in the loyalty, the virtue and the freedom of the burghers.'[38] That evening every window was lit up, and everyone agreed that Berlin had never before seen such a splendid illumination. A few students gathered around the houses of former ministers and the Mayor's house to send up a chorus of catcalls, but they were sent home by an armed division of the civil guard. Peace and order ruled in Berlin.

Festival of the Revolution

20 March was a festival day. Scarcely anyone was working. The town was without police, soldiers or administrators. Those officers and court officials who had stayed behind appeared in civilian clothing and the public buildings were occupied by armed burghers, students and members of the artisan associations. The population was promenading happily in the streets, with the women wearing the black, red and gold colours as ribbons in their hats or as pretty rosettes in their corsages, and the men as scarves, watch straps or cockades. The pawnshops were besieged by gatherings of people, since all pawned goods up to the value of 5 *Taler* had, by royal decree, been redeemed at the state's expense. Cigars and pipes were being sported openly, while floppy hats and high boots proclaimed Liberal sentiments, with barricades still on all sides blocking the way. They were removed only gradually, and at the state's expense. Political prisoners were released, among whom the Polish revolutionary Mieroslawski, a romantic and heroic figure, the darling of the Berlin ladies, who was now conducted through the streets at the head of a triumphal procession, holding a black, red and gold flag. The king was standing on the palace balcony with Arnim, Schwerin and Bornemann, the new Liberal ministers, beside him and as the procession drew near, the king removed his cap and waved it at the Polish revolutionary. His gesture was greeted with frenetic cheers and the Pole was moved to make a long speech praising the bond of friendship which would in the future bind a free Poland and a free Germany together.

Prussia merges with Germany

The next day a notice appeared, produced by Decker's privy court printing-shop, addressed 'To the German Nation', unsigned, curiously enough, and featuring these rousing sentences: 'A glorious new history is rising up this very day for you! From now on you are once again a great united Nation, strong, free and powerful, in the heart of Europe! Prussia's Friedrich Wilhelm IV, trusting in your heroic support and your spiritual rebirth, has placed himself at the head of the whole Fatherland for the salvation of Germany. Today you shall see him with the ancient and honourable colours of the German nation, riding in your midst.'[39] Sure enough, Friedrich Wilhelm IV appeared at midday on a gentle mare – he was not a good rider – wearing the uniform of the 1st Guards Regiment, an eagle helmet on his head and a wide black, red and gold band on his arm. The procession fell into position, with two generals on horseback in front, followed by three members of the new Liberal government. Then came a member of the civil guard on foot with a billowing black, red and gold banner, flanked by two armed burghers. Next came the king, accompanied by two town councillors. Behind him walked Urban, the veterinary surgeon who only shortly beforehand had been holding a barricade; he was now walking with measured tread, bearing a representation of the imperial crown. Last came the princes, with the exception of the king's brother, who had fled to England, much to everyone's satisfaction, and a few more generals, all decked out in the German national colours.

The procession wound its way through the inner city, stopping at several corners to allow the king to make a little speech. The tenor of the royal words was always the same: the unity of Germany was now the next step towards founding a constitutional German state. In front of the university a student called out: 'Long live the Emperor of Germany!' Friedrich Wilhelm turned away in vexation, murmuring so that only his closest entourage could hear him: 'No, no, that's not what I want, not what I like!' The whole affair resembled a festive procession, and was accompanied by a constantly growing crowd and general rejoicing. Young Theodor Fontane was there with his father, who was upset when they met up with the procession: '"There's something rather strange about it . . . to ride about like that . . . I don't know . . ."' 'As it was', his son tells us, 'I agreed with him. But then, it also impressed me and so I said "Yes, papa, now the old ways have gone once and for all. As for the buttoned-up ways, they won't do any more. Always at the forefront . . ." "Yes, yes". At which we turned towards Puhlmann's coffee-garden.'[40]

That evening the German national flag fluttered from the scaffolding of the as yet unfinished palace cupola. A notice hung from the walls, entitled 'To my People and to the German Nation', signed by the king and the new government, which collated every valid measure for reforming Prussia and Germany; the text culminated in the following peroration: 'My people, who do not shrink from danger, will not abandon me, and Germany will join me trustingly. Today I have assumed the ancient German colours and have placed myself and my people under the honourable banner of the German Empire. From this day on Prussia is merged in Germany.'[41]

II The German nationalist movement's road to the creation of the Reich

2 The background: Europe's transformation from an agrarian society to a modern civilisation of the masses

In the beginning was the demographic problem. After centuries of fragile equilibrium brutally maintained by wars, epidemics and famines, the population of Europe began, from the mid eighteenth century onwards, to increase rapidly. In 1750 the continent contained at a rough estimate around 130 million people; by 1800 they had already grown to around 185 million, by 1850 to 266 million, by 1900 to 401 million and on the eve of the First World War to 468 million persons. Germany was no exception; in 1750 there must have been around 17 million people living within the 1871 boundaries of the German Empire; by 1800 they already numbered 25 million, by 1850 they comprised 35.4 million, by 1900 56.4 and by 1913 67 million Germans. Not even the exodus of millions of emigrants in the last two thirds of the nineteenth century made any difference, and catastrophes which would in earlier centuries have brought about heavy setbacks, now had scarcely any effect on population growth. Silesia, for instance, lost about 50,000 inhabitants to the 1771–2 famine, but within 3 years they had been replaced by a further 70,000. Not only was the population steadily increasing, but so was its *rate* of growth, and this despite the fact that Europe in the 1800s was already the most heavily populated part of the world.

A whole bundle of causes was responsible for this population explosion. There was the sharp rise in agricultural production consequent on new methods of cultivation. The old three-field rotation system was replaced by modern crop rotations, improving the fertility of the soil everywhere. The introduction of the potato increased the food supply and both governments and landlords were gripped by the *'fanatisme de l'agriculture'*, as a contemporary put it, by a passion for ploughing. Heathland was put to the plough, moorland was drained, woods were cleared and meadows were turned into ploughlands. The great variations between harvests were steadily reduced, catastrophic famines occurred less frequently and finally stopped. People were better fed and were consequently more resistant to infection; new weapons in the struggle against illness and disease – such as immunisation and improved hygiene – contributed towards containing epidemics and to raising average life expectancy. Child mortality and for women, perinatal mortality, retreated; this was due not only to medical advances but to a changed attitude towards children and the family. Over large areas of Europe the restrictions on marriage imposed by feudal or guild regulations collapsed, and people were marrying more frequently and earlier; marriage partners were living together for longer, and numerous influences (which have on the whole not been sufficiently studied) combined to create a population surge not previously experienced anywhere in the world.

People began moving away. The old agrarian society of Europe was gradually breaking up, since despite rising food production, in many agricultural regions the population was growing faster still. The flow of emigration was partly towards the still unpopulated regions of the world, America, Australia and Canada, and partly towards places already inhabited by many people, namely the towns, which were growing furiously, and where, during the course of the nineteenth century, depths of social, hygienic and moral abuse were plumbed which defied description; Charles Dickens' and Eugène Sue's novels provide only a dim and romanticised notion of the crass and wretched reality.

This development might well have ended in a catastrophe of gigantic proportions. Thomas Malthus (1766–1834), a Scottish minister, had already provided the gloomiest prognosis: continuous population growth alongside unchanged resources must inevitably lead to collapse – a prediction supported by the massive impoverishment of many regions in Europe – the eastern provinces of Prussia for instance, or Ireland. The fact that this did not happen, that Europe as a whole did not collapse in a catastrophic famine, such as now stalks the Third World three centuries on, was due to the economic revolution, generally known as the Industrial Revolution, which took place simultaneously.

It is not really possible here to present the whole gamut of conditions necessary to get this process unique to world history moving – a theme furthermore, which is still very much the subject of learned debates. In any case, the process is unthinkable without its background of the scientific, philosophical, cultural, religious and institutional history of Old Europe since antiquity. Roughly speaking, it was characterised by four basic tendencies. In the first place, technological breakthroughs were achieved, above all in the form of machines which could work and produce energy – the steam engine with its multifarious applications was the trend-setter here; in the second place, the raw materials of iron and coal were for the first time demanded and used in massive quantities – the means of production were no longer restricted by the limits of human and animal muscle-power and of organic materials; thirdly, the factory system was established, the form whereby labour is organised into manufacturing production; and fourthly, free wage-labour became the chief way of earning a living.

This whole process first took place during the last decades of the eighteenth century in England, where special conditions for industrialisation were present: favourably sited coal and iron mines, and a dense infrastructure of roads, rivers, canals and coastal sea routes, which were not criss-crossed by trade barriers as in the rest of Europe. Close behind this came the highly developed readiness of the aristocracy to invest in manufacture, a far-reaching system of trade, banking and credit, a liberal economic policy which favoured the free movement of capital and labour, and more besides, which together made it possible for an extraordinary rise in production to occur within a few decades resulting in an economic growth which, although interrupted by crises, was able to carry on by itself. A process, which took over to the same extent those countries of Europe where comparable political, economic, social and, last but not least, intellectual conditions, were already present or were being established.

The growth in population and production was accompanied by a third secular revolution, in the means of communication. The transportation of goods and persons, as well as the transmission of news, attained wholly new dimensions. Whereas the speed of dispatch-couriers and later of mail-coaches had epitomised the relationship between space and time, now the proliferation of steamship travel and railways allowed the masses to travel in far greater numbers over longer distances in a far shorter time and at less expense. It meant that agricultural produce could be brought over seas and continents to the urban agglomerations without deteriorating, and that raw materials could be brought to distant processing-places. This made it possible to establish trade over extensive regions, the precondition for the growth and integration of the European economy. As long as economic islands limited to specific regions had existed due to the inadequate traffic conditions of the pre-industrial age, supply, demand and prices had been able to develop separately; the railway now ensured that competition became equally strong almost everywhere, which contributed decisively to the relocation of Europe's economic centres. The news of a military victory or of an economically significant event had previously taken weeks to cross Europe; with the invention of the telegraph, and later the telephone, all distances dwindled to nothing, and the hugely flourishing newspapers contributed their bit towards the massive dissemination of news.

All these demographic, economic and communications revolutions were closely connected and mutually determined. It was unavoidable that the European political system would react against this fundamental and previously unprecedented revolution. All the constitutions of Old Europe, whether monarchic or republican, had relied on the rule of small, closed aristocratic elites, legitimised by a God-given mandate as interpreted by ecclesiastical ordinance. The tendency however had for a long time been towards the regional and personal centralisation of power and its exercise; the reduction of the power of rival aristocratic groups in favour of a single ruler by introducing a bureaucracy based on merit, rationalising the administration of the state and making it more effective; the standardisation of the legislature; the extension of the ruler's monopoly of power over a variety of regional, social, economic and cultural spheres; the separation of the legitimate exercise of power from the forces of feudalism and the establishment of a central state monopoly of power. All this was also part of the preconditions to the Industrial Revolution, which, however, also altered the conditions determining political sovereignty. The absolutist state of the eighteenth century, which in its very different varieties and hybrid forms characterised that European age, was no longer able to perform adequately on the three decisive levels of the exercise of political power; those of participation, of political achievement and of legitimacy.

In political terms, the most serious aspect of the crisis of the political system consisted in the problem of participation, of power-sharing. New functional elites were everywhere gradually rising up alongside the powerful old aristocratic elites in Europe: positions of leadership in state and army were increasingly achieved by members of the middle classes, who were nevertheless excluded from the political and status-determining privileges of their aristocratic chiefs. Industrialisation produced a new social type, that of the middle-class industrialist, and later on that of the manager, the employed director, who exercised all in all considerable economic power and consequently insisted on applying this power in the political sphere as well. Not least of the state's problems in the age of the masses were those of taxation and of recruitment for the army; the American Revolution's cry of 'No taxation without representation' echoed through Europe and pushed through new forms of representation which contributed to the collapse of the feudal order and took account of the new ideologies.

As for the achievements of the political system, the unprecedented population growth, as well as the development of new means of communication, and not least the demand for a rationalised and more effective state system which was unleashed by industrialisation, led to the development of a centralised and hierarchical machinery of government and administration. Only thus was the state able to get hold of the nation's natural and social resources, preferably in their entirety, and to reach every layer and sector of the population. This enabled it to establish its monopoly of power and to meet the enormous social problems thrown up by the Industrial Revolution by ensuring a fair distribution of goods, values and life opportunities, in so far as this was possible.

Contemporaries, however, experienced the European revolution most profoundly as a crisis of legitimation, when the ancient myths and thought associations no longer held water, the God-given dispensation and the 'good old ways' lost their credibility. It is worth remarking at this point, that Europe's crisis of values had already begun before the population explosion and industrialisation had dissolved the feudal order of society. The de-Christianisation of extensive regions on the continent had already begun by the end of the seventeenth century, and could be observed not just as the elitist philosophy of the Enlightenment but also as a change in the widespread collective mentality of the uneducated classes (be it, for instance, altered theories about death, or the growing knowledge and practice of birth control methods, which were forbidden by the Church during the *Ancien Régime*).

Peoples' appreciation of reality also underwent a profound change, as did their attitude to the legitimacy of the order imposed by society and the state. Hitherto there had scarcely been any distinction between present, past and future times; people had been bound up firmly in their family, village or small-town circles and in the recurring annual cycle of agricultural production; historical developments hardly impinged on their lives; the future was anticipated in terms of a repetition of the past and the future order inevitably in terms of the 'good old order'. On the other hand, people felt that the present had speeded up furiously, giddily and dangerously; they felt deafened by the onslaught of new and unprecedented things which contrasted sharply with the earlier peacefulness of the unalterable and all-embracing sphere of ancient custom. Great migrations had hitherto always been associated with catastrophes, with war and famine, and those who left simply spread the epidemics further afield; they were the harbingers of death, a miserable downtrodden race. Consequently the massive shifts in settlement were also seen as catastrophic, or conversely (but with the same socio-psychological effect) they were viewed euphorically in the expectation of something wholly new. In any case, the daily existence of large masses of people was radically altered, leading to a weakening of old ties, myths and loyalties. The social body, once firmly entrenched in agrarian society, with its social orders and intellectual and religious foundations, was now broken up, releasing myriads of individuals, who sought for new forms of association, unless they were wholly preoccupied with securing a bare subsistence.

The times demanded that all values be reassessed, a call answered from many quarters. No one now believed in a God-given order, but in the right of the individual to freedom and happiness – 'the pursuit of happiness', the secular motto of European liberalism, as promised by the American Revolution, and (in its first phase) by the French Revolution as well. At the same time, the Idea of Nation acquired some substance as the unity of people and state, established by their will and decision or by their common language and history. Both these concepts, the freedom of the individual and the idea of nation, led to the concept of the sovereignty of the people. As indus-trialisation proceeded and a fourth social order emerged, the power of nationhood as a source of identity was challenged by a new rival, the class-myth, or rather the call for the solidarity of the masses against the self-interest of the ruling classes; the expression of self-awareness of a sub-class whose labour in the factories had made the growing prosperity of society possible in the first place. The old world mobilised its defensive forces, which in their turn formulated massively effective ideologies – conservatism lost its elitist character as the traditional line of defence of the ruling classes against mob rule and sometimes went so far as to adopt decidedly mob methods, as well as already associating with antisemitic elements. Political Catholicism, finally, stood for the reaction of a minority of the population less affected by society's lost bearings, to the demands for sovereignty of an aggressively invasive Liberalism.

Thus did Europe, at the end of the eighteenth and the beginning of the nineteenth centuries, give birth to a multitude of competing ideas about order and legitimacy, which circulated in 'movements' and parties. Every one was capable of inflaming crowds of people and bringing them out onto the barricades, without however being able to prevail completely over the other competing ideas. No political system was capable of permanent peaceful co-existence with a society which had split up into separate communities, with different beliefs and world-views, unless it could show that it was also capable of binding together a whole host of opposing ideologies.

The demographic and economic upheavals within Europe inevitably involved profound social, political and cultural changes, and the whole process of transformation from the ancient agrarian and feudal society of Old Europe to the modern mass democracy of the twentieth century did not take place at the same rate on every level or run a straight course. Given, too, that the many different trends of development could move faster or slower, seize up or even sometimes go backwards, and, finally, that the traditional elements of the old order were not generally subsumed into the new, inevitably led to revolutionary crises. Historians have long gazed in fascination on the myth of the French Revolution and have thereby often failed to observe that what was happening in France was simply a particularly spectacular version of a series of events from the last third of the eighteenth century to the twentieth, which, taken as a whole, decisively stamped and structured the history not only of Europe but of the Atlantic sphere as well. These revolutionary events could have very different characters; some revolutions led to profound changes, producing long-lasting myths and setting the political scene for generations. Among such are the American Revolution (1763–1775), the French Revolution (1789–1815), and the Revolution of 1848 which gripped the whole of Europe and yet was so remarkably unsuccessful. Other revolutionary events were more limited in space and time, involving only parts of the political and social whole or simply failing to fire the imaginations of contemporaries or historians to the same extent. Among such are the Geneva Revolution of 1868, the Belgian Revolution of the *Joyeuse Entrée* (1789/90), the Polish Revolution of 1781, or the French, Belgian and Polish Revolutions of 1830, to mention but a few. Finally, a closer inspection of the boundaries between revolution and peaceful transition show that they fluctuated. The Prussian reforms (1807–20) are described without further ado as a Revolution from above, in which not a drop of blood was shed, whereas the British constitutional history of the nineteenth century, which is generally presented as a model of peaceful change, is also the history of constantly recurring bloody revolts and outbreaks of violence.

Taken as a whole, the age of the greatest transformation of Europe was thus an age of revolution, and its individual revolutions should be seen as part of the whole transition process, as crises when the confrontations and contradictions of Europe's secular upheaval reached a peak. It is not, for this reason, particularly helpful to isolate individual revolutions from this dense web of activity, in order to describe them as 'bourgeois' or 'capitalist'. It is not remotely possible to reduce any of the European revolutions to such simple forms; in every instance, a multitude of economic, social, traditional, cultural and other tendencies and interests met and overlapped, and in no instance was a completely new system introduced. Instead, the existing development was simply speeded up, and sometimes even slowed down, as the process of industrialisation was in the case of the French Revolution. Consequently, when we come across atypical developments in Europe, including Germany, they cannot be attributed to the absence of a 'bourgeois' or other form of Revolution, since the revolutions as a whole did not constitute the driving-force behind historical progress, but simply more or less noisy rattles in the workings of European modernisation, at the end of which lies our present-day industrial society.

It is possible to establish constants for the whole of Europe, allowing us to refer to a predominantly uniform process of European dimensions, from which Germany cannot reasonably be excluded. In any case, the great European revolution which took place between the eighteenth and twentieth centuries, the pivotal period (Karl Jaspers) between Old Europe and the Modern Age, allowed for sufficient anomalies within the general modernisation process as well as regional variations for every nation and state to advance in its own unmistakable way into the twentieth century. The population of some regions started growing much later than in others, and the pace of growth varied considerably according to region. In France, for instance, the average rate of growth between 1850 and 1910 was 2.2 per thousand of population, whereas in England it was 15.3 per thousand; the figures for the rest of Europe lay somewhere in between the two. Some regions, France, for instance, or Bavaria (excluding the Pfalz) experienced very little in the way of population movement, whereas others, such as Prussia or England, experienced an enormous internal population shift from the countryside to the towns. Others, again, resolved their overpopulation problem chiefly through emigration, as was the case with the Upper Rhine area, Northern Germany and Ireland. All these trends could take place within the same region, whether simultaneously or serially. Industrialisation happened earlier in England than it did in Belgium or Switzerland; some countries had to undergo a very painful and brief period of industrialisation, as with Germany within the boundaries of the Customs Union, whereas others, such as France, experienced a relatively constant period of industrial growth extending over the whole century, albeit devoid of any clear thrust towards industrialisation. Conversely, France, thanks to the relatively modern administrative structure of the *Ancien Régime*, led continental

Europe in her system of roads and communications. In this, as with many other aspects of the modernisation process, the ongoing time-lag between Western and Eastern Europe was apparent.

These were but a few fundamental differences. To them may be added the different starting conditions; the geographical location, the relative modernity of the state administration, the level of literacy, the density of the road network, the mineral wealth, the area under agriculture, the economic and guild systems, the climate, the religious creed, the traditions, the economic attitudes and collective mentality etc . . . Enough, in any case, to permit us to talk about Germany and to trace the changes in her national order of legitimacy as a particular, characteristic variant in the general process of European history between the French Revolution and the creation of Bismarck's *Reich*.

3 The rise of a national culture

What are the Germans?' enquired the Imperial Privy Councillor Friedrich
Carl von Moser of his readers in 1766, replying to his own question as
follows: 'What we are, then, we have been for centuries; that is, a puzzle of a
political constitution, a prey of our neighbours, an object of their scorn
outstanding in the history of the world, disunited among ourselves, weak
from our divisions, strong enough to harm ourselves, powerless to save
ourselves, insensitive to the honour of our name, indifferent to the glory of
our laws, envious of our rulers, distrusting one another, inconsistent about
principles, coercive about enforcing them, a great but also a despised people;
a potentially happy but actually a very lamentable people.'[1] The grounds for
Moser's lament were obvious: the Empire was split up into 314 territories and
towns and into 1475 free lordships, all of which guarded the sovereign rights
guaranteed them by the European Powers after the Peace of Westphalia with
the utmost jealousy. Furthermore, Central Europe was divided by deep
confessional gulfs, since the conflict between Reformation and Counter
Reformation had not been resolved in Germany, unlike in most of the other
European states, but had been petrified by the principle of *cuius regio, eius
religio*' (whose the region, his the religion). Added to which there were
countless customs restrictions, an uncontrollable multitude of monetary and
measurement systems and a confused muddle of legal norms. For these
reasons, Germany's economic development lagged far behind Western
European levels; a gap only widened by war; for Central Europe was the
European theatre of war and the terrible destruction and losses of the Thirty
Years' War were still felt even a hundred years later.

The antiquated and rigid nature of the Imperial Constitution reflected that
of the *Reich*'s social structure. Whereas in France, the Netherlands and above
all in England, feudal restrictions had long ago started crumbling and an
increasingly powerful manufacturing and commercial bourgeoisie had
developed, demanding political participation and economic freedom, this
process had scarcely begun in the *Reich*, with the exception of a few, mainly
northern, trading towns. The feudal and guild order had survived nearly
everywhere in Central Europe, owing to the Empire's economic backwardness and internal divisions; even Prussia's new legal code, introduced by
Frederick the Great in 1794 and considered by all Europe to be a humane and

advanced body of legislation, proclaimed equal rights for all but also a strict distinction between the feudal classes: aristocracy, burghers and peasants were precisely distinguished by their separate duties and privileges.

One thing was new: since the mid eighteenth century the Empire had no longer had just one focal point in the form of the Emperor residing in Vienna, more as a *fata morgana* than as a political force. Since the two wars in Silesia (1740–2 and 1744–5) and the Seven Years War (1756–63) the Imperial power in the south had been confronted by an almost equal power in the north, with the Catholic Habsburg ruler being challenged so to speak by a Protestant anti-Emperor. The impoverished state of Brandenburg–Prussia, 'the Holy Roman Empire's sand-shaker', had been transformed, thanks to its rulers' lust for power, via a well-organised administration and a superior army, into a powerful modern state. On the other side, there was Habsburg Austria, desperately trying to retain her position as the leading German power and to restrict the northern upstart within its boundaries. However, the reforms implemented by the youthful Emperor Joseph II in an attempt to centralise and modernise his lands as his Prussian rival had done, were just as unsuccessful as were his attempts to strengthen the might of the Habsburgs on the battlefield.

Was there anything still German about this state, when two thirds of it lay outside the Empire's boundaries and the majority of its subjects could not speak the German language? Nevertheless, enlightened Germany had looked towards Austria during the first years of the Josephine reforms. The great Klopstock himself had proposed founding an academy of the sciences and arts in Vienna to promote German intellectual life, but his plan foundered, despite the Emperor's enthusiasm for reform, against the narrow-minded suspicion of the Austrian bureaucracy, fearful of a flood of north German Protestants and freethinkers. The Bavarian war of succession (1778–9) further served to demonstrate that the Emperor was no longer the Protector of Germany, as he had once been during the Empire's wars against French and Turks, but was a ruler like all the others, interested in nothing more than rounding off his own sphere of influence.

How different was his north German rival for the leadership of the Empire! It was the Prussian King Friedrich who had called the federation of German rulers into life in 1785 in order to fend off Habsburg attacks on the German *Reich*'s constitution. It was Frederick the Great, with his victories over Russian and French armies during the Seven Years War, who had provided the model for a German hero, and who, in Goethe's words, had saved 'the honour of part of the Germans against an allied world?' The Frederick myth had a profound effect, especially among the *Reich*'s young men, who were still ignorant of any national German consciousness (the word not having yet been invented) and instead felt 'Fritzisch' – as the young Goethe did. It did not matter in the slightest that Frederick stood against everything that smacked of German culture, despising it profoundly. His world, the world of the intellect, of culture and good taste, was a French world; for him, things German meant his father's deeply detested court, that dull, unintellectual, bigoted and uneducated milieu, reeking with beer and tobacco fumes. In 1786, shortly before his death, Mirabeau, the French ambassador asked him why he had become a German Caesar but never a German Augustus, and Frederick replied: 'But what more could I have done for German culture than I did do, by having nothing to do with it?' As for the federation of German rulers, Frederick was certainly not thinking in terms of Germany, but of Prussia's hegemonial position *vis-à-vis* Austria; 'But that', he wrote to his brother Heinrich, 'must be concealed like a murder.' Thus, Frederick was no German hero, but a German myth – history is, however, often made not by men but by their myths.

Well might one speak of the irony of history, of the 'cunning of Reason' (Hegel): the German nation grew up out of the confusion of a splintered territory, out of petty principalities and the desire for power of a hundred little *serenissimi*. There was a tendency innate in the whole of the European continent at that time, whereby small, closed aristocratic elites lost their sovereignty through the concentration of regional and personal sovereignties. The imprecise term for this is absolutism, whereby rival aristocratic groups lose their power to a single ruling individual; laws and constitutions are standardised; the ruler's monopoly is extended over all regional, social, economic and cultural sectors, and the executive power of the state is centralised and legitimised. Extending the state also involved extending its administration, which had to overcome increasingly complicated problems. The absolutist state could no longer be ruled by the traditional instruments of feudal power. Apart from the fact that it was in the rulers' interest to keep their aristocracy as far away as possible from the direct exercise of power, by summoning them to court or putting them in uniform and restricting them to military service, the administration of a state required abilities far above the educational level of the average nobleman. The new official had to be capable of performing his duties effectively and rationally; he had to be educated in the law, since the state had been reorganised along legal lines; he had to possess technical skills, above all in agriculture, since improving manufacture and agricultural production were the preconditions for a prosperous state and thereby of its ruler's glory and power.

In a word: the state administration required educated officials. The determining factor was no longer birth; but abilities and knowledge were now demanded. State examinations were introduced in Prussia as early as 1755 for all lawyers, whether of noble or middle class origin; fifteen years later state examinations were made obligatory for all higher officials, and the state provided secondary schools, academies and universities to educate them. Since every territorial ruler jealously defended the autonomy of his own administration, insisting on his own territorial educational institutions, there were more universities in Germany than anywhere else: from Kiel to Graz, from Königsberg to Freiburg there were in 1775 no fewer than 40 – twice as many as in France.

In this manner, middle-class careers were possible and much desired; Clemens Brentano, the romantic poet, ends his poem in which he paints every detail of a childhood spent in narrow middle-class conditions with the following consoling verse:

> When the toiling and moiling is done,
> By the state you're at last taken on;
> It heals every wound and you're sure that
> You'll finish your days a *Geheimrat*.

The nobleman was also forced to match the middle-class level of education if he wanted to move up in the administration. This led to the emergence all over Germany, especially in the capitals, in the university and trading towns, of an educated, non-feudal, noble and bourgeois class, freed from military service and taxation, and directly subject to their ruler's jurisdiction. The higher echelons of the bureaucracy formed the core of this educated middle class, which comprised evangelical pastors and professors as much as lawyers, doctors, book-dealers and writers, all of whom had one thing in common: the exercise of their offices and professions was based not on status but on ability – evidence of which was provided in every case by their academic training.

This new bourgeois class was not vastly different from the third estate of West European provenance. Its emergence was not founded on economic or political, but on administrative and cultural grounds. Furthermore, this emergence was coupled with another important development: the development of an authentically German national culture during the same period. It was only then that the German local idioms and dialects developed into the language of German high culture that is, into *Hochdeutsch* (High German), whose roots are middle German, low German and Lutheran. German national literature, music and theatre created a unity of taste and judgement which transcended territorial boundaries. Anyone writing in German did so not only because the literary market demanded it, but also because he was thereby proclaiming his allegiance to the unity of an enlightened middle-class spirit, which stood above territorial boundaries and consciously distanced itself from the French language and culture prevalent in court life. It was these cultural boundaries which gave the German educated elite its national identity, and Justus Moser was already encouraging it in 1785 to be no longer the 'apes of foreign fashions'.[2] Klopstock was already singing his *Ode to the Fatherland*:

> No other land has ever dealt as uprightly
> With foreign lands as you!
> Do not be too upright. Their minds are not noble enough
> To see how fine is your mistake![3]

The German nation, or simply the nation to which Klopstock was referring, was to be found solely in the heads of its educated members. At a time when four out of five Germans were rooted in a peasant environment and understood higher politics in terms of church prayers for the ruling aristocratic family or, perhaps, of the turmoil of war and the billeting of and pillaging by foreign soldiers; when urban youth felt *'fritzisch'* as the young Goethe did and worshipped the Prussian King Frederick who had bequeathed them the example of a national hero with his victories over the Russian and French armies, there simply wasn't the basis for a popular concept of nation. According to estimates by the enlightened Berlin book-dealer Friedrich Nicolai, in about 1770 around 20,000 people were participating in the national debate, albeit without producing any political results. German identity was first and foremost wholly one of language and culture. The growing density of communication between educated people in all the German territories; the enormous wave of new books and new editions; the considerable increase in news organs; the flourishing of Reading Societies down to the small towns, all created a new sort of critical and inquiring public. Madame de Staël, the French authoress, pointed out however at the beginning of the nineteenth century: 'The educated people of Germany argue amongst themselves with the greatest vivacity in the sphere of Theories, and as a result are fairly keen to leave the whole reality of life to their earthly rulers.'[4]

The reason for this lies close to what has been said earlier: in spite of all its criticism on principle of aristocracy and rulers, in spite of all its enlightened and philanthropic basic tenets, this class was to a considerable extent bound to the state and the monarchy. Added to this, the bitter feelings about under-privilege and social disadvantage, which had created a fertile soil for the emergence of a revolutionary bourgeoisie in France, played a lesser role here; although the French Revolution was welcomed by nearly all the bureaucracy and educated middle classes, they were equally almost wholly certain that there was no need for similar events in their own German states – German Jacobins were definitely a peripheral phenomenon and Adolph, the Bremen official and well-known *Aufklärer* Freiherr von Knigge, was not contradicted when he postulated the following: ' . . . I claim, that we have no reason either to fear a revolution in Germany nor to wish for one . . .'[5] The existing territorial state was seldom questioned by educated people; they felt, whether Prussians, Bavarians, Saxon-Goths or Schwarzburg-Sonderhauseners, thoroughly *'Teutsch'*. Their *'Teutschheit'* was, however, in direct compe-tition with a widespread and enlightened cosmopolitanism as well as with their scarcely questioned loyalty to the then reigning territorial ruler; when they referred to such concepts as 'nation', 'fatherland' or 'patriotism' they could be thinking of any sort of vaguely defined Germany as much as of the actual state in which they lived; they could also mean both of these at once.

4　What has become of the German Fatherland?

Following the French Revolution and the revolutionary wars the picture of Central Europe was profoundly altered. In Germany, the events in France were at first greeted with unanimous approval by the intellectuals; scarcely any German poet or philosopher failed to applaud the young French Republic with enthusiasm. But the enchantment was soon broken. The ideal of fraternal and peaceful coexistence between free and equal citizens could not be reconciled with the news from Paris; the Revolution had turned bloody and the revolutionary Terror, mass murder in the name of various virtues pertaining to the Enlightenment, was deemed a catastrophe by the horrified citizens of Germany.

Nevertheless, the example of the *nation une et indivisible* had a profound effect on educated Germans, who had experienced the whole extent of the Empire's impotence during the course of the revolutionary wars. While the French armies were occupying the whole of the left bank of the Rhine and then driving further on into South Germany, the counter-revolutionary coalition of German rulers crumbled. Prussia gave away the Rhineland in April 1795 at the separate peace of Basel and turned to the East to carve up Poland between herself, Austria and Russia, for the third time around. Two years later even the Emperor followed Prussia's bad example with the Peace of Campo Formio, when he sacrified the integrity of the Empire to the particular interests of the House of Habsburg. The last word did not even belong to the German rulers but to France and Russia as the powers guaranteeing the Empire's existence. Their plan envisaged the final ceding of the whole left bank of the Rhine to France, with the German rulers being indemnified at the expense of the smaller German territories. The *Reich* Deputations main resolution of 25 February 1803 consigned the world of small German states to the past; the number of immediate territories sank to around thirty. The most loyal subjects once pertaining to Emperor and Empire, the Imperial towns, Imperial nobility, and Imperial churches were almost all mediatised – their possessions were transfered to the middle and larger sized German states, who for their part thought that their future lay in a close association with France. The Empire's death-throes continued for three more years; on 12 July 1806 the representatives of sixteen South and West German states signed the Rhine Confederation Charter, according to which they accepted the French Emperor as their protector and cut themselves off from the *Reich*. A few weeks later, Franz II divested himself of the crown of the Holy Roman Emperor, thereafter entitling himself simply Emperor of Austria. His coach-driver's quarrels, Goethe commented, were of greater interest to him than this news, and like him, the rest of the world merely shrugged its shoulders over the demise of the almost thousand-year-old Holy Roman Empire of the German Nation on a point of order.

It was not the demise of the Empire which led to the development of a new and stronger idea of the identity of the German nation; the real father of the German nation was more probably Napoleon. Although the south German states were France's allies, the French troops tended to behave as if they were the actual rulers of the land; in August 1806 a Nürnberg book-dealer called Johann Philipp Palm was shot by a French trooper for having distributed a brochure entitled *Germany in Her Deep Humiliation*. This text was hardly read at all but Palm's death became a symbol of the first modern dictatorship in European history.

Napoleon had greater cause to fear words than weapons as subsequent events were to demonstrate: after a long period of diplomatic manoeuvring, Prussia finally declared war on France in September 1806, since Napoleon obviously wanted to provoke the quarrel by making persistent inroads into Prussian territory and by demonstrating a clear disregard for Prussian interests. The haughty Prussian officer corps was still living in the age of Frederick the Great and his past successes and was utterly sure of its ability to teach the Corsican upstart a sharp lesson. Napoleon, for his part, wrote to his wife from his field headquarters on the eve of the decisive battle: 'With God's help, I believe that within a few days everything will take a decidedly painful turn for the poor King of Prussia.'

The Prussian defeats at Jena and Auerstedt on 14 October 1806 were so overwhelming that there was no possibility of another big battle taking place. Napoleon advanced almost unopposed, almost every Prussian stronghold surrendered without a single shot being fired and, a fortnight after the battle, Napoleon marched into Berlin, to be greeted with enthusiasm by masses of Berlin citizens, while King Friedrich Wilhelm III retreated to the furthest corner of north-eastern Prussia where, abandoned by his Russian ally, he was finally forced to sign the victor's dictated peace. From being a major continental power, Prussia had dwindled almost overnight to a second-class middle state, and it looked as if she would eventually disappear off the map of Europe.

This catastrophe was the first spark which set German nationalism alight. The latent anti-French *motif* which had pervaded the culture of the educated middle classes in Germany since the late eighteenth century now contained a new and sharper chord; the people and their language were discovered as the only and final legitimising basis for the nation. Enlightened persons such as Thomas Abbt, Friedrich Carl von Moser, Johann Jacob Buhlau and Justus

Moser had previously understood the concept of nationalism in terms of a state, which, along the lines of the American or even the French Revolution at its beginning, would effect the greatest happiness of the greatest number of its citizens. However, when this concept was confronted with an aggressive French nationalism, Gottfried Herder's idea about the fundamental social individuality of the *Volkstum* based on language now grew virulent. In the winter of 1807–8 Johann Gottlieb Fichte delivered his *Lectures to the German Nation* to an enthusiastic audience in a Berlin under occupation by the French: the German people is the original, unadulterated people, which is fighting for its freedom and identity against military and cultural subjugation by France, and is thereby acting in the service of a higher historic mission. This new and romantic concept of '*Volk*' was rounded off and elevated by a religiosity principally coloured by pietism. In Herder's time German national characteristics were already imbued with religious fervour, and since then both the religious and the secular spheres had become intertwined and inseparable: from worshipping God in the manner of the nation it was only one step to worshipping the Nation through God. Friedrich Ludwig Jahn, the 'father of gymnastics' who urged German youth to practise gymnastics so as to be fit to fight Napoleon, felt that the Germans were a 'holy people' and the poet Ernst Moritz Arndt preached: 'Let the unanimity of your hearts be your church, let hatred of the French be your religion, let Freedom and Fatherland be your saints, to whom you pray!'[6]

This was the tone struck, albeit in varying sharps and flats, in the intellectual circles of the age, a tone which could be heard as clearly in sermons and lectures as in discussions held in the Reading Circles and salons. It developed into an intellectual circle in which terms such as 'Fatherland', 'Volk', and 'Nation' became political key words under the impact of the Napoleonic occupation. It is clear, however, that the growing hatred of the occupation regime had not predominated from the start. Even Karl August Hardenberg, the future Prussian State Chancellor, who hoped for good relations with France so as to avoid any increase in the burdens weighing on the Prussian State, complained as late as 1808 in a letter to Altenstein, the Minister of Finance, about the lack of 'a sense of self-sacrifice quite especially among educated people', which he attributed to the 'prevailing cold cosmopolitanism'.[7]

However, it was soon general knowledge that Napoleon considered Germany chiefly as a base for Imperial recruitment to his *Grande Armée* and as the object of financial and economic exploitation. The burdensome billetings and devastating marches through the country by foreign armies, the financial burdens, which Prussia in particular had to bear after the Peace of Tilsit, and which entrained the impoverishment of various sections of the population, were followed by a tariff system which protected the French economy at the expense of the remaining European states, entailing price rises and economic collapse. Thus, the population's original indifference was transformed within a few years into hatred of the occupying power. During the years between the Austrian war against Napoleon of 1809, which was conducted by Archduke Karl the Austrian commander-in-chief in the name of the 'German People' and which ended with the French victory at Wagram, and the War of Liberation of 1813–14, groups of conspirators formed (mainly in Prussia) to organise and encourage a hesitant and often apparently treacherous state leadership to combat the Corsican upstart. These conspiracies involved discussion circles and dinner parties, organised in the tradition of the educated bourgeoisie as reading associations or citizens clubs but with new aims.

There was, for instance, the *Deutsche Bund* (German Confederation) founded in the middle of November 1810 in Berlin by the student Friedrich Friesen and the teacher, Friedrich Ludwig Jahn, a rigorous organisation, (albeit enjoying a negligible membership) disseminating propaganda aimed at 'The Survival of the German People in its Originality and Self-sufficiency, the Revival of German-ness, of all slumbering forces, the Preservation of our Nationhood . . . aiming at the eventual Unity of our scattered, divided and separated Volk'.[8] The Berlin Central Club (*Hauptverein*) numbered around 80 members in 1812, with branches in at least seven Prussian villages, as well as four outside Prussia. The 'Society for the Practice of Public Virtue' (called the *Tugendbund* for short) spread out from Königsberg, and its demands included, alongside plans for reforming the state, love of the Fatherland, *deutsche Selbstheit* (German selfhood) and military and physical prowess in order to raise all Germans into a liberally constituted unitary German state under one Emperor as the sole German sovereign. These were the early 'points of crystallisation' of a German national movement, insignificant and initially circumscribed as they were, given their small membership and their illegality. They were followed by Jahn's *Turngesellschaft* (Gymnastics Society), founded in 1811 on the Berlin Hasenheide. It was formed initially of 200 gymnasts, mostly high school pupils and students, who were subsequently joined by numerous burghers. They performed gymnastics, according to Jahn's programme as laid out in his *Deutsches Volkstum* of 1810, to strengthen not only their physiques, but also their willpower, their communal spirit and their characters. They also undertook night marches and military manoeuvres and practised fencing and crossbow-shooting so as to be ready for the uprising against the forces of occupation. It was, however, by maintaining a high profile and by setting an example in how to mobilise that the Gymnastics movement was most effective in the national pedagogical endeavours.

Firmly as the national idea had been and was entrenched in the sphere of the educated bourgeoisie, as its influence slowly increased, and third pillar of the Nationalist Movement could also be seen emerging alongside the Clubs and the Gymnastics movement: the *Deutsche Burschenschaft* (German student fraternities) was formed in close association with the German

Confederation. Established in Friesland and approved by the members of the Confederation, the 'Order and Institution of the German *Burschenschaften*' rejected the previously territorial organisation of German university students and instead promoted a union of various students in every institute of higher education to combat particularism and to promote national unity. Among the students' duties was that of 'esteeming above everything the German people and the German fatherland, and he must be German in his words, deeds and life'.[9] This programme was quickly supported by the student body of the newly founded University of Berlin, as well as the University of Jena, where the historian Heinrich Luden was an active supporter of the German Confederation.

Thus, on the eve of the War of Liberation, at the time of Napoleon's defeats in Russia, a political atmosphere was forming in which terms like 'German', 'Fatherland', 'Volk' and 'Patriotism' had become keywords. As before, the social class conducting this discourse was a small elite, but it was effective in propaganda terms over a far wider social spectrum than that of a few educated burghers and enlightened nobles.

One of the leading Prussian reformers, Colonel Neidhart von Gneisenau, had corrected the king when the latter dismissed the suggestion of an army of town burghers as 'mere poetry', with the words: 'the safety of the throne is founded on poetry'.[10] There was no shortage of poetry; it had been around for a long time, inspired by the hatred and bitterness of the patriotic educated circles, albeit suppressed by a rigorous censorship fearful of French oppression. Censorship was lifted at the beginning of the War of Liberation in March 1813, and a flood of suitably nationalist poems deluged Germany in brochures, sheets, songbooks, exhortations, magazines, pamphlets and newspapers. There was scarcely any German poet who was not gripped by the new *Zeitgeist*, and did not temporarily abandon the search for the blue flowers of romanticism to compose gruesome lyrics about hatred and killing, from Heinrich von Kleist:

> Bleach every space, field and town
> White with their bones;
> Spurned by crow and fox,
> Deliver them unto the fishes;
> Dam the Rhine with their bodies;
> Let her, swollen with their limbs
> Flood the Pfalz with foaming waves,
> May she then be our frontier!

to the gentle Clemens Brentano:

> Bayonets
> Vie with one another
> To cast the chains
> Down onto the river bed
> That no foe of Germany may survive!

These sentiments were disseminated a hundred thousandfold among the people and aroused mass enthusiasm on a totally unprecedented national scale.

'The King called, and everyone, everyone came' was how the War of Liberation later came to be viewed from the perspective of Wilhelmine Germany, and indeed, mass enthusiasm comparable in many ways to the spontaneous uprisings of the French Revolution, was indeed aroused when Frederick William III, after lengthy and timid dithering, issued his appeal 'To my People' and called on 'Prussians and Germans' to join the struggle. However, even then only specific social classes were caught up in this enthusiastic frenzy, as the muster-rolls of the Prussian Volunteer Units clearly reveal: schoolboys, students and men from the educated classes and the higher echelons of the bureaucracy provided about twelve per cent of the volunteers; which, given that these formed two per cent of the whole population, meant that the educated classes were over-represented by a factor of six. The same applied to the class comprising the remaining state employees: the middle and lower echelons of the bureaucracy, the secretaries, former soldiers, agriculturalists, rangers and foresters, to whom loyalty to the king may surely be attributed rather than any broader nationalist motive. Most glaringly apparent, however, was the considerable over-representation of another class of population, one which had not previously appeared exceptionally orientated towards nationalism: the artisans. They comprised seven per cent of the Prussian labour statistics, but provided a full forty-one per cent of the volunteer soldiery, and were thus over-represented by a factor of almost six. Written testimonials dealing specifically with this class are too few to allow any certainty about their motives, but the following may be mooted: there is much to be said for the case that this enormous mobilisation of mainly artisan apprentices had to do with the introduction of manufacturing freedom in Prussia in 1810 and the removal of obligatory guild membership, the almost complete freedom of settlement and the liberalisation of the manufacturing market. A sense of optimism about the future derived from these reforms may well have rendered this section of population particularly susceptible to the prevailing nationalist anti-French feeling.

Conclusive evidence is, finally, provided by those who were not moved by the volunteers' enthusiasm. Every other professional class was represented in the volunteer units approximately to the same extent as in the population as a whole, except for one: the peasant and sub-peasant group, which still formed at this time around three quarters of the whole population, but which contributed only eighteen per cent of the volunteers. On closer examination, these were mainly day-labourers and menservants, who presumably entered the ranks of the volunteers primarily to escape their miserable lot. The other bare five per cent of peasants came almost to a man from regions west of the Elbe and outside Prussia, whose peasantry was mostly free, whereas the only recently freed former serfs from the regions east of the Elbe scarcely ever appear among the Volunteer statistics. It may be concluded that the idea of nationhood in 1813 in Prussia – no comparable statistical source exists for the other German states – was the concern of part of the urban population, which itself comprised around twenty per cent of the whole population; as before, this included the educated classes, the higher bureaucracy, and, for different motives, the artisan class, especially the apprentices.

During the short one-and-a-half years of the War of Liberation, the volunteer bands felt themselves to be 'the nation in arms'. The emergent nationalist movement had its martyrs, more prominent among whom were the fallen poet Theodor Körner and Eleonore Prohaska who, disguised in men's clothing, fell before the enemy. The political aims of the youths and burghers who gathered together in the Freikorps appear obvious, when one looks at the prevalent programmatic lyrics, mostly rendered in song form, which were these volunteers' favourite means of expression: their subjects were mainly 'Fatherland', 'Germany' and 'Freedom' – but did they offer anything concrete? 'What is the German's Fatherland?' asked Ernst Moritz Arndt in 1813:

> Is it Prussia? Is it Swabia?
> Is it along the Rhine where the vine resides?
> Is it along the Belt where the seagull glides?
> O no! No! No!
> His Fatherland must be greater still!

It *must* be – Germany is presented as will and idea, in a purely optative form. Arndt's *Song of the Fatherland* employs felicitous couplets to run through provinces and countries in complete innocence:

> Is it the land of the Swiss? Is it Tirol?
> That land and people pleased me well.

He also rejects 'Austria, rich in honours and victories':

> The Fatherland must be greater still.

Arndt then concludes:

> As far as the German tongue rings
> And to God in Heaven Lieder sings
> That's where it should be!
> That, bold German, pertains to thee!

Germany: once again a nation determined by language, without clear frontiers, and in any event expressed only in vague poetic terms was an expression of culture, which did not project even the outline of a German nation state. A concept of nation in the sense of later unification oaths had not yet been precisely formulated in this period: the German Fatherland of the War of Liberation had no firm shape, it was poetic, historical and utopian, an ideal, which in its earthly incarnation occasionally bore the name of Prussia or Austria. Friedrich Wilhelm's appeal to his people to be 'Prussians and Germans' (which ironically enough earned him condemnation as a Jacobin by the rulers of the Rhine Confederation), characterised the temporarily unproblematic merging of Prussia and Germany.

'Freedom' was also a thoroughly ambivalent term. Contrary to later testimonials, when employed in the poetry and programmes of the War of Liberation, this term at no time expressed a longing for liberal constitutional reforms, but entirely one for national liberation from oppression by the enemy. While certain forms of expression, such as Max von Schenkendorf's extraordinarily popular song *Freedom, which I mean*, could indeed be understood two ways, and lines such as 'I enter the battlefield for the sake of Heavenly wealth and not for princes' rewards and glory' (Max von Schenkendorf) or 'It is not a war that crowns know about, it is a crusade, it's a holy war' (Theodor Körner), permit conclusions to be drawn about bourgeois self-awareness and underlying anti-aristocratic motives, nowhere are demands for freedom, despite the temporary absence of censorship in the sense of an inner political programme to be found. Consequently it is thoroughly debatable whether the nationalist movement during the War of Liberation should be seen (depending on the point of view) as evidence of a Liberal opposition, or as the precursor of the 'little Germany' nation state. The blinkered view of the years between 1813 and 1871 as a one-way street to the Bismarckian Reich, consistently maintained in historical studies, is actually based on a teleological misinterpretation. There is much evidence that the course of history could have been different, if the German rulers and, above all, the Prussian King had proceeded with the reforms and had carried out their promise to allow a representative body, at least of the educated and propertied part of the citizenry. It is possible that the loyalty of the politically active population towards their existing rulers could have been maintained; the legitimation oft he German territorial states would have been well-founded, and the future might possibly have belonged to them and to the German Confederation.

5 The nationalist movement's road from an elitist to a mass phenomenon

The opportunity to bind the loyalty of those classes participating in the political debate to the individual German states was lost in the years following the War of Liberation and the Congress of Vienna. This became apparent immediately after the war. The enormous collective spiritual impetus was followed by disenchantment and the poetry gradually faded. Above all it was the Volunteers, mainly students and artisans, who had been drawn into the war with unprecedented enthusiasm and were driven not only by a considerable need for action, a search for excitement and for a new adventurous existence, but who also attempted to equate their experiences with the words of their songs, words such as 'God', 'Freedom', 'Fatherland', 'Germany', 'Altar', 'Dedicated', 'Volk' and 'Holy'. These songs, sung and composed by them, gave rise to a new forcible and direct language, which summoned up vistas of sworn companionship and harmony, of readiness for sacrifice and a quasi-religious transcendence of the individual into the nation as a whole. The taking of Paris and the final victory over Napoleon at Waterloo marked a sudden end to this intoxication; the young people were supposed to become sensible, to return to their lecture halls, their counters and workshops. They were supposed to trust in the wisdom of the bureaucratic and princely authorities, now conferring in Vienna about how to restore Europe's ancient order, how to talk away the young Germans' dream of the unity and freedom of their Fatherland, and, in the eyes of many, how to betray it. On the economic side too, there were problems. The harvests of 1816 and 1817 were miserable, the price of wheat and bread shot up and, while the middling and great landowners were living through golden years in spite of the failed harvests, the public's purchasing power, already exhausted by the war, sank still further. The depression produced a massive number of bankruptcies among businesses which had expanded unwisely following the manufacturing reform, and it was precisely those artisan apprentices who, spurred on by their expectation of a free-enterprise future, had hastened to join the Volunteer bands in 1813, and who now saw themselves cast into an even more oppressive poverty.

The nationalist movement's change of mood was manifested for the first time at the Wartburg Festival of 18 October 1817, on the occasion of the three hundredth anniversary of Luther's nailing up of his theses at Wittenberg.

Present were mostly representatives of the German *Burschenschaften* from almost every part of Germany, who assembled on the Wartburg beneath the black, red and gold standard, the regimental colours of the Lützow Free Corps. The festival was celebrated like a divine service, and its expressive symbolism bore a clear message: should Germany not be reformed by means of a bold deed? Was it not once more a matter of freedom from foreign, oppressive powers? For the first time the issue was not freedom from the Corsican tyrant, but from the many native tyrants; the rulers were criticised in the festival speeches, albeit very moderately, for having failed to carry out the promises they made under duress to establish liberal constitutions and a united Germany. A minority went a step further: 'A big basket was then brought to the fire', a witness reported, 'filled with books, which were there publicly, in the presence of the German people, consigned to the flames in the name of Justice, the Fatherland and the Spirit of Community. This was supposed to be a righteous judgement over the wicked books, which dishonoured the Fatherland and destroyed the spirit of community; it was supposed to frighten the evil-minded and all those who, with their banal superficiality, had – alas! – marred and attenuated the ancient and chaste customs of the Volk. The title of each of those books was read out by a herald; and every time a great cry rose from those present, expressive of their indignation: Into the fire! Into the fire! Let them go to the devil! Upon which the *corpus delicti* was delivered up to the flames.'[11] Besides the 'Fatherland's books of shame' – alongside works by the playwright August von Kotzebue, accused of being a Russian agent, by Ludwig von Haller's *The Restoration of Political Sciences*, as well as the Napoleonic *Code Civil*, a Hessian wig, Prussian stays and an Austrian corporal's staff were also thrown on the fire as symbols of illiberal reaction. The merging of nationalism and Liberalism, which was to determine the development of the German nationalist movement, could already be seen here.

The Wartburg Festival publicly established the *Deutsche Burschenschaften* and their sympathising Professors as effective propagandists for the nationalist movement. They were organised mainly in the Protestant German universities and were numerically still pretty insignificant. Of the some 10,000 German students, in 1817 around 10 per cent belonged to the *Burschenschaften*. Nevertheless, the authorities considered the movement dangerous and when a Jena student called Karl Ludwig Sand murdered the writer August von Kotzebue two years later for having poured scorn on the students' ideals, the federal and state authorities reacted by issuing the Karlsbad Decrees, providing for preventive censorship, prohibition of the *Burschenschaften*, as well as of Jahn's associated Gymnastics Movement, and the dismissal of professors deemed revolutionary, such as Fries in Jena and Oken in Bonn, and supervision of the universities.

This dealt the organised nationalist movement its death blow. Although the Karlsbad Decrees were carried out very differently in the various member states of the German Confederation – hesitantly and slackly in Bavaria, Württemberg and Saxony-Weimar, for instance, yet extremely severely in Prussia, Austria and Baden – and in some states, as in the two Mecklenburgs and in the Hanse towns, gymnastic clubs managed to survive and *Burschenschaft*-like groups in the universities persisted in secret and sometimes worried the state and federal authorities. None of this mattered, however: the efficacy of the gymnastic and student bodies lay in their public appearances, their propagandist activities, their ability to render nationalist thinking perceptible by means of symbolism, and give it actuality by their example. All this now collapsed, and when even wearing traditional German costume and smoking in public, the sign of resistance against police oppression, were threatened with draconian punishments and when whole crowds of 'demagogues', 'Jacobins in bears' pelts' as the enthusiasts for German unity were called, were herded into prisons and strongholds, resignation and readiness to retreat into the prevailing Biedermeier idyll of inwardness soon set in. For a whole decade there was no organised nationalist movement in Germany, if one disregards the beginnings of apolitical pan-German organisations, such as the 'Society of German Natural Scientists and Doctors' founded in 1822 or the 'Exchange Association of German Book Dealers' of 1825.

Although people still hoped for the creation of a German nation-state, this hope had no political perspective ever since the European powers had agreed at the Congress of Vienna to arrange central Europe as they had after the Thirty Years War, not as a compact and powerful state, but as a politically splintered field balancing European interests. The German Confederation, which first saw the light of day when the Federal Act of 8 June 1815 was signed, was a loose association of 39 sovereign German states and towns and as such the proper heir to the old Empire, but it lacked legitimacy. In an age, when the norm was the powerful nation-state with the propertied classes gaining an increasing share of the power; when the idea of the *nation une et indivisible* reverberated as an echo of the American and French revolutions, and together with belief in the individual citizen's entitlement to freedom and happiness was the common property of educated Europeans, the German Confederation, actually visible only in an anachronistic Congress of Delegates in Frankfurt and in a 'Central Commission for Investigating Revolutionary Activities' in Mainz, was patently an antediluvian monster. At best, its multitude of customs restrictions, currencies and systems of measurement hindered trade and traffic; at worst it was an instrument of repression in the name of princely legitimism and a splintered nation.

The German nation on the other hand was changing more and more into an utopian projection of the past. Imperial Baron vom Stein had already demanded in his memorandum of 18 September 1812 that the constitution of the Peace of Westphalia be replaced by the renewed medieval Empire, and Max von Schenkendorf had composed the following:

German Emperor! German Emperor!
Come avenge us, come and save us,
Free your people from their chains,
Assume the crown that's meant for you!

By this he meant not the Habsburg ruler in Vienna, but Frederick Barbarossa, the Hohenstaufen Emperor buried in the Kyffhäuser mountain. Medieval history experienced a powerful boost: Freiherr vom Stein founded the *Monumenta Germaniae Historica*, a truly gigantic collection of medieval German written sources which is still being continued today. The *Niebelungenlied*, the Teutonic *Iliad*, started on its victorious progress as the monument of German national poetry and a Jena professor called Heinrich Luden (who was condemned by the authorities as a demagogue and enemy of the state) published his twelve-volume *Geschichte des deutschen Volkes*. The history of the Middle Ages, he claimed, must begin with the Germans and constantly return to them, since of all peoples they were the most worthy, and their culture was superior to all others. Johannes Voigt's *Geschichte des deutschen Ritterordens*, Friedrich von Raumer's *Geschichte der Hohenstaufen*, Gustav von Stenzel's work on the Frankish Emperors: all these were produced in the 1820s and went into numerous editions.

In this manner did nationalist themes retain their hold on public opinion, albeit in an apparently apolitical manner. Public discussion about German unity came to a complete standstill in the doldrums of that decade, and the strictly limited political debate of those years (between the demands for constitution and participation made by Southern German and Rhineland pre-Liberalism and the conservative outlines for the state drawn up by restoration-minded theorists such as Adam Müller, Friedrich Gentz and Carl Ludwig von Haller) referred exclusively to the existing particularist arrangement of the states within the German Confederation. Tendencies were however present which paved the way for the approaching disturbances inspired by demands for the nation-state. On the one hand, public life, meaning those groups of persons who took part in the political discussion about the state and society, about the economy and history, acquired a broader base. This was related to the growing rate of literacy; between 1820 and 1850 the number of pupils attending Prussian primary and middle schools rose to about 80 per cent; in the sphere of secondary education it rose by as much as threefold. The number of new books and newspapers appearing every year doubled over the same period and bookshops sprang up everywhere, even in the smallest towns. It is estimated that adult literacy rates rose from about 15 per cent in 1770 to around 40 per cent in 1830: this was indeed a 'reading revolution' (Rolf Engelsing), which ensured that opinions, programmes, catchwords and appeals could now strike not only at the educated middle class elite, but at a huge public.

All this resulted in a huge gulf opening up between state and society. The reforms in individual states petered out; economic modernisation by means of agrarian, manufacturing and tax reforms entailed considerable social costs. Alongside the descent of countless smallholders and peasants with inadequate titles to their land into an increasingly destitute agricultural proletariat, it became obvious that it was precisely the urban class which had been most optimistic about the manufacturing reforms, i.e. the artisan class which, once deprived of the protection of the guilds, had been helplessly exposed to market forces and were to a large extent threatened by economic and social decline. Within the social body, dangerous lines of tension and cracks were building up beneath the surface of bourgeois self-sufficiency, to such an extent that the Prussian reformer's recourse to the 'arsenal of revolution' (Gneisenau) did not remain unpunished. It was not possible to introduce universal military service, to improve national education and manipulate public opinion so as to raise it to a pitch of wild excitement during the War of Liberation, and then to count on the people knuckling down permanently under the educational measures of an enlightened bureaucratic elite. These growing social tensions were accompanied by bitterness over the broken promises about a constitution and over a ruling class which, horrified by the radical tones of the opposition's public voice and fearful of a repeat of the French Revolution on German soil, tightened the screws of censorship and tried to control by police methods the demand that economic freedom be tied to political participation.

The July Revolution of 1830 in France, which electrified all Europe, drove the question of nation to the fore again. While the reactionary Bourbon King Charles X and his Prime Minister Polignac were replaced in Paris by the bourgeois King Louis Philippe of Orléans, the United Kingdom of the Netherlands, which had only been formed in 1815, was split in half when the overwhelmingly Catholic Flemish and Walloon part of the population revolted and combined to form a neutral Belgian state with a Liberal constitution. A rising in Poland in the winter of 1830–1 drove the Russian troops out of the country for a few months, and bloody rebellions broke out in the central Italian states. Central Europe did not remain unaffected by the revolutionary changes at the continent's periphery; the events in France and even more in Belgium had a direct impact on the Rhineland, and the Polish example enthused German Liberals to such an extent that the Prussian authorities were worried. In Germany, as everywhere else in Europe, social, Liberal-constitutional and nationalist tendencies were all interconnected. Social tensions found an outlet in a series of violent local conflicts – from Jülich to Prague and from Chemnitz to Vienna riots over price-rises and unemployment were unleashed and the Liberal privileged classes in those north German towns which had remained without a constitution used the disturbances to demand moderate constitutional reforms of their intimidated governments. In Braunschweig, Saxony, Hanover and Kurhessen, they managed to get their delegates recalled and to introduce a Liberal constitution as well as agrarian and administrative reforms of varying effectiveness. For its part, Prussia scarcely felt the effects of the July Revolution – some pressure may have been removed by the introduction of provincial parliaments (*Landtage*) in 1823, and the Prussian burghers' loyalty dating from the time of the War of Liberation had not yet been quenched.

Two factors became apparent during the 1830 movement: first, that the Liberal movement was a pan-European phenomenon, and that to that extent the fears of the sovereign rulers at the Congress of Vienna which had resulted in the formation of the 'Holy Alliance' had been justified; second, that the Liberal, constitutional and social currents of the time were all pursuing a common cause, that of the national principle. The whole of Europe was now repeating what had started with the French Revolution in 1789: the traditional, anti-national states of the later absolutist era appeared administratively cumbersome and weak in legitimacy in an age of accelerated social change. Freedom in the Liberal sense, unity in the national sense: these were the ideologies which permeated collective views of the world and carried the promise of future felicity.

The political shocks of the 1830s dispelled the mood of resignation which had characterised political life in Germany during the previous ten years. In some states, especially Baden, censorship was eased and an intense journalistic debate broke out. Demands for a German nation-state with a single executive head, and above all for a national parliament could be heard on all sides; Wilhelm Schulz, a Darmstadt journalist, published a much-read text on *Germany's Unity through National Representation* and Paul Pfizer, the Leader of the Opposition in the Second chamber of the Baden Landtag, advised Germans to take a lesson from the French: 'Germany has long been ill served by the mere principles of bourgeois freedom . . . The longings of individuals for freedom notwithstanding, Germans will always play a despicable role and, for all their enthusiasm, they will, on account of their weak compliance, earn only a pitying smile from foreign countries for as long as they do not desire freedom as a Nation and even appear to believe that dependence on foreign countries is what the Germans mean by Liberty.'[12] This struck a new tone: Germany as a nation-state grounded on the sovereignty of the people – in stark contrast to the nationalistic dreams of the 1813 patriots. Even more of a contrast was his view of France, not as Germany's enemy, but as her model.

The extent to which the nationalist movement had turned around became apparent two years later at the *Alldeutschesfest* ('All-Germans festival') held on the ruins of Schloss Hambach at Haardtrand bei Neustadt. The invitations had been issued by the 'German Press and Fatherland Association', an association called into being under nationalist-unification and Liberal-constitutional auspices by journalists Johann August Wirth and Johann Jacob Siebenpfeiffer, and composed of *Landtag* delegates, journalists and liberal dignitaries mainly from the Pfalz. This organisation was in the mainstream of traditional middle-class associations, and for a few months it became the focus of Liberal and nationalist public opinion in the South-Western area, with local branches as far afield as Thuringia and North Germany. Various forces and tendencies of the opposition gathered together on the Hambach castle – while a purposely simultaneous solemn celebration in memory of the proclamation of the Bavarian constitution took place in Munich. This was the 'first political popular assembly in the history of modern Germany' (Theodor Heuss), at which not only dissatisfied burghers, artisans and students came together, but also thousands of protesting Pfalz peasants, who demonstrated beneath a black banner. Alongside speeches demanding a Liberal constitution, radical and democratic voices hostile to princes and aristocrats were also raised, as if the ghosts of the 'German Jacobins' of the 1790s had returned; talk about the social revolution could also be heard. What bound these thoroughly heterogeneous voices, groups and interests together was nevertheless the idea of nationhood. 'Freedom, enlightenment, nationality and popular sovereignty' were demanded by the main speaker Johann August Wirth both for Germans and for other oppressed and divided European peoples, but he also made it quite clear where his priorities lay: first with the unity of the Fatherland; the ruin of the aristocratic ruling class would inevitably bring about popular sovereignty, and Alsace and Lorraine would automatically find themselves back within the united and liberated Fatherland.[13]

Moderate Liberals such as Karl von Rotteck, the Freiburg historian and Baden parliamentarian, were already apprehensive that the radical democratic and nationalist undertone to the Hambach Festival would inevitably summon the forces of reaction onto the scene. And that is indeed what happened. After the news of the events in Hambach had given rise to similar announcements in other places, with scattered attempts at insurrection as well, the German Confederation replied by introducing 'Regulations for Maintaining Peace and Order as required by Law' on 28 June and 5 July 1832. Thus was the brief and false spring of the July Revolution brought to an end; the Federal authorities tightened censorship, vetoed the Liberal press law in Baden and prohibited every form of freedom of association and assembly. Although the signs had already been present in 1830, it became increasingly obvious in the light of the strengthened repression that the Liberal and nationalist party was split. On one side was a wing consisting of wealthy Liberal burghers which was principally supported by the Liberal factions within state parliaments; it was biased towards a monarchical constitution and looked for a solution to the nationalist question within the framework of the existing constitution. This side also included an early industrial elite located overwhelmingly in the Rhineland, linked to the higher Prussian, Hessian and Bavarian bureaucracies. On the other side were the radical newspaper-editors, lawyers, student societies, artisans and peasants, who had come together during the struggles of 1830 and at Hambach castle. Their demands for a German nation-state were already couched in democratic and republican language. The idea of nation bound both these factions together: it was coming increasingly into the foreground as the fundamental opposition idea of the age.

If the events of 1830 and 1832 had already demonstrated that the influence of the national question spread far further than its former elitist public, ten years later on nationalism was finally established as a mass phenomenon. The breaking point was provided by the Rhine crisis of 1840, which was unleashed when the Thiers government in France attempted to compensate for the hard blow dealt to France's eastern policy and the ensuing crisis of nationalist fervour by instigating an aggressive eastern policy and propagating for the first time since 1815 the re-establishment of the Rhine as a 'natural' frontier.

The German reaction was very measured – to start off with. The cabinet ministers of the leading states in the German Confederation, headed by Prince Metternich, the Austrian Court and State Chancellor, conducted themselves wholly in the tradition of the Congress of Vienna by attempting to 'de-nationalise' the question of the Rhine frontier and to treat it as a matter involving all the European powers. Metternich in particular had reason to fear the nationalistic motives behind French policy, in which he could see the revolutionary principle directed against the European system of peace. German public opinion responded equally moderately on a purely academic and rhetorical level, as always when the national question was raised. The Rhineland newspaper reports about the debates in the Paris *chambre des députés* and about the signs of a French mobilisation were almost devoid of emotion, whereas the South German press was already engaged in a lively campaign against 'our neighbour's treacherous intentions', explaining in innumerable articles that France's demands for a new frontier affected not only Prussians, Badeners or Bavarians, but all Germans.

During the autumn of 1840, however, given the open demands for war by the leftist French press and the news of concentrations of troops in Alsace, the general concern grew, especially in Western and Southern Germany. Government ministers in Berlin and Vienna did all they could to calm the situation by their obvious restraint. The German Confederation's preparations for its common defence, above all in south-western Germany, were characterised by their Biedermeier cosiness and inadequacy. Along with the population's fear of a re-enactment of the horrors of war, which had overwhelmed the Rhineland a generation ago, the national impetus grew. Since public opinion was throttled by censorship of the press and the prohibition of assembly, the dammed-up tide of popular emotion was at breaking point. This is how the social and psychological phenomenon of the 'Rhine-song-movement' can be explained, by which the idea, to use Karl Marx's terminology, gripped the masses for the first time and was transformed into a material force. On 18 September 1840 a poem by an unknown assistant clerk-of-the-court, Nikolas Becker, was published in the *Trierische Zeitung*:

> The German Rhine
>
> . . .
>
> They shall not have it,
> Our free German Rhine,
> Though like greedy crows
> They hoarsely cry for it.
>
> So long as it softly wells
> And bears its green mantle
> So long as a rudder splashes
> Cleaving a path through its swell!
>
> They shall not have it,
> Our free German Rhine,
> So long as hearts are beating
> Along its glowing vines,
>
> So long as in its stream,
> The rocks still stand firm,
> So long as lofty domes
> Are reflected in its mirror!
>
> . . .
>
> They shall not have it,
> Our free German Rhine,
> Until its flood has buried
> The limbs of our last man!

The poem was unremarkable both as literature and as original thought, but it provided the right words at the right moment. Within a month, there was not a German newspaper which had not printed it; a real Rhine-song fervour united the upper and lower classes; the song was sung in streets and salons from Cologne to Königsberg, from Hamburg to Stuttgart. The number of tunes set to it was legion, and competitions brought in hundreds of entries. Nor did the greatest composers of the century, from Robert Schumann to Konradin Kreutzer to Heinrich Märschner, shrink from setting the Becker hymn to music. In spite of the innumerable tunes set to it, the Rhine song was soon hailed as the German national anthem, as a 'German Marseillaise', and in its wake came a flood of further nationalist compositions and songs about the *Volk*, among which Max Scheckenburgher's *Wacht am Rhein* (Watch on the Rhine), which achieved its greatest success in a slightly altered form only in 1870. Hoffmann von Fallersleben's *Deutschlandlied* was also created in the wake of the Rhein-song movement.

The emotions of the masses were aroused, much as they had been in the spring of 1813. The themes, the terminology and the enemy were the same, and the Rhine motif developed into a hugely effective symbol of the nationalist movement and epitomised the aspirations of a generation attuned to romantic and heroic themes. The parallel with 1813 was also apposite in that the idea of nation lost its inner political and oppositional profile during the Rhine crisis, thus allowing the semblance of unity between rulers and people to be re-established. The new Prussian King Friedrich Wilhelm IV and the Grand Duke of Baden voiced their sympathies for the newly awoken mass nationalism, and for the first time in German history the government cabinets of the Federal states felt a sort of push from below, which forced them to take political action. Metternich sensed the danger emanating from mass opinion and he opposed the urgings of Prussia and several middle states to reform the Confederation's military constitution and to instigate countermeasures. The two leading powers of the German Confederation ended nevertheless by agreeing in November 1840, with express reference to the 'nationalist attitude' and its demands, on a common plan of operation in the event of war. In the following year the Federal Parliament decided to establish federal strongholds at Rastatt and Ulm.

The Rhine crisis of 1840 petered out when the Thiers administration was sacked by the king at the end of October and replaced by the Guizot government, which returned to the politics of an European balance of power. In Germany however, more had been set in motion than the strategists of the Vienna system had hoped for. Nationalism had been revealed as a political force of the first rank. Now, beyond the song movements and lyrical fashions, could be discerned the motifs, which during political crises could provide mass-unrest with the catchwords and explicit content capable of bunching all the different tendencies together. Although the left wing of the nationalist movement, which had set the tone at the Hambach Festival, was still fiercely critical of the boisterous German unilateralism and the emotional anti-French feeling of the Rhine-song movement, the leaders of the Liberal democrats (mostly resident in foreign lands) such as Georg Herwegh, Karl Gutzkow or Robert Prutz, for whom Germany's domestic political freedom came before national unity, and whose models were French liberal traditions, broke away. It was precisely those renowned protagonists of the left wing, such as Johann August Wirth, who had organised the Hambach Festival, and Jakob Venedy and August Ludwig von Rochau, the émigré publicists and poets, who now provided glowing declarations of solidarity.

Hence the new emphasis of the nationalist question in the public mind of the 1840s, when this theme appeared to have sunk into resignation since the vigorous Liberal actions of the July Revolution and the Hambach Festival. National organisations could now no longer be prevented: in 1842 the

Prussian prohibition of gymnastics was raised and the gymnastic movement spread out over the whole of Germany, and with it Jahn's ideological mixture of physical fitness, character training and nationalist aspirations. On the eve of the 1848 revolution there must have been about 300 gymnastic clubs in Germany, with a total membership of 90,000: a considerable potential; disciplined, physically fit and capable of political mobilisation.

Parallel to this was the spread of the singing societies; their emphasis upon the supreme importance of music and lyricism for the massive dissemination of programmatic terms and catchwords was conducive to the nationalisation of German public opinion. Patriotic singing societies, choral societies, and glee clubs started off as regional organisations, but already by 1845 the first 'German choral festival' took place in Würzburg, with 15,000 members of 95 singing societies from all parts of Germany. Further pan-German choral festivals in Cologne and Lübeck followed. The first pan-German learned congress, the 'Germanist Days' in Frankfurt in 1846 and in Lübeck the year after, stressed the unity of learning and the idea of nation.

The forties were also flourishing years for the national-monument movement, which was carried mainly by middle-class associations, albeit also dependent on subsidies from princely treasuries, whether the project was plans for the Hermann monument in the Teutoburg Forest or the Walhalla near Regensburg, which was opened in 1842, or the Hall of Liberation near Kelheim, which began to be built in 1842. The Cologne Cathedral Building Association, which, as a German national monument, promoted the completion of the largest German ecclesiastical building, was organised on the basis of local associations as far afield as Austria and East Prussia, and the Cologne Cathedral Building Festival of 1842 demonstrated a transient, but (given its potential) increasingly visible unity between crowns and people, Catholicism and Protestantism, the Prussian state and Rhinish self-awareness, under the banner of national unity.

This was one aspect of the *Vormärz*, the pre-March period: the growing formation and organisation of the nation as a cultural entity (*Kulturnation*). At the same time, however, the crisis of the political and economic systems sharpened. As in 1815 and later 1830 the liberal burgherdom had counted on a general introduction of constitutional conditions in the years 1840–2, and it was once again frustrated in its expectations. This disappointment was aired in a widespread public discussion about the question of a constitution, which was already almost generally envisaged within a national framework. In 1847 the highpoint was reached when the *Deutsche Zeitung* was founded to act as the mouthpiece of nationalist and constitutional demands on the part of bourgeois Liberalism. Alongside this was ranged the growing political opposition of the Liberal factions within the second chamber of the South German Parliaments and in the Prussian provincial ruling bodies. Political Catholicism was also being organised as the opposition to Prussian administration and cultural policy in the Western provinces and in Silesia.

Here too, within the sphere of the *Historisch-Politischen Blätter für das katholische Deutschland* (*Historical and Political newsheets for Catholic Germany*) founded by Joseph Görres in 1838, demands for an united German nation state, albeit with emphasis on the ancient Empire and under the leadership of the Catholic Habsburgs, were fermenting. In the second half of the decade, democratic radicalism rose anew in south-western Germany and Saxony, which put no trust in constitutional guarantees to safeguard freedom, and envisaged Germany as a democratic republic. In Baden and the Pfalz especially, this line of thought found significant support among the lower middle classes and the agrarian population.

This multiform national opposition received its explosive charge from the growing impoverishment of the society and economy. Pauperism in all its misery, essentially due to the Malthusian consequences of overpopulation, came to the fore. During the years 1815–48 the total population of Germany had grown from 22 million to 35 million persons, that is, by a good third within a single generation. Agriculture, in spite of being modernised as a result of the reforms, was incapable of taking on, let alone feeding, this mass of people. The misery of the landless peasant population – cottagers and day-labourers – assumed immense proportions, without the authorities being able to assuage it. Those who made the move to the city fared no better; they simply swelled the army of unskilled casual workers, who were happy if they could earn enough to pay the rent for their pitiful mass accommodation hastily erected by speculators, and so avoid being driven into the workhouses. The frequently horrendous poverty was exacerbated by the changing social structure, shifting from an artisan to an industrial base. Whole sectors of artisan production, in particular domestic manufacturing, were unable to meet competition from cheap factory products – inhuman hours of work, child labour, starvation wages and scarcely imaginable living conditions were the result.

Social catastrophe (its impact was to diminish only during the intensive industrialisation of the second half of the century) was matched by economic misery. Towards the end of the forties two crises occurred: one (1846–7) was the latest economic crisis of the 'old' type, a starvation and manufacturing crisis unleashed by failed harvests and the ensuing enormous rise in price of basic foods with wages remaining level. On top of this came (1847–8) a 'modern' crisis of industrial growth, conjured up by the collapse of the consumer-goods economy.

As always when economic crises coincide with a crisis of political legitimacy, the protest movement gained considerably in strength. Of the three main opposition ideas; nationalism, the Liberal constitution and the social protest movement, it was the idea of nation as a prevailing standard of legitimacy which served to bind together the other, in part contradictory, factions making up the party of protest. There was constitutional Liberalism, whose leading exponents met up on 10 October 1847 at Heppenheim on the

Bergstrasse to demand a German federal state with a powerful central government answerable to parliament. There was democratic Radicalism in the aftermath of the 1830s movement, which announced its programme on 12 September 1847 at a gathering in Offenburg when plans for a republican nation state were laid. There were also the first socialist clusters around Friedrich Hecker, Wilhelm Weitling, Moses Hess and the radical German émigré associations in Switzerland, France and England. This chorus of many voices was held together by the all-embracing demand for the establishment of a German nation-state. The March Revolution of 1848, notwithstanding its social and liberal driving forces, was principally a national revolution.

7 1848: The whole of Germany it shall be

As in 1831 it all started with the news from Paris: once again a king had been dethroned, and there had been fighting at the barricades and revolutionary martyrs. Rioting broke out in the streets of almost every German capital. In the parliaments the moderate Liberal and democratic radical opposition was demanding freedom of the press, freedom of assembly, authorisation of political parties and the arming of the people (the establishment of citizen militias, to provide a bourgeois counterweight to the individual states armies, the guarantors of the old order). Finally, they crowned this subversion by demanding a German National Parliament. These March demands were followed by the March governments – everywhere, from Saxony to Baden, from Bavaria to Oldenburg, new cabinets consisting of Liberal dignitaries were formed. In Heidelberg delegates from the Liberal factions in the south German parliaments met up to found a pre-parliament, the first step to a national representative body for all Germans. Once again the nation succumbed to the optimism of spring and, without encountering very considerable opposition, the black-red-gold banner of the national move- ment waved over nearly all Germany.

Everything now depended on how the two leading powers of the German Confederation, Austria and Prussia, proceeded. The events of the March revolution in Berlin have been extensively told. They ended provisionally with the humiliation of king and army, the pillars of the absolutist régime, with the armament of the burghers, the appointment of a Liberal ministry and Friedrich Wilhelm's statement: 'Prussia is henceforth merged into Germany.'

In Vienna events went at first much as in the German middle states; already by mid March, however, the moderate Liberal element had been swept aside by a flood of more radical revolutionaries. Radical democratic students formed the spearhead of a broad popular movement, which secured the withdrawal of the army and Metternich's resignation. Meanwhile a workers' revolt was raging in the Vienna suburbs; pawnbrokers' shops, factories and tax offices were stormed and shops were looted. Although the movement took a radical turn similar to events in Berlin, it was not appeased as it was there by the monarch's clever response. Metternich fled to England, the Austrian court escaped to Innsbruck, while in Vienna a sort of revolutionary alternative government in the form of a hydra-headed 'security committee' was installed. In the Italian provinces, in Hungary and in Bohemia national movements rose up against the central authority of the Habsburgs, which combined rebellion against Metternich's repressive system of government with revolt against German hegemony in a state made up of many peoples. Within a few weeks, Austria, the predominant power within the German Confederation and the guarantor of Metternich's 'System', was politically unviable and it was apparently only a matter of time before it collapsed.

In spite of being wholly spontaneous and unplanned, events developed at first according to the schedule envisaged by pre-March Liberal theory. After internal freedom was established in the separate German states, the foundations of national unity were laid by the German National Assembly, which met at Mainz on 18 May 1848, in order to draw up a Liberal constitution for the whole of Germany and to elect a national government. The 585 delegates formed a parade of the greatest names of intellectual and Liberal Germany. Poets like Ludwig Uhland and Friedrich Theodor Vischer were elected, as were leaders from the time of the War of Liberation, Ernst Moritz Arndt and Friedrich Ludwig Jahn. Remarkable too was the number of historians represented, people like Friedrich Christoph Dahlmann, Johann Gustav Droysen and Georg Gottfried Gervinus, as well as priests like Wilhelm Emanuel Freiherr von Ketteler, Bishop of Mainz and a social theorist. It also included the leaders of political liberalism in its various hues, old Liberals like Heinrich von Gagern as much as republicans like Gustav von Struve or Jakob Venedey. Three quarters of the delegates were academics with one in five a professor, another one in five was a judge or a lawyer, and only around a sixth of the delegates came from commercial professions, that is to say, were shopkeepers, bankers or manufacturers. Even by the middle of the nineteenth century, the educated classes were still the real champions of the idea of national unification.

The first task undertaken by the National Assembly was the only one to be carried through successfully. By 28 June 1848 they had already agreed on establishing a provisional German central government, with the Austrian archduke John at its head as the *Reichsverweser* (Imperial Administrator), 'not because, but in spite of his being a prince', as Heinrich von Gagern, the Parliamentary President, stressed. The *Reichsverweser* immediately nominated a *Reichs* ministry under the prime minister-ship of the Liberal prince Karl von Leiningen: the first German government to be legitimised by parliament. The next two steps ensued automatically. The National Assembly had to provide the new German nation-state, founded on popular sovereignty and human rights, with a constitution, and the provisional nature of the Empire's central authority obliged it to establish its mandate in Germany. It was however poorly equipped for such a task. When the *Reich*'s war minister, Eduard von Pecker, himself a Prussian general, arranged for all German troops to pay their solemn respects to the *Reichsverweser* and to adopt the German colours, he was obeyed only by the majority of the small and medium states, while Austria, Prussia, Bavaria, Saxony and Württemberg abstained discreetly from the proposed undertaking. In September too, the agreed proportional contributions supposed to finance the *Reich*'s expenses, proceeded slackly and were wholly inadequate. The central authority of the *Reich* was hardly more than an assembly of a few idealist Liberals, whose power extended no further than the session-chamber door.

Not only in Germany, but all over Europe national movements were rising up and demanding independence. The Revolution of 1848 was an European revolution against the principles established in 1815. The Congress of Vienna's dispositions for peace in Europe had been the last attempt at arranging the continent in terms of the international balance of power by means of rational policies made in cabinet. This peace had lasted a whole generation, longer than ever before in the history of Europe, but the longer the rigid system of the Holy Alliance was sustained, the more it conflicted with the fundamental dynamism of the social and economic forces which had been released by the waning of feudalism and the onset of industrialisation, and which were calling for a new order and the introduction of new ways of thinking. The European state system relied on a splintered Central Europe and on the counter-revolutionary alliance between the three non-national and reactionary pillars of the pentarchy – Russia, Austria and Prussia. The full force of the new secular creeds – nationalism and liberalism – was consequently directed against the survival of these Empires and against the European system of peace in particular, among whose guarantors were France and England, the western pillars of the pentarchy. The problem was further complicated by the creation of a big nation-state within Europe, whose very existence contravened the principles established in 1815, and whose nationalist impact was felt deep within the spheres of interest of other regions and other nationalities.

Take for instance the Schleswig-Holstein affair. The State of Denmark also comprised many peoples; besides the Danish regions of Jutland and the islands, it included the dukedoms of Schleswig, Holstein and Lauenburg, which were tied to the Danish crown through personal union, but were inhabited by a majority German population and were endowed with their own common law and inheritance rights, thus giving them limited autonomy. Since the beginning of the 1840s the nationalist Liberal 'Eiderdanish' movement had been demanding Schleswig's integration in the Danish part of the kingdom; the conflict between the German and Danish populations in the dukedoms was followed with passion (and even incited) by nationalist public opinion in Germany as well as Denmark, both ready to flare up. Following the accession of a new Danish ruler in January 1848 and the ascendancy of the Eiderdanish party in Copenhagen, the Estates of Schleswig-Holstein proclaimed their independence of Denmark on 24 March 1848 and appealed to the Federal Parliament (*Bundestag*), and then to the National Assembly at Frankfurt for help.

German public opinion was very deeply concerned about the Schleswig-Holstein affair. The German '*irredenta*' lay to the north of the Elbe and, in the eyes of the German nationalist movement, national representation, that is, the National Assembly and its provisional central authority, could only be legitimised when it had succeeded in absorbing the dukedoms within the nation. But the National Assembly had no powers and had to borrow Prussian troops which then carved their way deep into Jutland. Their action summoned the other European powers onto the scene, whose attitude towards German efforts at unification had been sceptical from the start, and who now saw their fears substantiated by the German nationalist movement's acquisition of lands pertaining to the Danish Crown. The British Ambassador in Berlin lectured the Prussian government and told it that its policy must be 'adjusted to the system of international law, the best guarantee of peace, which the enthusiasts of German Unification seek so eagerly to overcome, and which the apostles of disorder strive with such great success to consign to contempt and oblivion . . .'[14]

Disorder: this, in the eyes of the European cabinets, was German unification; an outright rebellion against the principles of the European balance of power. British warships appeared in the North Sea, Russian troops performed manoeuvres at Prussia's eastern frontier and French envoys demanded guarantees for the continuing sovereignty of the individual German states. Massive pressure by the European powers forced Prussia to withdraw its troops from Schleswig-Holstein and to make peace with Denmark, despite vociferous protests by the Frankfurt Parliament.

Whole worlds lay between nationalist enthusiasm and nationalist reality, as was revealed by the debate over the purview of the forthcoming *Reichsverfassung* (constitution). 'The whole of Germany it shall be'; the debate took place beneath Arndt's motto, and, as with every professorial debate, it made all sorts of extravagant claims. 'Austria is not to be considered for inclusion in the German federal state which is to be established', pronounced Heinrich von Gagern, whose solution was a 'little Germany' along the lines of the existing *Zollverein* (Customs Union), for which reason he also voted for the Prussian king as the future German Emperor. Such were the firm frontiers, the clear outlines and sensible solutions proposed – had Austria's power not been broken up into a state of many peoples by revolutionary confusion, had Friedrich Wilhelm IV not acknowledged his adherence to the ideals of German unification and freedom? This solution could appeal only to the mind, not to the heart; since 1813 Germany had extended 'as far as the German tongue rings out' and consequently all factions within the National Assembly were roused to opposition. They conjured up a variety of references to the 'palisade of the

Carpathians', the 'insurmountable barrier of the Tyrol', Bohemia 'the head and front of Germany', as well as to the civilising German missions to the East and the Balkans. The fact that other nations were also fighting for freedom and independence in these places carried scarcely any weight in the Paulskirche debates.

Then there was the Polish question: the National Assembly decided, in spite of opposition from part of the leftist faction, on integrating all the parts of Posen mainly settled by Germans into the German state – given the medley of tongues prevailing in the eastern provinces of Prussia there was undoubtedly no solution which could have done equal justice to the nationalistic demands of the Germans and Poles living there, but the principle of 'when in doubt, for Germany' governed the German National Assembly's decision, as it did with the Bohemian question. On 28 October the National Assembly decided (with only 80 votes against) that the Austrian states within the German Confederation should belong to the new Germany: the Czech nation's demands for autonomy were dismissed by delegates of the Right with mainly power-political arguments, and by those of the Left with cultural and humanistic arguments. The Italian Tyrolese demands for automony were rejected with considerable annoyance with reference to the history of the Empire ('a near betrayal of the nation', according to Heinrich von Gagern), and the Duchy of Limburg, a possession of the Netherlands, was proclaimed an exclusively inner-German area. Great Germany under the Habsburg Emperor, the newly awakened old Empire anointed with a drop of the holy oil of Liberalism and popular-sovereignty; that was the aim, which the majority of the dignitaries assembled in the Paulskirche had dreamt up.

This was, however, little more than shadow boxing, with no practical results. In a revolution the victory goes to whoever can solve the question of power to his advantage, and the Paulskirche was completely powerless. This became clear even to the most entrenched idealist when democratic radicalism, which had hitherto been upstaged by bourgeois Liberalism, threw down the gauntlet, demanding the republic and popular sovereignty, an united state and egalitarian democracy. These were the demands of the second revolution, carried by Liberals of the extreme left, but also by intellectuals and artisans, who were already calling for a social and red Revolution. The call for direct action grew louder, and references to parliament as a Liberal talking-shop began circulating for the first time in German history. On 18 September 1848 radical democrats tried to storm the Paulskirche; two conservative delegates were killed in the milling crowd and the terrified people's representatives had to be hauled out by Prussian and Austrian troops. These events proved to be but a smaller version of the future course of the revolution. All at once, the educated and propertied Liberal middle classes realised they had taken on the role of the sorcerers apprentice, who is incapable of dismissing the forces he has conjured up. Unity and freedom had been on the agenda, not revolt, bloodshed and danger to property; faced with radical uprisings in the Rhineland, the Pfalz, in Hessen, Baden and Central Germany, they were inclined hastily to consolidate what had been achieved and to combine with the old powers to ensure security and order.

Austria and Prussia, the old powers, had in the meantime recovered from the shock of revolution. After the events of March, the end of the Habsburg monarchy had seemed to be nigh, but the revolutions in Austria had finished by paralysing one another – the constitutional, social and national movements all intermingled and the collapse of the Empire and loss of German supremacy seemed to the German middle classes intent on the black-red-gold banner to constitute a greater disadvantage than did compromise with crown and army. This allowed Field-Marshals Windischgrätz and Radetzky to ignore the danger in their rear and to deploy their armies, with some assistance from Russian troops, in Hungary, Bohemia and Northern Italy, to defeat the rebel armies there, and finally, at the end of October 1848, to take Vienna from the radicals.

In Prussia, the course of events was similar; here too, a Prussian National Assembly had laboured throughout the summer and deep into autumn to draft a constitution, a Liberal charter with a strong parliamentary flavour, a reduced royal prerogative and the creation of a popular militia. All this displeased Friedrich Wilhelm IV, and when labour riots also broke out in Berlin, and the moderate Liberal citizen militias found themselves fighting at the barricades against the forces of 'street democracy', it was easy for the military party to win the king over to coup-like proceedings against the Prussian National Assembly. On 8 April 1848 troops under General von Wrangel moved unopposed into the capital and drove the parliament out of town. The king authorised a constitution, which was firmly biased towards the original draft constitution. By the end of 1848 the counter-revolution had prevailed in Berlin and in Vienna, the centres of real power in Germany, and the terrified middle classes were only too ready to be reconciled with the old powers in exchange for constitutional concessions.

The rest of the story is tragi-comedy. In Frankfurt an agreement had been reached in the meantime to restrict the whole-German constitution to the territory of the German Confederation as determined in 1815. Paragraph 2 went as follows: 'No part of the German Empire may unite with non-German states to become one state.' Six months previously this might well have been a realistic proposition, but the newly strengthened Austrian government was not in the least prepared to hand over its recently acquired victory to the non-German nationalities in the multi-national state for the sake of the proposed German nation-state. This left only the unpopular solution of a 'little Germany', the unification of Germany under Prussian leadership. On 3 April 1849 a profoundly moved delegation from the Paulskirche Parliament appeared before Frederick William IV to present him with the German Imperial crown. He, however, had forgotten his nationalistic sentiments of the previous March, but not the humiliations to which he had been exposed, and he rejected the 'hoop of mud and clay' hung about with 'the carrion stench of revolution'. Not all his reasons were so silly. Apart from his hatred of revolution, apart from his belief that the right to rule rested not on parliamentary majority decisions, but on God-given legitimacy, and apart from his respect for the Habsburgs' more ancient historical claims to the Imperial crown, there was also his well-founded fear that such a step would lead to war with Austria. As a peace-loving king, who avoided all forms of conflict, he was not prepared to engage in a new Seven Years War.

With this the German revolution folded, the Paulskirche assembly fell apart, and the ghostly re-appearance of a rump parliament in Stuttgart was put a stop to by Württenberg dragoons on 18 June 1849. Four weeks later the German Confederation's Congress of delegates, the *Bundestag*, convened again in Frankfurt just as if nothing had happened.

When the revolution collapsed, so too did the dream of establishing an all-German nation-state based on Liberal principles. However, the revolution had also brought clarity to many things; for the first time, Germans realised that their nationalist hopes were one thing, and the reality in Europe another. In the eastern part of Central Europe, it had been demonstrated that a clear-cut divide between German, Polish and Czech ambitions was not feasible, and that by despising the nationalist wishes of its eastern neighbours, the German national movement had lost its innocence. The national question in eastern Europe was, however, not to be solved unless by renunciation or indeed conquest, when supra-national ideas of order had lost their legitimacy. Furthermore, it had been exemplarily demonstrated how narrowly the limits of toleration for the German nationalist movement were drawn within the European framework. Every attempt to found a German nation-state at the expense of the European balance of power established in 1815 foundered against the determined opposition of other European states.

Finally, too, the verbal battles within the Paulskirche had thrashed out the question of what the German Fatherland was. The alternatives were either great-Germany under Habsburg leadership and incorporating the Austrian part of the German Confederation, or little Germany, without Austria and under Prussian hegemony.

8 On the road to a national economy

The revolution was over, great hopes had evaporated leaving only disenchantment and the rejection of unsuccessful 'idealistic' policies. A book appeared in 1853, which was written by a former *Burschenschaft* member and revolutionary called August Ludwig von Rochau and entitled *Principles of Realpolitik, with reference to political conditions in Germany*. Those radical democrats who had not chosen the path of emigration turned into sensible observers of the prevailing conditions; the Liberal middle classes came to terms with the state of affairs and settled down into commercial or learned professions or, as loyal servitors of both the people and the crown, got themselves elected to the second chambers of the various Parliaments (*Landtage*). One thing had however been achieved. In every German state, in Prussia especially, the rulers had committed themselves to constitutional norms and had come to share their legislative power with the parliamentary forces.

In any case, the liberalism of the propertied middle classes had also won, in so far as the economic revival benefited from the political doldrums of the fifties. After all, was not involvement in economic matters also a means of drawing closer to their nationalist goal? This is what Friedrich Motz, the Prussian Minister of Finance, had realised as early on as the twenties, when he attempted to remove the nuisance of an economically splintered Germany and the muddle of the different customs duties and currencies in the 39 states. An economic alliance 'resting on shared interests and natural foundations' should be established between the states of the German Confederation, Motz pointed out in a memorandum addressed to Frederick William III, since only then would 'once again a really united, and a truly free Germany, both inwardly and outwardly, rise up and flourish under Prussia's care and protection'.[15] Motz then used a combination of stick and carrot to rationalise northern Germany in economic terms, similar to the earlier attempt to standardise her military and political frontiers. Since 1828 Hessen-Darmstadt and a few Thuringian dukedoms had belonged to the Prussian Customs Union. Württemberg and Bavaria on the other hand, as well as Hanover, Saxony and Hessen-Kassel, had all (particularly the latter group) entered into regional customs unions with one another in order to obstruct Prussia's economic power, in which they were also supported by Austria and France.

However, the advantages of the Prussian Customs Union were obvious and the enthusiasm (as broadcast by a publisher in Stuttgart called Johann Friedrich Cotta) of both southern German kingdoms for entering into a customs union with Prussia increased so much that the Central German Commercial Association, which was entirely opposed to Prussia's commercial and political hegemony in northern Germany, found itself in serious difficulties. At the same time, Motz was pursuing his policy with a careful eye to the interests of the smaller partners, even when these sometimes ran counter to Prussian interests. The problems of the age, as the Prussian Minister of Finance repeatedly pointed out to his fellow negotiators, were not to be solved by individual German states on their own; they required the co-operation of all the German states, but, given her inner disintegration, her growing economic backwardness and her involvement in trade outside Germany, the exclusion of Austria.

In 1834, therefore, the Prussian, central and south German customs unions all combined to form the German Customs Union (*Deutsches Zollverein*). This united economic region acted as a magnet so that, by 1842, 28 of the 39 German federal states belonged to it. Metternich, the upholder of the 1815 European 'system', saw the danger clearly; a 'State within the State' was threatening to emerge, he remarked in a report to Emperor Franz I, 'Prussia's preponderance' was strengthened, the 'extremely dangerous doctrine of German unity' was being encouraged, and although its future contours were still unclear, 'nevertheless, the lessons of history and statesmanship will not allow the unprejudiced observer to doubt that Austria's relations with the other German federal states . . . will eventually loosen and finally break off entirely.'[16] As so often before, this great Austrian conservative minister was more clearsighted than many of his contemporaries. The German Confederation, presided over by Austria, certainly formed and was to form the larger framework of German policy, supported by international agreements and interests as well as by the claims of tradition and legitimacy. The German Confederation was, however, an instrument of the status quo and of stability, but also of reaction; the last bastion of Old Europe. The Prussian-led Customs Union, on the other hand, was an entity which looked to the future; its economic power and financial clout were growing steadily and acting like a magnet on the states surrounding it.

This newly-created Prussian/German economic sphere resented the old fashioned, slow and unreliable traffic conditions; river boats and pack-horses made the exchange of goods difficult and ineffective, although the highroads and canals had been much improved since the Napoleonic era. More than any others, the Liberal economic theorist Friedrich List and a few Rhineland industrialists were responsible for the eventual opening of the first German railway line on 7 December 1835, after a lengthy and wearisome struggle against conservative prejudice hostile to the new technology: all of six kilometers from Nuremberg to Fürth. Belgium already had 20 railway kilometres, France 141, and Great Britain 544. This was however just the beginning; railway lines spread out from the industrial regions and the capital cities to interconnect and cross the borders – by 1840 469 kilometres of railway had been laid and there were exactly 5,000 within the Customs Union on the eve of the Revolution; more than twice as many as in France, and four times as many as in Austria. Above all, the railway established the Customs Union's market because supply, demand and prices had previously been able to develop quite separately from one another, given the inadequate means of transport and the existence of economic islands restricted to specific regions. Now, however, the railway ensured that competition was equally strong in the various parts of the Customs Union. As a result, the economic centres began to spread out, with Silesia, formerly Prussia's wealthiest province, falling behind and the Rhine and Ruhr industries growing apace.

All sorts of industries were involved – rails, engines and waggons were needed; machine factories flourished, and a highly diversified distribution industry sprang up out of the ground with (when they could deliver the raw materials) the coal and iron mines lagging not far behind. The railway lines which had already been laid made it possible to transport raw materials cheaply to far-flung processing places; to carry agricultural produce hundreds of kilometres to urban conglomerations without it spoiling; and to transport masses of people, both troops and work-seekers, right across Germany. People's awareness of time and space was altered in consequence, and the telegraph did its bit by reducing distance to a matter of no account. Politics, economy, culture and war had previously been conducted within narrowly prescribed regions, measured by the speed of despatch-couriers and post-coaches. From now on, however, all these things would happen on a massive, unified and controllable scale over the whole length and breadth of the continent.

Thus it was that, in spite of the collapse of political unification during the 1848 revolution, there was one strong bond uniting the nation – economic integration. Whereas politics fell for a decade into a 'Sleeping-Beauty' state of suspended animation and the victorious powers of reaction held ever more tightly to the reins of power by reviving censorship and the political police, Germany entered the actual take-off stage of the Industrial Revolution. Her political exhaustion guaranteed not only Germany but the whole of Europe a hiatus in which peaceful and long term investment projects could be developed alongside the enormous growth in capital, boosted by the discovery of Californian and Australian gold. Borrowing was consequently cheap and, with rising prices and a growing demand, these were golden days for the commercial middle classes. New banks were opening all over the place; between 1851 and 1857, there was a near threefold increase in the circulation of bank notes, in the stock of bank deposits and paid-in capital, and there was no shortage of investment opportunities. Railway construction was booming, the railroad network doubled in size between 1850 and 1860, engine and machine construction was at its peak, resulting in a whole gamut of technical innovations from metallurgy to signalling and the transmission of news.

A further reason for the economic boom lay in the low cost of labour. The new factories, mines and steelworks sucked people in from an inexhaustible reservoir of labour. These miserable and pauperised human masses were happy to obtain any sort of regular work and secure pay, and we should remember this despite all contemporary and subsequent criticism of the dreadful living conditions and miserable pay meted out to this first generation of factory workers. Compared to the wholesale poverty prior to industrialisation, the average worker was now better off; unemployment, underemployment, female and child labour and practices such as undercutting wages by putting work out and keeping wages low on account of English and Belgian competition; all these now diminished. Although the price of wheat rose swiftly following poor harvests between 1852 and 1855, this time there were no revolts. Pauperism, which only a decade earlier had been considered an inevitable fate threatening the future of European society, was reduced; by 1873 at the latest, when the first phase of economic growth was over, it was no longer a subject for concern.

In the first instance, all this benefited the states which had combined in the Customs Union. Between 1853 and 1856 Customs Union exports leaped from 356.9 to 456.1 million *Thaler*, while Austria's exports over the same period dwindled from 184.3 to 150.3 million *Thaler*. Whereas the Customs Union's volume of trade grew faster than the turnover of world commerce, Austria took no part in this economic boom. There were many reasons for this separate development, the most important being the Habsburg monarchy's unfavourable geographical position, cut off from traffic with northern Germany by the Alpine region, and looking towards the far distant Adriatic ports with their particular lines to world trade and economy. Added to this were Austria's inadequate coal resources – the vital raw material in the initial phase of industrialisation. Above all, however, it was Austria's conservative and protectionist policy, fearful of technology and industry, as demonstrated by the first important railway line on the continent; the 130 kilometre-long stretch between Budweis (České Budějovice) and Linz was ready as early as 1832, and was extended a further 70 kilometres to the salt mines of Gmünden in 1836. However, when the money ran out, they simply failed to build a proper substructure, an essential requirement for running a railway. Instead, the stretch was used as a horse-tramway path right down to the sixties – 'A peculiarly Austrian application of technical innovation, which emphasised short-term ostentation at the expense of growth-potential' as an American economic historian has commented.[17] Nor did it help when, from 1850 onwards, Austrian diplomacy attempted with increased enthusiasm to squeeze Prussia out of her leading economic role in Germany. While Count Schwarzenberg, the Austrian Foreign Minister, was demanding that Austria be admitted into the Customs Union, Freiherr von Bruck, the Viennese Minister of Trade, was proposing a plan for a central European customs union, which would unite all Habsburg lands with the Customs Union and all the hitherto commercially and politically unaligned German states. This was the first appearance of a Central European project, which would later on frequently be mooted as an alternative to the German nation-state.

However, they were too late. The commercial, currency and customs structures of the Customs Union were already too well established, and its economic lead over the Danube kingdom was too great, as a glance at the map showed. The density of traffic systems, especially railway connections, of the telegraph network, of banking services and industrial centres rapidly diminished south of the Saxon and Bavarian frontiers; apart from a few South German factory-owners, who had profited from the expansion of the internal market to cover the Alpine regions, interest in the Customs Union was meagre. Furthermore, clever tactics on the part of Prussian diplomacy, if one leaves out of account the psychological impact of the (albeit politically and economically ineffective) Postal Union (*Postverein*) treaty of 1850, which standardised postal services and tariffs between the Customs Union and Austria, also ensured that Austria was kept out of the Customs Union.

By the end of the fifties, Austria found herself practically on her own in the Federal Parliament, since Prussia's economic preponderance simply drew the central German states to herself. Looking at the economic logic alone, it is clear that there was no turning off the road to a Prussian-led 'little Germany'.

9 Speeches and majority decisions.

The doldrums of domestic policy ended with the advent of 1857, when the Prussian throne changed hands; the mentally deranged Friedrich Wilhelm IV was replaced by his brother Prince Wilhelm who assumed the regency on 7 October 1858 and, contrary to the image of 'Cartridge-Prince' which the Prince Regent had cultivated in March 1848, dismissed Manteuffel's conservative ministry, appointing in its place a conservative/Liberal cabinet of the 'new era', under Count Karl Anton von Hohenzollern-Sigmaringen, reputedly a nationalist and a progressive. However, it was not only the Liberal turn of affairs which enlivened politics but also the economy. Once again, economic growth had slowed down. The initial spurt of the fifties had created an over-optimistic climate for investment at a time when the market's capacity for absoption was temporarily exhausted. Commodity prices sank, and the economic depression was worsened by the news of a banking crisis in New York, which also affected north Germany via London.

On top of this the question of an united Germany was thrown up again by the Italian crisis staged by Napoleon III, and brought back into the wider political scene. Louis Napoleon, the great Corsican's nephew, who, like him, had become Emperor of France by means of a coup, was the greatest cause of unrest in Europe in the fifties and sixties. As the heir to Revolution and Ceasarism, his legitimacy did not rely on the concept of Divine Providence, which had presided over the European 'system' of peace established in 1815, but on the consent of the masses, and thereby on alignment with the massively effective ideologies of the new age. He saw himself as the protagonist and protector of European nationalities against the supra-national powers of the Vienna concord. By personally supporting Polish and Italian nationalism, he established France's quasi-hegemony in the struggle against the order established by the Holy Alliance. However, although his policy was principally directed against Austria, Napoleon's revisionist programme also included winning back France's 'natural' frontiers, including the Rhine boundary, and was clearly aimed against the German nationalist movement (in spite of his role as the defender of European nationalism).

The theatre of war in Italy opened with an adroit dalliance conducted between Napoleon and Count Camillo Cavour, the Prime Minister of Piedmont. By means of provocative threats of war and revolution Austria, trusting in Prussian assistance and English support, was induced to issue an ultimatum to Piedmont-Sardinia on 19 April 1859 and to follow it up with a declaration of war when, as anticipated, the ultimatum was rejected. While this did result in an alliance between Piedmont and France, to the surprise of the diplomats in Vienna, it did not result in any help at all for Austria from the German Confederation, let alone from Prussia. The Prussian Foreign Minister argued in the Frankfurt Parliament that the war in Italy was an extra-German affair and that if the German Confederation were to enter it on Austria's behalf, the result would be war with France over the Rhine frontier.

While Austria was waking up to her international isolation (Russia had just agreed to a moratorium with France, and England's sympathies lay wholly with the Italian Liberals' and Patriots' struggle for unity), nationalist feeling in Germany was running high for the first time in ten years. While the Austrian armies in Lombardy were losing battle after battle to the Piedmontese and French allies during the early summer of 1859 and finally sued for a cease-fire on 8 July, a war of words was raging in the German newspapers, as if the solution to the question of German unity lay directly before them. At first, the voices attacking the anti-Austrian party and calling Prussia to arms to fight in a final, decisive war against France prevailed. A new wave of Rhine songs washed over Germany. 'O Germany, high in honour', by Ludwig Bauer, much sung later on during the First World War, was born during the throes of the Italian crisis:

> Let the banner wave on high,
> Let us loyally and boldly go
> With the peoples of Austria!

Upper Italy appeared in these hues as the main prop of the ancient Staufen Empire, and the protagonists of the modern idea of nation-state had no difficulty in reconciling it with the memory of an Imperial entity presiding over all the ancient nationalities, which was now interpreted wholly in the sense of German rule in Italy.

However, as the defeat of the Habsburg monarchy became increasingly obvious, this nationalist movement panned out into a new mood: could Austrian involvement in extra-German trade not be exploited, in order to throw out the ballast of the multi-nation state and found a 'little-German' *Reich* under Prussian leadership, without the Habsburg ruler? Ferdinand Lasalle, who had founded the first German Workers' party four years later, demanded point-blank that Austria be sacrificed on the altar of national rebirth: 'When Austria falls apart, Prussia will collapse as a separate entity, just as two opposites will cancel each other out. Once Austria is destroyed, Prussia and Germany will be one.'[18] Similar thoughts were expressed by Liberals like Constantin Rössler, as well as by radical democrats like Arnold Ruge or Ludwig Bamberger. While German conservatism was wholly, and old Liberalism mainly ranged on Austria's side, condemning Prussia's waiting game, the leftist faction of the nationalist movement was in the front line advocating separation from Austria and a national war against France to win back Alsace. Yet another was arguing in the same way against the Prussian government's restraint: Otto von Bismarck, the Prussian delegate to the Federal Parliament, who was relieved of his post on account of his anti-Austrian attitude and was sent to St Petersburg as ambassador. On 5 May 1859 he wrote to Adjutant General von Alvensleben that it was now time to solve the 'German question' by force in alliance with France and given Russia's benevolent neutrality, to transform Prussia into a 'Kingdom of Germany'. 'The present situation once again holds out the chance of first prize for us, if we let Austria's war with France consume itself quickly, and we then launch ourselves with the entire armed forces southwards, carrying frontier posts in our packs, to set them up again either by the Bodensee [Lake Constance] or anywhere where the Protestant religion ceases to predominate . . .'[19]

However, whether for or against Prussia, with or without Austria, the German nationalist sensibilities, suppressed for a decade, now burst out in a rash of new societies, poems, festivals and newspaper articles. The new wave of nationalism reached its highpoint at the centenary of Schiller's birth on 10 November 1859, which was celebrated in every German-speaking land. Every town conducted their own Schiller festival; in every case the celebrations were financed from the burghers' own pockets, the male choirs and civic guard associations did most of the organising and the whole population, from the workers to the town dignitaries, took part in it. The festival would be opened by a triumphal procession, enlivened by floats bearing scenes from Schiller's plays; flags and festival banners would wave above the heads of a crowd carefully sorted into different professional and artisan groups. The festival procession would generally break up in the market square, where speeches would be made and Schiller and the German nation would be cheered. *Tableaux vivants* and symbolic representations played a considerable part in all this; alongside the statues of Schiller were generally found figures of Germania – since the Rhine Crisis of 1840 she had been the poetical symbol of German unity (with a decidedly anti-French bias). Few indeed were the Schiller festivals which did not display a banner based on Lorenz Clasen's popular painting of *Germania on the Watch on the Rhine*. Schiller and Germania, Freedom and Unity were the concepts covering over the old tensions of the German nationalist movement, which nevertheless broke out in a few place, as in Berlin, where democratic speeches were made beneath the Schiller memorial and the police were called in. It was however now clear that Liberalism and Nationalism still represented two sides of the same coin, and that they had now grown into a broad popular movement.

This became even more obvious in the following years. The Liberal 'new era' saw the disappearance (or slacker application by the authorities) of legal restrictions on associations. Old organisations representing the nationalist movement experienced an enormous boost. In 1861 the first national parent organisation of the 'German Riflemen's Confederation' (*Deutsche Schützenbund*) was formed, followed a year later by the 'German Singing Confederation' (*Deutsche Sängerbund*); the Committee of the German Gymnastic Clubs formed a national association in 1861, which ended up as the 'German Gymnastic Society' (*Deutsche Turnershaft*). Pan-national performances brought truly masses of organised patriots together – more than 8,000 civic guards turned out in 1862 for the 'German Riflemen's Festival' (*Deutsches Schützenfest*) at Frankfurt am Main, and in the following year, 20,000 gymnasts appeared at the 'German Gymnastics Festival' in Leipzig, and the 'German Song Festival' of 1864 in Dresden featured 16,000 singers from every part of Germany, Austria and even from German-speaking Switzerland.

The German national movement, which had previously constituted an ill-defined conglomeration of middle-class societies, Liberal publicists, economic and civic intiatives and parliamentary opposition, had remained united as a common bastion. Although questions about frontiers, the constitution and the predominant role of a German nation state met with an almost unmanageable mish-mash of different points of view, during crises, however, all the quarrelling gave way to a general call for German unity. Even in the Paulskirche gathering of 1848–9 there had been no firm alignments over the question of Austria and Prussia's role in the unification of Germany, but a freely fluctuating series of majority groupings, which constantly varied according to the day's political events and the varying opinions of leading delegates. The question of a 'great' or 'little' Germany was perceived increasingly as a tactical problem; in any case the overwhelming majority felt that its solution lay in a great Germany, and this majority could be counted on at any time by any faction offering the most viable solution to the question of a nation-state.

Now, however, this was all changing. The Italian crisis of 1859 had clearly shown up the German Confederation's inability to act and both its leading powers had, in the eyes of public opinion, turned out to have no clothes; Austria on account of her defeat in war, and Prussia on account of her delaying tactics. Nevertheless, after the Habsburg monarchy's defeat, the thought of a federal state under Prussian leadership as an alternative to the German Confederation, with its inability to act and weak claims to legitimacy, was revived. By mid-September 1859 the German National Society came into being, founded by Liberals and moderate Democrats from all non-Austrian German lands. It was led by the Liberal leader of the opposition, Rudolf von Bennigsen, a Hanoverian; by Hans Victor von Unruh, the former president of the Prussian National Assembly; and by Hermann Schulze-Delitzsch, the founder of the artisan fellowships. The National Society's seat was Coburg, capital of the Liberal and nationalist-minded Duke Ernest II of Sachs-Coburg-Gotha. Its programme was linked to the

Reichs Constitution of 1849; the question of establishing a central authority remained unanswered, as did that of relations with Austria, but the accompanying music made its bias towards Prussia, as the leading power, obvious. A new tone dominated in yet another respect: 'First cast off the yoke of foreign rule from Germany, and subdue the insolence of our national enemy', Schulze-Delitzsch wrote in the National Society's first broadsheet, 'first establish our Fatherland's independence, our People's participation in the questions of its national existence, before even considering the development of individual internal conditions: before anything else, then, a German central authority with a popular representation at its side . . .'[20] First a central government, then a national parliament – this too was *Realpolitik* with an insight into the nationalist movement's weaknesses during the revolution of 1848; a decisive step on the road to the later national Liberalism, to solving the German question from above.

The German National Society consisted, thoroughly in the tradition of German associations, solely of high-ranking persons; there was, however, no need at all to propagate the notion of a 'little Germany': Protestant Germany especially had long been prepared for Prussian leadership in the event of national unification. Especially effective were the Prussian stories and legends which filled the school books and enhanced the older people's memories: Menzel's illustrations for Kügler's biography of Frederick the Great – the flute concert at Sans-souci, Old Fritz on horseback – were already part of the national heritage, pictures which everyone called to mind when Germany's greatness was evoked. German historiography with very few exceptions also concentrated on Prussia. A whole generation of political teachers, such as should never again appear in Germany, entered German schools: Dahlmann in Bonn, Häusser in Freiburg, Duncker and then Treitschke in Berlin, Droysen in Jena and Sybel in Munich, all of them Liberals, convinced of Prussia's German mission, of monarchical constitutionalism's suitability for Germany, and of the depravity of south German, ultra-montane and 'anti-national' Catholicism. These men no longer agreed with Leopold von Ranke, who had roundly denounced the use of history for instructing the present. They were all politically active, as delegates in the parliaments, as co-workers on the leading newspapers, as university-teachers – 'lectern prophets', as Max Weber was later to call them – and above all as writers, developing the German people's view of history. Johann Gustav Droysen achieved the greatest public success as early as 1833 with his *History of Alexander the Great*, an account of that semi-barbaric empire in northern Greece, which was nevertheless capable of firmly imposing order on the chaotic little states in the South. Thus unified, the Greek empire then formed the point of departure for Alexander's fantastic progress towards the East in the name of a higher, Greek, form of humanity. Droysen's Alexander book was to be found in every middle-class library, and everyone understood its message: Macedonia was Prussia, Greece was Germany, and Asia, Europe. The middle classes were supposed to recognise in Bismarck a new Alexander, whose rise and success were already instilled in peoples' minds by the historical sciences.

Not all succumbed, however. Onno Klopp, the Catholic Hanoverian, wrote in 1860 that Friedrich II of Prussia had destroyed German history, pointing to the Prussians' greed for conquest and extolling the legitimacy of the house of Habsburg. The quarrel between Julius von Ficker, a Catholic from Westphalia working as a professor in the University of Innsbruck, and Heinrich von Sybel became notorious: whereas Sybel criticised the Staufen Emperors for their universalist policy, viewing their Italian policy as a cancerous sore on the national integration of the Empire, Ficker insisted on the legitimacy of a trans-national imperial rule, which he wanted to see prolonged into the present and the future. Theirs was only superficially a learned dispute since it was highly relevant to present-day affairs, and was understood as such by the public.

Opposition to the concept of a little Germany also grew. Liberal enthusiasm for Prussia should be understood against the background of the 'new era' in Prussia; consequently, when they exhorted Prussia to secure her moral ascendancy in Germany, the leaders of the National Society saw no contradiction between their Liberal ideals and the national ideal, given that they also felt sure that the spirit of Liberalism would be strengthened by the influence of the middle states in a 'little Germany' dominated by Prussia. Such hopes were however squashed by the outbreak of the Prussian army conflict of 1861, which panned out into a fundamental constitutional conflict between Prussian Liberalism and the monarchy, with Liberal sympathies for Prussia ebbing swiftly. Furthermore, the National Society's activities were received by most of the governments of the 'third Germany' with the utmost coolness.

In 1862, therefore, the 'great Germany' wing of the nationalist movement responded to Prussia's claims to hegemony by forming a 'German Reform Society' along with Liberal/separatist and conservative/clerical forces as well as disappointed partisans of a Prussian hereditary imperial rule who, when Bismarck's cabinet was appointed in 1862, could see in its policy only great-Prussian and reactionary goals. Whereas the National Society managed to build up an united and closed organisation of local associations, with a capable leadership, well thought-out financial management, regular meetings and their own Society newspaper, the Reform Society stuck fast in an organisational morass. It was not just the heterogeneity of its political aims which beset the 'great Germany' movement, but also its pitiful membership of 1,500 at the most. Unlike the National Society with its 25,000 members, the Reform Society never managed to establish a firm connection between its organisational superstructure and its multitude of local associations.

However, the National Society was changing too. Those friends of Prussia who belonged to it were, given the sharpening conflict over the Prussian constitution, no longer keen openly to take the part of Prussian rule. Contributions towards a navy, a *Reichsflotte*, which the National Society was collecting and had until 1861 handed over to the Prussian government for fitting out their fleet, were now retained, and in the following year the Society openly attacked the Prussian government by formulating its own programme in the Schleswig-Holstein affair and even allying with its opponent, the

Reform Society, to see it through. By the mid sixties very little indeed of Prussia's moral ascendancy could be sensed in German public opinion. The National Society now announced, thereby openly breaking with its previously proclaimed idea of Prussia's mission, that a general German parliament, above the representatives of the German central authority, had first to be designated. On the eve of Koniggrätz the prevailing tenor of the National Society's press was that of deep resignation; the neutrality of the middle and small states, as the National Society's weekly paper explained on 14 June 1866, was 'the nationalist policy's only appropriate solution' since 'the banner of the Nation' was not flying over the Prussian or the Austrian bastions.

10 Blood and Iron

When the *Reich* was established in 1871 it seemed superfluous to pursue the question of whether the German nation-state would then have to be established and if so, whether under this form. Bismarck's state appeared to contemporaries and to two subsequent generations as an inevitable historical necessity, with people generally inclining towards Hegel's dictum about the Rationality of the Real, of things as they are and, moreover, towards the tendency since 1871 (mocked by Jacob Burckhardt as the 'victorious German gloss on history') to consider the nineteenth century as a providential one-way road from the old *Reich* to the Second *Reich*. Was there not a lot to be said for this view? Were the Germans not simply catching up with what most European nations had long ago put behind them – a 'delayed nation'? Did not the power of growing national awareness as the decisive mass ideology speak out as much for Bismarck's solution to the German question as did the process of economic modernisation, and the development of economic structures? Should the question of historical alternatives be posed at all?

Yes, it must be posed, since it is only by reconstructing past possibilities and opportunities that teleological and fatalistic historical clutter can be dispensed with and a proper assessment of actual historical developments be made. Seen from the perspective of a political observer prior to the unification of the *Reich*, what actually happened was only one of many possible series of events and maybe not even a very likely one.

There were many models for a solution to the German question. The German Confederation of 1815 was one of them, and weighty factors spoke in favour of it: the remnants of Imperial traditions; existing ruling interests; the Confederation's ability to offset the two leading powers, without however having a majority vote over the other states; and, last but not least, the European powers' interest in maintaining the balance of power, which appeared to be endangered by every unification process in Central Europe. That the German Confederation proved nevertheless incapable of permanency was due in the first place to the stalemate situation between Austria and Prussia, which prevented any modernisation of the Confederation or centralisation of power. It was due in the second place to the ideological backwardness of this construct of states, whose system for legitimising and maintaining power was in direct contrast to the century's massively effective and influential trends.

The second possible solution was tried out in 1848–9: establishing a modern, German and centralised nation-state based on popular sovereignty and human rights. However, this model also proved unviable – it collapsed beneath the social and ideological heterogeneity of its Liberal and national representative classes, as much as beneath the European powers opposition, viewing an aggressive foray over the frontiers of the German Confederation by German nationalism as a revolution against the European balance of power. However, no German national parliament which renounced the 'liberation' of German '*irredenta*' in the west, north and east, could hope for legitimation in the eyes of German patriots.

When the 1848 revolution collapsed there was no shortage of other solutions, which had been heatedly discussed since the re-awakening of the nationalist movement, each solution having its own stronghold. There was, for instance, the 'great Germany' concept, by far the most intoxicating solution, being the most comprehensive and emotionally the most appealing by recalling a glorified imperial past. Nevertheless, this concept was also the most hopeless, as viewed from the perspective of the early sixties; it was not necessarily Prussian claims to hegemony which spoke against it – that was mainly the affair of the top Prussian bureaucracy, whereas both the king and the super-conservative aristocracy held the Habsburg claims in great respect. However, given the advanced economic integration of the Customs Union, it was on the one hand the relative backwardness and antediluvian mercantilistic economic policy of the Danube monarchy which spoke against the concept of a great Germany, and on the other it was Austria's long-since initiated exit from Germany, her involvement in the Balkans and in extra-German conflict in Italy, and her multi-national constitution which, in the event of the dissolution of the Habsburg empire, would have led to insoluble problems.

A further possibility lay in a dual hegemony of both the leading powers of the German Confederation, which Prussia occasionally favoured and tried to insert within the concept of Federal reform. It involved dividing Germany along the axis of the River Main, with a Prussian/north German confederation in the north and a south German/Danube federation ruled from Vienna in the south. Bismarck proposed this solution to the German question as late as 1864; it would also have solved the century-old standing conflict between Prussia and Austria. This would indeed have presented a realistic alternative to German history, but it failed because Austria did not trust (and not without grounds) this Prussian self-restraint and feared a spate of new demands from the Berlin government.

Then there was the *Trias* idea put forward by the German middle states, who were as horrified by the notion of a Prussian hegemony as by that of a Prussian–Austrian duumvirate. The concept of a 'third Germany' had been one of the great formative elements of German history for centuries: it encompassed the union of the smaller and middle-sized territories with the aim of repulsing hegemonial offensives by the great powers and of defending their traditional liberties. The 'third Germany' had always been loyal to the *Reich*, in the sense that the existing *Reichs* constitution was best disposed to guarantee the rights of individual states. Alongside this was the attempt to align with a great power in order to resist pressure by another power – which recalled both the League of the German Princes of 1785 under Prussian patronage, and the various alliances with a non-German power, from the Heilbronner Confederation of 1633, which was dominated by Sweden, to the Rhine Confederation of the Napoleonic era. After 1859 the 'third Germany' rose up again in an attempt to reform the Federal constitution in the sense of strengthened federal rights, and to strengthen the Confederation's effective powers against Prussia and Austria. It rapidly became obvious that the Bavarian, Saxon and Baden plans for reforming the Confederation were so different that the middle states would never co-operate, but the *Trias* was still strong enough to manoeuvre between Austria and Prussia and to play off the two great German powers against each other in the Federal Parliament. Furthermore, according to the Federal act of 1815, every individual state was entitled, as before, to enter into alliances with non-German powers, and a new version of the Rhine Confederation policy was still thinkable.

A little Germany under Prussian leadership was only one of many options considered as solutions to the German question. However, if the Customs Union, Austria's weakness and temporary Liberal sympathies gave it an advantage, it was doomed never to be realised. Two things had to happen; an exceptional international situation, in which the intervention mechanism of the European balance of powers in the event of a concentration of powers in Central Europe was undermined, and a Prussian leadership capable of seeing their opportunity and acting accordingly. The former occurred when the concert of Europe actually was disrupted by the Crimean War (1853–6). The European flanking powers, England and Russia, lay far apart from one another and a common intervention such as took place in 1848 on the occasion of the German offensive against Denmark was now less likely. Also, Napoleon III's France was courting Vienna and Berlin with fine impartiality and was hoping, in the event of a decisive German struggle, to be able to watch it from a safe distance. Prussia's manoeuvrability had also increased, without the new limits to her movements being clearly drawn. The risks of crossing frontiers, given that the punishment for it was reduction to the status of a second-ranking power, were still enormous.

It lay, however, totally outside the nature of Prussian policy to exploit this constellation of events with the aim of solving the German question under the auspices of Prussian hegemony. Although the Prussian and Austrian struggle for mastery of Germany had become a determining element of German history since the wars in Silesia, Frederick the Great's successors had always been chary of fundamentally contesting Austria's presence in the German Confederation or even the higher legitimacy of the Habsburg crown; their hegemonial conflicts were fought out on the diplomatic or economic level, but every Berlin cabinet had hitherto done its best to avoid a military confrontation with the Danube monarchy – not out of an overriding love of peace, but because the risk of losing a war seemed to the Prussian state to be too great.

This changed with Bismarck's appointment as Prussian Prime Minister on 24 September 1862. According to Liberal and national public opinion he stood for the counter-revolution and was the tool of the army and of super-conservatism with the task of ending by every means at his disposal the constitutional conflict between the crown and the Liberal majority in the Chamber over the army budget, and of forcing parliamentary Liberalism to its knees. To start off with, King William I and his military *camarilla* viewed him in the same way. However, all sides had judged Bismarck wrongly in their assumptions about his motives for his policy. He did not consider the Prussian Prime Ministership as an end in itself, but as a means of achieving a higher purpose. He was concerned with broadening Prussia's power base and consolidating her position in a revolutionary Europe, a road which he was convinced could only be followed by establishing Prussian hegemony in Germany at Austria's expense, but in unison with the other European powers' interests. His means were revolutionary, but his aim was conservative: this 'white revolutionary' (Henry Kissinger) and his principle of 'creative anti-revolution' (Michael Stürmer) could not be grasped in terms of the nineteenth century. On top of this, there was his readiness to go to extremes, and his passion for taking every crisis to the limit. His astonishing ability to juggle with many balls at once, to take in all the complexities of a situation every time, to separate tactical means and strategic aims strictly and yet to keep them both in mind, and finally his almost self-destructive tendency to risk everything when a situation had been carried too far – in this lay his superiority over internal and external political opponents.

'It is not by speeches and majority decisions that the great questions of the age will be decided – that was the big mistake of 1848 and 1849 – but by blood and iron.'[21] This insight of Bismarck's, which horrified all Liberals of every hue, was only the logical conclusion to be drawn from the experience of past defeats. His 'Blood and Iron' metaphor did not spring from any kind of warmongering *Junker* mentality, but from a poem by Max von Schenkendorf, one of the volunteers in the 1813 war, who later formed the core of the student movement for Unity and Freedom:

> For only Iron can save us
> And only Blood redeem us
> From the heavy chains of sin
> And the Devil's arrogance.

This had been a revolutionary avowal, and it was Bismarck's adoption of this concept, when Schenkendorf's Liberal successors shrank back from the *ultima ratio* of their policy – putting hand to hilt – which made it clear that the forces of change were not to be found in the first instance at grassroots level among the populace. Revolution in Germany, as elsewhere in Europe at that time, did not happen from beneath but from above.

It is striking in retrospect to read how people in Liberal and nationalist movement circles reacted to Bismarck between 1862 and 1866. Their writings reek with dismissive arrogance (Bluntschli to Sybel: 'He would be very serviceable in a subordinate, ancillary post, but he is absurd and unbearable in a ruling position'[22]) and even pure hatred (Baumgarten to Sybel: 'People, who despise the Constitution, Reason and Right, must like naughty boys be made to tremble. One must arouse in them a lively concern that they will one day be struck down like rabid dogs'[23]). There were good grounds for scorn and hatred, given that Bismarck had taken office to end once and for all the Liberal opposition's struggle in Prussia for the parliamentarisation of the authoritarian state. Since national unity and inner political freedom were indivisibly entwined in the nationalist movement's programme, in spite of all its internal arguments over individual concerns, the Prussian Prime Minister was seen, in the words of the *Wochenschrift des Nationalvereins*, as 'the keenest and last bulwark of the Reaction of Divine Providence'. If one compares the deep gulf between Bismarck and the nationalist movement with the well-functioning cooperation between the Piedmontese prime minister Count Cavour and Italy's nationalist forces over the unification of Italy, one might well feel that the unification of the German *Reich* had been rendered hopelessly difficult.

The opposite, however, was the case. Nothing would have hindered Bismarck's plans more than an alliance with the nationalist movement, whose anti-establishment ambitions were obvious and which was regarded with the utmost suspicion by the governments in London, Paris and St Petersburg. He used his hostility to the Liberal and nationalist forces in Germany precisely in order to conceal his strength and his aims behind the scenes of this conflict, and thus be able to act all the more surprisingly when the right moment came. In 1863, when an uprising in Russian Poland aroused the sympathy of all European Liberals for the oppressed Polish people, Bismarck alone, with an eye to Russia's benevolent neutrality in the event of an Austro-Prussian conflict, sided with the Tsars, to the overwhelming disgust of German public opinion. The National Society went so far as to threaten 'the man at the head of the Prussian state, condemned by his own people, working for the ruin of Prussian supremacy' with revolution.[24] The nationalist movement turned even more acutely hostile when Bismarck next set himself to tackling the Schleswig-Holstein problem.

Since the revolutionary year of 1848, the Schleswig-Holstein *irredenta* had constituted one of the German nationalist movement's favourite themes, and the public's displeasure welled over when the Danish parliament of 1863 decided on the complete annexation of the duchy of Schleswig (which had hitherto been joined to Denmark only by personal union), within the unitary state of Denmark. The Liberal German press hastened to promote the question of an autonomous Schleswig-Holstein under a German ruler, the Duke of Sonderburg-Augustenburg, as a national and political imperative. Schleswig-Holstein associations were started up in every small town and in Frankfurt, 500 delegates from all the German Parliaments demanded that the Duchy be liberated. As in 1848, Prussia was once again prepared to intervene with the army – but not for the independence of the Elbe duchy and for the rights of the Augustenburg claimant. Although he could claim his rights of inheritance, he did not have the international agreement stipulating Danish indivisibility on his side.

Unimpressed as he was by all this nationalist uproar, Bismarck recognised the right to rule of the Danish king of the house of Sonderburg-Glücksburg, which satisfied the other European powers, but he also planned an armed attack on the Elbe duchy on account of its infringement of Schleswig-Holstein's special rights, a cause to which he also knew how to win Austria over. The difference between the nationalist movement's demands and those of the great German powers who, to everyone's surprise, suddenly appeared arm-in-arm, was a purely legal one, but what the German patriots could not bear was Bismarck's formal recognition of the Danish king's rights and thereby of the European order of peace. When Prussian and Austrian troops advanced into Holstein in January 1864 to occupy the whole of Jutland by the middle of the year, the fury of Liberal public opinion knew no bounds – and not without good reason, as the peace agreement of 30 October 1864 demonstrated, when the liberated duchy did not enter the German Confederation as an independent German state, but in the form of a condominium administered by the two victorious powers, Austria and Prussia.

It also became apparent that Bismarck's scorn for the 'chatterboxes and swindlers of the movement party', as he called the patriotic Liberals, was not unfounded. In the light of his success, the anti-Bismarck bastion began to crumble, with prominent historians like Heinrich von Treitschke, Heinrich von Sybel and Theodor Mommsen now openly siding with Bismarck's seemingly senseless yet obviously successful policy, and even a democrat like Franz Waldeck, a man of the extreme Left in the Prussian House of Delegates, declared unashamedly that he could no longer see any alternative to Bismarck's concept.

The Danish war, later to be viewed as the first war of German unification, showed up the Nationalist movement as strong on noise but powerless. When the Austro-Prussian conflict sharpened, with both sides poised to attribute their opponent with responsibility for the outbreak of war; when the spearhead of the Prussian army finally crossed the Bohemian border on 21 June 1866, Liberal opinion was shocked, paralysed and incapable of action.

When the outcome of the war was settled by the Battle of Königgrätz on 3 July 1866, with Prussia victorious and Austria out of the German power-game, the nationalist movement as an independent political force literally broke up overnight. On 1 May 1866, the Liberal lawyer Rudolf von Ihering could still write to a friend: 'Perhaps no war has been broached with such shamelessness, such horrible frivolity, as has the war which Bismarck is presently trying to raise against Austria. One's innermost feelings are revolted by such an outrage against every principle of law and morality . . .'[25]

Three months later, after Königgrätz, he wrote: 'I bow before the genius of a Bismarck, who has performed a masterpiece of political combination and ability. I have forgiven the man all that he has done up till now, yea, more than that, I have convinced myself that it was necessary to do what seemed to us uninitiated folk to be outrageous presumption, and which has sub-sequently been established as the indispensable means to the end . . . For one such man of action I would give . . . a hundred men of Liberal persuasion, of impotent honesty. Nine weeks ago, who would have believed I would yet write a dithyramb about Bismarck?'[26]

1866 has been called the 'fateful year for Liberalism'; it was also a fateful year for the German nationalist movement. The consent of the great majority in the Liberal bastion to Bismarck's policy, eased as it was by the ending of the conflict over a Prussian constitution by the offer of indemnity and Bismarck's admission that he had acted unconstitutionally, cannot be viewed as mere opportunism. It was far more the case that once again, it was proven that the forces of change from above could be influenced only to a limited extent by the opposition. Bismarck's plea for indemnity was in any case a semi-victory for parliament, a compromise, which was to point the way for the further constitutional development of the north German Confederation and of the *Reich*. In the light of the decision about the leadership of Germany taken at Königgrätz, in the light of its acknowledgement that this indicated the further road to the German nation state, by far the greater part of German Liberalism was now engaged in *Realpolitik*. Apart from a few 'Great-Germany' minded publicists and socialistic politicians, the German nationalist movement now perceived that its goal was near at hand, albeit not through its own doing. In the autumn of 1867, half a year after the constituent *Reichstag* of the North German Confederation had met, the German National Society was formally dissolved, having been pushed aside and superbly out-played by Bismarck. The majority of its members turned up again in the newly founded National Liberal Party, which was to be Bismarck's most important prop in the decade to come. Resignation was balanced by the feeling that new ground was being broken; Hermann Baumgarten, the national Liberal historian, wrote the funeral oration for the independent German nationalist movement:

'Having found out that, in a monarchical state, the aristocracy constitutes an indispensable part, and having seen that these much-abused Junkers know how to fight and die for the Fatherland, in spite of the best Liberals, we will restrict our bourgeois fantasies a little and apply ourselves to claiming an honourable position alongside the aristocracy.

'We thought to transform the German world from the ground upwards with our agitation; but we were simply on course to turn ourselves inside out. I think that we should take this lesson to heart.'[27]

11 Revolution from above and below

Were one to describe the development of the German nationalist movement on the level of political history and the history of events until its dissolution in 1867 as the history of an attempt to influence the great political decisions of the age, one would produce an impression of great helplessness and uselessness. The history of Germany in the nineteenth century is presented as a history of revolution from above, in which the state, or rather a few statesmen, inaugurated, against a background of set economic conditions and determinants, changes such as an elite of political journalists, cut off from the sphere of political action, could only dream of. This wholly conventional picture of a state separated from society, with the former exercising an uncontested jurisdiction over the latter, might suffice were it not that in the long term, politics had progressed precisely towards the realisation of the nationalist movement's basic aims, while the opposition of powerful pre-revolutionary and pre-industrial elites was gradually eroded. The results show that the state and the nationalist movement were far more closely linked and interrelated than a superficial study of successive historical events would indicate. Might it not even be possible, on another level, to write the history of the constantly collapsing nationalist movement as success story?

Let us recall our introductory comments about the transformation, unique in the history of the world, from the old agrarian society of Europe to the industrial mass-civilisation of the outgoing nineteenth and the twentieth centuries, which people experienced in terms of the breakup of the feudal order, the loss of social and religious ties, the collapse of their social milieu and the absurdity of traditional loyalties. The power-sustaining myths and symbols of the *Ancien Régime* were no longer accepted, new communities and new legitimations for authority were established to replace the old ones, and the new idea which proved most effective on a massive scale was that of the nation: it was this awareness which incarnated the common will, and to which every ruling body had to justify itself.

This tendency applied to the whole of Europe, but in Germany's case, despite the nationalist enthusiasm aroused by the struggle against Napoleon, the nation had not achieved identity as a state and, although the memory of the national community envisaged during the War of Liberation lived on, no proper framework for the nationalist dream had been outlined. It was precisely because there were so many untested and wholly Utopian theories about the reality of a German nation, her boundaries and internal order, that German nationalism became so attractive and put other competing ideologies and world-views in the shade. Nationalism was open to all kinds of content; it could be made religious, Liberal, democratic and egalitarian and could fit in with demands for any number of drafts for a state or a constitution – in short, it formed the ideal vehicle for every kind of anti-establishment creative idea. Therein lay its weakness; all sorts of heterogeneous ideologies, interests and classes came together under the banner of the Nation, and consequently the German nationalist movement as a whole was quite incapable of coming to a clear-cut revolutionary decision – one reason why the revolution of 1848 failed. It was also a reason for the confusing observation, that there were very few individuals within the nationalist movement who did not change their political alignment several times over; the change from republican barricade-fighter in 1848 to national-Liberal Bismarck-worshipper eighteen years later was just as common as was the opposite development from moderate democrat before the Revolution to revolutionary socialist not much later on. For this reason too, the German National Society could tackle the German question in 1859 by proposing the 'little Germany'/'great Prussia' solution, and yet ally with the 'great Germany' Reform Society against Bismarck a few years later. Given the all-embracing nature of the nationalist idea, a tactical U-turn of this kind was a negligible quantity.

That the Utopia of a German nation state was able to survive the defeats and frustrations of 1815, 1830, 1840, 1848–9, and 1859 proves furthermore that it clearly met a massive need. The nineteenth century was a time of upheaval, when whole sections of the population were uprooted, society was atomised and its values turned upside down, and nationalism offered two things: community and transcendence. This community was not only asserted but also experienced; in the memory of the War of Liberation as well as of a multitude of interlocking myths, which linked an imaginary future with a glorified Greece, Germania or Medieval period. Public festivals and celebrations, from the Festival of the Battle of the Nations in 1815 to the Wartburg Festival and the Hambach Festival, and to the abundance of nationalist celebrations in the forties and again from the late fifties onwards, all served to create an authentic experience of community and confirmed the individual's sense of participation in the whole. These celebrations invested a strict ritual with strong religious echoes; in many cases, as at the Wartburg Festival, the rite of Mass was paralleled down to its ceremonial and liturgical details. Such proceedings revealed the function of nationalism as a substitute religion quite clearly, and were possibly a reason why traditional Catholic regions were converted to mass nationalism to a much lesser degree than was Protestant Germany. Since nationalism was not a reality in terms of state, it had to be believed in: the nationalist movement was a religious movement.

Being a religion, it needed symbolism as the visible sign of the myths it subscribed to. Symbols established its identity as a community; the black, red and gold flag was derived from the regimental colours of the Lützow Free Corps and quickly crossed with the supposedly medieval Imperial German coat-of-arms to form the colours of the Jena *Burschenschaft* at the Wartburg Festival in 1817. These were then adopted by the German *Burschenschaft* and, by the time of the 1830 riots, they already stood for all the opposition groups which fought for the idea of a Liberal constitution under this banner. The black, red and gold flag was the *'teutsche Tricolor'*; it was clearly revolutionary in aspect and was prohibited by the Frankfurt Federal Assembly. After the 1848 revolution, which took place under the nationalist colours, the black, red and gold tricolor turned up again as the armband of the *'Reichsarmee'* – the German troops fighting on the Austrian side against the Prussian army.

Nationalist symbolism included not only a flag, but a song, which was changed from time to time. Lacking as it did firm forms and institutions, the movement needed a theme tune as well as a liturgical chant. Added to this were further symbols expressive of the German national movement, such as the tree, either the oak or, with a different content, the lime-tree, as the symbol of Germanic virtues but also as the *pars pro toto* of the German forest, whose wealth of meaning can only be hinted at here – it stood for all things Germanic and ancient and served as a polemical argument against unnatural French rationalism, and incorporated the German *Urvolk* as conjured up by Jahn and Fichte. Then there were Blood and Iron, the pledges of willingness to sacrifice all for the nationalist cause. There was also the Flame, signifying the victory of light over darkness, of truth over falsehood, of nationalist hopes but also of cleansing. All that is unclean, whether the corporal's staff, the corset and wig, or the written evidence of the spirit of anti-nationalism, is consumed in the holy fire, and the cleansed nation, rung in by bells, rises phoenix-like from its ashes.

This wealth of mythological and symbolical meanings serves to clarify the advantage which the idea of nation held since 1813 over all competing dogmas. By the 1840 Rhine crisis at the latest, it was clear to everyone that nationalism was the legitimizing ideology *par excellence*. Government cabinets and the *Bundestag* felt that they were being forced by an unprecedented mass movement to adopt a political stance quite opposed to the cool calculation of previous cabinet policy. Nevertheless, the demands of publicists like young Friedrich Engels to repeat the 1814 march on Paris went far beyond the hesitant measures taken by the German Confederation. Metternich feared a *levée en masse*, the outbreak of a national revolution fostered by a renewal of the enthusiasm of the War of Liberation. This even led to the Prussian proposal for reforming the Confederation being pigeonholed. Nevertheless, plans for mobilisation were renewed, two new federal strongholds were built, and a few states responded even more closely to the mood of the masses.

This was the model according to which outbreaks of nationalist protest were henceforth to be handled. It always came to a compromise between the forces of inertia and those of the movement. This had already been the case in 1830, when a few middle-German states had reacted to the disturbances by introducing constitutions and relaxing censorship and the prohibition of assembly; it happened in 1849, from the authorised Prussian constitution to the Constitution of Union at Erfurt in 1850, and it occurred again in 1859, when, under the pressure of public opinion, manifold proposals for the reform of the German Confederation were put forward – absurdly enough, the plans for increasing the Prussian army, which led to the military and constitutional crisis also go back to the Prussian mobilisation and the experiences arising from it, which, in their turn, had been initiated by pressure from public opinion.

On the other hand, it was also the case that tendencies directed against the nationalist movement after 1840 at the latest had in the long run no chance of succeeding. After that date, political legitimacy was derived solely from the concept of a nation-state, which was the most important reason, apart from the Austro-Prussian conflict, why the German Confederation remained a lifeless construct. For in spite of its institutional framework, within which the desire for national unity could have been fulfilled, it incorporated all that was hostile in terms of domestic policy to the nationalist movement. The 'great Germany' solution to the German question also suffered from a lack of legitimacy, as was already apparent in the Paulskirche parliament and was confirmed later on by the organisational and numerical inferiority of the Reform Society as opposed to the National Society.

Thus the road to the foundation of the *Reich* can also be described as a team-game between Bismarck and the nationalist movement, or in any case as a team-game *malgré soi*. The gulfs between Bismarck and the Liberal publicists were undoubtedly deep; he was not only their chief reactionary opponent in the struggle for a constitution, but he was also suspected of conducting not a national, but a 'great Prussian' and particularist policy. The road, which ended by leading the greater part of the nationalist movement (along with its nationalist and Liberal core) to Bismarck, had its starting point in the nationalist movement's old criticism of the German cabinets' foreign policy, which was seen as weak and defensive, and above all of the Prussian government. The call for a stronger foreign policy was as much patriotic as it was liberal; it was taken up by Bismarck, who until 1866 played only gently on the instrument of nationalist emotion, but thereafter increasingly stongly: 'Prussian interests', he wrote, 'are fully in accordance with those of most of the Federal states, apart from Austria, but not with those of the Federal government.'[28] This gives us a glimpse at the well known and long maintained theme of a division of interest between people and government, which can be so effective on a demagogic level and in the Bismarck era was quite simply revolutionary.

Public opinion was already so powerful that not only Bismarck but every German government (even after the 1848 revolution) tried to win over this source of influence and amended their own political stance accordingly. It became particularly obvious that since the crisis of 1859 at the latest no middle-German state dared to form an alliance with a non-German state, although the Federal Act had not done away with the right of any German state to ally itself with non-German powers. The policy of a 'third Germany', a federation of individual states with French backing along the lines of the Rhine Confederation, would have entailed incalculable risks in the field of domestic policy.

So the model of the 'revolution from above' for the German unification process must at least be relativised. While the German *Reich* was certainly not united by speeches and majority decisions but by blood and iron, this did not lead to the success which mass nationalism gained in the long term. Bismarck himself had pointed this out in his memoirs: 'Although German unity was not to be established by parliamentary decisions, newspapers and sponsorship festivals, Liberalism did exercise a pressure on the rulers which made them more inclined to make concessions for the Reich.'[29]

Although Bismarck's policy apparently destroyed the nationalist movement, the movement was basically successful in forcing, if not its means, at least its ends on him. Without the diffuse but nevertheless legitimising power of the unification movement there would have emerged not a German *Reich* but a Great Prussia. By putting the nationalist movement on a lead Bismarck was playing a dangerous game, as was probably made clear to him after his fall in 1890. His successors, however, were to prove incapable of continuing to keep this tiger leashed.

III Documentary appendix

1 Johann Kaspar Riesbeck. The German is the Man for the World

This figures as a summary at the end of a fictional traveller's account, supposedly composed by an enlightened French citizen, writing to a brother in Paris about his experiences in Germany a few years before the start of the French Revolution. It belongs to the tradition of texts criticising society by observing domestic conditions through the eyes of foreign visitors with their alien points of view. The author was born in Hoechst in 1754 and was part of the southern Catholic Enlightenment, i.e. was among those publicists who provided the accompanying music to the Josephine reforms. In this text Germany appears as a wealthy and potentially powerful country, and, thanks to her princes, as more enlightened and more inclined to philosophy than her neighbours but unfit for national unity, because the German national character runs counter to it. At the turn of the eighteenth and nineteenth centuries it was taken for granted, mostly with reference to ancient Greece, that a high level of culture and a dismembered state were mutually dependent.

Source: Johann Kaspar Riesbeck, *Briefe eines reisenden Franzosen über Deutschland* (Zurich 1783), ed. Wolfgang Gerlach (Frankfurt a.M. 1967), pp. 330–6.

Germany, including Silesia, is around one fifth larger than France. The total area comprises 12,000 German square miles. The country's soil is very different, however; a large part of it is so productive that no other state in our part of the world, apart from Southern Europe and France, is as fertile. The huge craggy masses in the southern regions of the Bavarian and Austrian sphere and the sandy tracts in the north – namely almost all the lower Saxony region, Brandenburg, Pomerania, Lausitz and the parts of Westphalia which point to the north – are indeed not as susceptible to cultivation as the other German *Länder*; but their very difference would entail great advantages for the whole country, if the same could concentrate its interests there. The mountain masses in the south produce nearly every sort of metal of the first quality and in enormous quantities, and the sandy plains in the north produce the best wood for ship-building, tar, hemp, fish and wool to excess.

Bohemia, Moravia, Silesia and the Archduchy of Austria, Bavaria, Swabia, Franconia, the Rhinelands, including those of the Wesphalian sphere, the

Austrian Netherlands and the region of the upper Saxony region, which do not belong among the King of Prussia's possessions, produce so much corn, cattle, wine and all sorts of the primary requirements of life, that they could adequately supply not only those regions of Germany which lack these things, but could also carry a considerable amount abroad. In short, Germany is the only European state capable of independence from the whole of the rest of the world for every requirement necessary for the defence of a cultured and wealthy people. France is short of wood, of cattle, especially horses, of the most vital metals and of linen, and Russia needs to import wine, wool, draft horses and some other articles besides from abroad. Germany has every requirement, which these two very different countries, which are so rich in some products, produce, as well as those which they lack, and to excess.

The King of Prussia reckons in his treatise *De la Littérature Allemande* that Germany comprises twenty-six million souls, and this figure seems to me to be the most reliable of the lot. The Empress of Russia says in her manifesto to the Court in Vienna concerning the latest Bavarian quarrel, 'all the powers in Europe must agree that the equilibrium in Germany must not be upset, since given the strength of this empire and its situation, the equilibrium of the whole of Europe would be upset at the same time.' This is indeed an irrefutable truth. Only France and Italy can compare with Germany as regards the ratio of their population to the size of their country.

This broad empire has not remotely attained the degree of cultivation it is capable of; not even the degree which our *patrie* has already attained. The Peace of Hubertusburg (1763) was the era of its cultivation. It is only since that time that agriculture and industry have become general. Germany is taking far faster and bigger steps in her cultivation than any other European kingdom. All at once, she is straining all her forces to fill the gaps which the devastating wars since Gustav Adolf have made in her bosom.

Even her dismemberment, so disadvantageous in the external application of her forces, encourages internal development. For the princes of Germany are competing with one another in improving their justiciary, their police, education, in promoting industry and commerce, as they once competed in splendour and empty pomp. Nowhere are people so enlightened about the value of individuals and their various employments and nowhere do people try harder to vindicate this esteem than in Germany. In most parts of this empire a benevolent light has been extended over the legislature and the interest of a state, which not only exposes its deficiencies, as in many countries especially in France, but also incites the princes and their servants to make good what is lacking.

It is incontrovertible that Germany, as does all Europe, has much to thank the present King of Prussia. He is the first practical philosopher of recent times to sit on a throne. He provided the solution to that happy revolution which had regenerated Germany twenty years ago. He it was who taught his neighbours that the ruler's interests run parallel to those of his subjects. He began to strip off the veil covering religion, justice and politics. He overthrew the petty tyrants, the religious and the nobility, who were gorging themselves at the expense of the burghers and peasants and, however military the constitution of his state appears to be, Germany has lived in peace for twenty years thanks to this so very frightful constitution and its imitations; only then, after centuries, could Germany begin to nourish feelings for herself.

Germany's legislation is now her greatest pride. She is also incontrovertibly the summit of philosophy and all human knowledge. Philosophy alone can make us happy. Religion, education, yes even the climate are at her disposal. She alone creates the social person and establishes his worth. And how proud Germany must be of Frederick, Joseph and Catherine, three simultaneous law-giving geniuses, when even thousands of years could hardly produce even one such! Besides these great rulers, the cause of happiness for millions of our countrymen and foreigners, Germany has several more geniuses of this kind, who are only distinguished from the former by their restricted sphere of action.

Philosophy appears to be an especially German concern. Cold and accurate judgement, allied with untiring diligence, distinguish them from all other Europeans. First they cast light over mathematics and physics, for which we have so much to thank them, then they illuminated theology, then history and finally legislation with the same philosophical intellect. They do well, too, in leaving wit to other nations, a game in which they can engage only with difficulty.

If Germany could vindicate herself completely; if she were united under one ruler; if the separate interests of individual princes did not so often run counter to the common good; if all parts were nicely joined in one body, so that the superfluous juices of one part could be easily conducted to the other members, then the Empire would be able to take much faster steps towards its culture. But then Germany would be able to prescribe laws for the whole of Europe. How powerful are the Houses of Austria and Brandenburg already, whose greatest strength rests on their German states and yet who own not even remotely half or even the best part of Germany! Imagine this Empire in a situation, where no excise duty impeded the internal commerce of the various provinces, no customs duties restricted exports to the rest of the world; where the huge sums for foreign wares, wares which Germany herself produces, were saved; where she could develop into a maritime power, for which she has both a favourable position and a surplus of all the requirements; where the colonists which she produces so frequently for foreign states are employed by herself – which European state could then measure up to the Germans?

The character of individuals is mostly the result of their government. The character of the Germans is on the whole as lacklustre as is the constitution of their Empire. They have naught of the national pride and love of the fatherland which characterise the Britons, Spaniards and our countrymen, however much their poets have for some time now been lauding these character-traits. Their pride and feelings for the fatherland relate solely to that part of Germany where they were born. The rest of their countrymen are as much strangers to them as are all foreigners. On the contrary, in many regions of Germany people are incomparably more partial to a few foreign nations than they are to their own countrymen.

Their national pride is obliterated by the smaller (German) peoples' sense of their weakness. The reason is simply that, because Germany cannot deploy her forces in unity and let other nations feel her power, her inhabitants are despised by other peoples, whose advantage over her is no more than a firmer cohesion among themselves or a derisory vanity. We seldom judge people according to their inner worth, but merely according to their outward appearance. We esteem the Russian, the Briton and such-like according to the weight of his whole nation, but not according to his peculiarities; and though he be ten times more barbaric than the German, yet the strength of his united countrymen in relation to other nations makes him the more estimable in our eyes.

Although the character of the Germans does not have the lustre of other nations, it does have its good inner content. The German is the man for the world. He can settle under every sky and can overcome all natural obstacles. His diligence is insurmountable. Poland, Hungary, Russia, the English and the Dutch colonies have much to thank the Germans for. The leading European states also owe part of their Enlightenment to Germans.

Besides diligence, sincerity is still a general character trait of the Germans. The customs of the country folk and the burghers in the smaller towns have also not deteriorated as much as in France and other countries. This is also a primary reason why Germany is still so populous in spite of heavy emigration. Furthermore, sobriety on the part of Protestant and ingenuousness and kindness on the part of Catholic Germans are fine character traits.

2 Christian Ulrich Detlev Baron von Eggers, Germany's Expectations of the League of the Rhine, 1808

The fact that the Rhine Confederation with its bias towards France was a creation of Napoleon's which did not survive his Empire has resulted in this institution being presented by German historiography wholly as a betrayal of the German nationalist cause. The fact is, however, that during the Napoleonic era the German question was still so open that even the Rhine Confederation, whose reform measures were far more liberal than the Prussian or Austrian ones, could be envisaged as a framework for future national unity, as this pamphlet by the lawyer von Eggers, who as an advisor to the Austrian government cannot be suspected of separatist leanings, proves. The text must be understood against the background of the tradition of a 'Third Germany', that of the German middle-ranking states and the Imperial towns, which had since the mid eighteenth century been in constant danger of being outranked by the great powers of Prussia or Austria. This 'Third Germany' was to preserve for a long time yet an older Imperial patriotism and a pride in the fact that they, unlike the leading German powers, contained exclusively German territories.

Source: *Die Erhebung gegen Napoleon 1806–1814–15*, edited by Hans-Bernd Spies (Darmstadt 1981), pp. 60–70 (excerpt).

One should try above all things to awaken and to nourish the idea of the unity of the state in all the subjects of the princes of the Rhine Confederation.

This idea is of the greatest importance for the power of the Confederation, for the culture of the nation, for the well-being of individuals. In a certain sense this idea itself lies in Nature, however much or often political arrangements are distractions from it.

Bavarians, Saxons, Franks, Swabians, Rhinelanders, Westphalians – do they not all talk and write German, do they not share many common customs, needs, ties? Now a single political bond embraces them all, one that gives them back the unity of the state against outsiders, which Germany had lost as long as three hundred years ago. This event is decisive and can have the most important consequences, if the rulers use it appropriately in all its emanations.

All these states have from now on only one common interest against outsiders: among themselves they possess only that of concord, of felicity. Can a happier federal bond be imagined?

What is there now to prevent the *Völker* (peoples) from considering themselves as the branches of one race? as born-again Germans?

In this the governments ought to try to be effective, each within its sphere. Nothing may be neglected which can lead to this great purpose. In this respect nothing is indifferent that has an influence on opinion.

We should now change the very names. The Rhine Confederation was formed for a far more restricted circle. It is now the true Germanic Confederation. The *Länder*, which would otherwise still belong to Germany, have now been absorbed into other states, apart from a few which are still awaiting their final destination. Their inhabitants have stopped being Germans. Austria and Prussia are now so very concerned that their subjects should view themselves only as Austrians and Prussians that the princes of the Rhine Confederation must wish that their subjects believed themselves federal Germans again, yea, considered themselves the only Germans.

The subjects of individual princes must all be esteemed as citizens of one state; all must enjoy the same rights in the other *Länder*. There must be no indigenous laws, no exclusive rights of citizenship, no right of withdrawal among the federal states.

It would be most desirable to insert shared institutions into the Constitution Act, which would constantly and clearly convey this Idea of Unity.

I have already mentioned the Federal Tribunal above. Its seat would have to be in the first prince's capital.

This capital would serve as the principal town of the Confederation. General assemblies would always be held there.

One would have to erect a Germanic Academy of the Sciences. Could there be any more favourable time for this than the present, when a Dalberg could assume its presidency?

An annual Federal Festival should be celebrated in every individual *Land*.

One could also found a common Order of Chivalry, to reward exceptional service of every kind. Each prince would be entitled to award the order to fewer or more people, according to the total size of his state.

Naturally these are but instances – thrown up in order to render the Idea perceptible. He who knows people and is interested in the Confederation, will find them not unworthy of his attention.

3 Johann Gottlieb Fichte. Extract from his fourteenth Lecture to the German Nation

Fichte's public *Lectures to the German Nation* in the winter of 1807–8 were the sensation of the Berlin Season; educated people of all classes, soldiers, burghers and officials, sat at his feet and were enthused. The lectures were published almost simultaneously and, in spite of the interventions of the censorship, the print-run immediately ran into huge figures. Fichte envisaged the eventual downfall of old Prussia and the onset of a new age, introduced by the Napoleonic occupation. Fichte felt that the German '*Urvolk*' now had the opportunity, through national education, of developing its nationality. Once the Germans had achieved national autonomy, their task would be that of liberating mankind. Fichte's lectures roused the stirring spirit of nationalism in Prussia, but met with rejection in Court and in conservative circles, on account of their emphasis on the priority of *Volk* and Nation over the State. The *Lectures to the German Nation* were prohibited reading from 1814 to 1824.

Source: *Fichtes Reden an die deutsche Nation*, edited by Rudolf Eucken (Leipzig 1915), pp. 249–54.

Centuries have gone by since you were last summoned together as you are today; in such numbers; in such a great, urgent and common concern; so thoroughly as Nation and Germans. Nor will you ever again be offered this. So if you do not pay attention, or retreat within yourselves, or allow these lectures to pass over you as an empty tickling in your ears or as a strange aberration, no man will ever rely on you again. Do listen, for once, do at last come to your senses. Just this once, do not leave your place without having reached a firm decision: and may each one who hearkens to this voice reach this decision by himself, just as if he were on his own and had to do everything alone. If truly many individuals think thus, then a great whole will soon stand there, merging into a single close-knit force. On the other hand, if each one excludes himself and pins his hopes on the others, leaving the cause to the rest, there will not be any others and all together will remain as they were before. Make this decision here and now. Do not say, leave us in peace a while, to sleep and dream a little longer, until better things somehow come along by themselves. They will never come by themselves. Anyone, having already failed the events of yesterday (which would have been even more apt for reflection), even today still cannot summon the will and tomorrow will be even less capable of it. Each delay renders us even more sluggish and pushes us still deeper into amiable accommodation with our miserable circumstances. Nor have the outward inducements to come to our senses ever been stronger or more compelling. He who is not roused by the present has surely lost all feeling. – You have been summoned together to form a final firm decision and resolution; not in the least as an order, a task or an exhortation to others, but as an exhortation to yourselves. You should reach a decision, which each one of you can carry out only on his own and by himself. It is not enough, somehow simply to concur in every idle resolution, every wish, or every dreary acquiescence, to which one would commit oneself if only one could do a bit better; but of you is demanded such a decision, as will immediately affect both life and inward deed, and which will endure without fluctuating or cooling, until it has attained the goal.

Or has perhaps the root from which alone such a life-affecting decision can grow, been fully extirpated from you and vanished away? Has your whole being really and truly been drained and reduced to an empty shadow without juice or blood and the ability to move, to a dream in which colourful faces appear and mingle busily but whose bodies remain lying there, deathlike and rigid? The age has long been told to its face, and had it repeated in every way, that this is more or less what one thinks about it. Its spokesmen have thought that one only wanted to denigrate it, and they have felt compelled to cast their own slurs, at which the whole business starts all over again. What's more, not the slightest change or improvement has been felt. If you have hearkened to it, if it has been capable of rousing your ire: well then, chastise those who think so and talk about you, chastise the lie through your deed: show yourselves to be different before the eyes of the whole world and the falsity of such accusations will be disclosed to the whole world. Perhaps it was precisely because they meant to rouse you, and because they despaired of rousing you by any other means, that they spoke thus harshly of you. How much better inclined to you were they than those who flattered you, in order to keep you in this dreary quietude, and in this feckless unthinking state.

Weak and powerless as you may be, it is nevertheless in this time that you were enabled to think clearly and peacefully as never before. That which actually upset us in the muddle of our situation, in our thoughtlessness and in our blind complaisance, was our sweet self-satisfaction, and our way of staying put. We had managed so far, and would continue the same; to anyone urging us to consider, instead of refuting them, we pointed triumphantly to our existence and continuance, which happened without any consideration on our part. But this was only the case because we had not been put to the test. We have since then undergone the test. Since this time, have the deceptions, the illusions and the false comforts with which we have all been confusing each other tumbled down? – Are our inherent prejudices, which like a mist in nature, derive from nowhere in particular and spread over everything, shrouding everything in the same twilight, now supposed to have disappeared? This twilight no longer holds our eyes, nor can it serve us any longer as an apology. We now stand there, clean, empty, divested of all foreign veils and vestments, simply as what we ourselves are. It must now be shown what this self is, or is not.

One of you ought to step forward and ask me: what gives you, among all German men and writers, the particular task, vocation and right to assemble us and to harangue us? Hasn't each of the thousands of Germany's writers the same right as you; but not one of them pushes forward save you alone? I reply that in any case each one would have had the same right as me; that I am the one to act is precisely because none of them has done it before me; I would keep silent if another had done it earlier. This was the first step towards the goal of a thoroughgoing improvement, and someone had to take it. I was the first to become vividly aware of this; that is why I was the first to do it. After this step, any other step can be the second; all have the same right to take it; once again, however, only one person will take it properly. One person must always be the first, and whoever can do it, well let him then do it!

Without worrying about this circumstance, let your glances dwell on the view which we pointed out to you earlier, of the enviable condition in which Germany and the world would be if the former knew how to use her fortunate situation and how to recognise her advantage. Then lift your eyes to that which both have since become, and let yourselves be penetrated by the pain and revulsion that must grip every noble spirit. Then return within yourselves and see that you are they, who must free the age from the mistakes of the previous world, from whose eyes it wants to remove the mist, if you allow it; that it is given to you, as to no race before you, to undo what has been done and to delete this dishonourable interval from the book of German history.

Let the different conditions, between which you have to make a choice, pass before you. If you retreat still further into your stupidity and listlessness, all the evils of servitude, despoliation, humiliation, of the victor's mockery and arrogance will then await you; you will be driven from corner to corner, because you are everywhere in the wrong and in the way, until you, by sacrificing your nationality and language, will buy yourselves some subordinate little place, and until in this manner our *Volk* will gradually be extinguished. But if instead you brace yourselves and take note, you will firstly be granted a tolerable and honourable continuance and next you will yet see a race flourish among and about yourselves that promises the most lasting renown for you and for Germans. You shall see in spirit the German name raised by this race to the most glorious of all the peoples, you shall see this Nation as the regenerator and restorer of the world.

It depends on you, whether you want to be the end and the last of a race unworthy of respect, one despised by posterity, yea even more than its due, the end of whose history our successors (should indeed the barbarian race which will then spring up ever achieve history) will rejoice over, congratulating fate on her justice; or whether you want to be the beginning and the starting point for a new age, glorious beyond all your imaginings, and to be people from whom posterity will count the years of its salvation. Think ye, that you are the last, in whose power this great change lies. You have still heard the Germans called One; you have seen a visible sign of her Unity: a *Reich* and a *Reichs*-union, or you have heard of it. From time to time there can still be heard among you voices enthused with this lofty love for the Fatherland. What comes after you will become accustomed to other concepts: it will accept strange forms and a different routine and way of life; and how long will it be until no one is left alive who has seen Germans, or heard tell of them?

What is demanded of you is not much. You should only value it above yourselves, pluck up your courage for a brief while and think about that which lies directly and openly before your eyes. About this you should form a firm opinion, remain true to it and even express it and speak it out in your familiar surroundings. This is the precondition, this is our firm conviction, that the success of this thinking will turn out in the same way with all of you, and that, if you only really think, and do not retreat into your former listlessness, you will think in agreement; that, if you only summon up a little spirit and do not persist in mere vegetable existence, the unanimity and harmony of the spirit will come by itself. However, once we have reached this stage, then everything else that we need will occur of its own accord.

4 Wilhelm von Humboldt. Memorandum concerning the German Constitution, December 1813

Wilhelm von Humboldt was more of a philosopher and philologist than a politician, and at the time of writing this memorandum he was Prussian Ambassador in Vienna. He was chiefly responsible for Austria's entering the War of Liberation on the side of Prussia and Russia. Napoleon's defeat is already in view, and the victorious powers are about to assemble in Vienna to reorganise Germany and Europe. In this memorandum to Freiherr vom Stein the author outlines his picture of a German cultural nation, which was still wholly imbued with the spirit of the classical German educated elite. As such it was in a state of permanent and unresolved tension between its dream of national unity and its attachment to provincial and regional autonomy as a stimulus for educational and cultural development. Consequently, the bond between the German states should not exceed that of a confederation of states, in which Prussia and Austria, the only federal members to count as truly military, would together hold the leadership. Some of Humboldt's proposals did in fact contribute to the founding concept of the German Confederation. In any case, Humboldt's calculations still reckoned with the patriotism of German citizens as the legitimising basis for the coming German State Union, and not with the subsequent opposition between the German Confederation and the nationalist movement.

Source: Wilhelm von Humboldt, *Werke in funf Bänden*, edited by Andreas Flitner, Klaus Giel, vol. 4 (Stuttgart 1964), pp. 302–22 (extract).

A truly assured community can only be effected through physical coercion or moral obligation. Government, however, is so determined that it can rely but little on the latter unless it displays the former in the background, and how necessary and effective this display is depends, always and everywhere, on the chance combination of circumstances. So our governments should never think of means which have to be absolutely secure, but only of those which can best adjust to the particular combination which seems politically most probable and can control it most naturally. In the event of uncertain success one must always admit and not forget that the spirit which founds an institution is continually needed to maintain it . . .

However, when one talks about Germany's future condition, one must be very careful not to adhere to the limited view point of wanting to secure Germany against France. Although Germany's autonomy is in fact threatened only from that quarter, such a one-sided viewpoint should never serve as a plumbline for laying the foundations for the lasting and beneficial condition of a great nation. Germany must be free and strong, not simply so as to be able to defend herself against this or that neighbour, or against any enemy whatever, but for this reason, that only a nation which is also outwardly strong can preserve within herself the spirit from which all blessings flow inwardly; she must be free and strong, even though she may never be put to the test, so as to be able to nourish the necessary self-confidence, to further her development as a nation peacefully and undisturbed, and to establish a lasting claim to the beneficial place which she occupies in the midst of the European nations.

Seen from this aspect, is not the question as to whether the different German states should continue on their own or form a common whole rather dubious? The smaller princes of Germany need a prop and the bigger ones an alignment and it would benefit even Prussia and Austria to see themselves as parts of a greater and, generally speaking, even more important whole. This relationship, which is made up of generous protection and modest subordination, involves greater fairness and universality in its attitudes towards its own interests. As well as which, the feeling that Germany constitutes a whole cannot be deleted from any German breast, since it rests not merely on customs, language and a literature held in common (given that we do not share them to the same extent with Switzerland and Prussia proper), but on the memory of laws and liberties enjoyed in common, of glory won and dangers overcome in common, on the remembrance of a closer alliance, which bound our fathers, and which lives on in their grandsons' yearning. The German states' dismembered existence (even if one were to join the very small ones to bigger ones) would, each state being left to itself, increase the mass of states either partly or wholly incapable of supporting themselves and would thereby endanger the European Balance of Power and the bigger German states, even Austria and Prussia, and might in the end completely bury all German nationality.

The manner in which Nature unites individuals into Nations, and divides the human race into Nations must be considered; a wholly profound and mysterious means of keeping the individual, who in himself is nothing, and the race, which is valid only in the individual, on the true road to vigorous development. And although the government never has to agree with such views, neither should it fail to run counter to the national condition of things. Though Germany's frontiers may be extended or restricted according to circumstances, she will always remain One Nation, One *Volk*, One State in the feelings of her inhabitants and in the eyes of foreigners.

The question can therefore only be this: how is Germany to be restored to unity?

If the old constitution could be re-established nothing would be as desireable as this, and were it only a foreign power which had suppressed her inherently sturdy vigour, it would resiliently have risen up again. Unfortunately her own slow dying was itself the chief cause of her destruction by an external power, and now, when this power is disappearing, no part of her is straining to rouse her unless it is by impotent wishful-thinking. From a close alliance, from a strict subordination of the members under the leader, and as a result of such and such a part pulling away, she had become a looser-knit whole, one in which every part had been struggling against the others more or less since the Reformation. How is the opposite struggle, which we now so urgently need, to emerge from that?

There are only two means of binding (Germany) into a political whole; a real constitution or a mere union. The difference between the two (at all events where our present purpose is concerned) lies in this; that in the Constitution legal powers to proceed against infringements are vested on some states, whereas, in the case of the Union, all must have this power against the violator. A Constitution is unarguably preferable to an Union, it is more solemn, more binding and more lasting . . .

The question: should Germany adopt a true constitution? can, in my opinion, only be answered thus. At the time when this question must be decided, if the head and members declare that they want to be head and members, then one should conform to the announcement and merely guide and restrain. Should this not happen, and nothing is expressed except the cold and rational judgement, that there must be one alliance for the Whole, then let one keep humbly to the lesser part and merely form an Union of states, a Confederation. . . .

Should we then ask ourselves what the binding and supporting principles for the Unification of Germany should be when it involves merely protective alliances? Then I can simply name the following very forceful, albeit mostly moral, instances:

The agreement between Austria and Prussia; the interests of the greatest among the rest of the German states; the impossibility of the smaller ones prevailing against them and Austria and Prussia; the re-awakened spirit of the Nation, to be maintained by peace and autonomy, and the guarantees given by England and Russia.

The firm, thoroughgoing and never interrupted agreement and friendship between Austria and Prussia is the sole keystone to the whole building. This agreement can be secured as little by the Union as the Union could be maintained did the agreement not exist. It is the best point outside the Confederation, which must be arranged so as to include it; and being thoroughly political it also rests on a purely political principle. Precisely, but by introducing to the Austro-Prussian relationship absolutely nothing more committing than that contained in any other alliance and by making this relationship the basis for the prosperity of the whole of Germany, which includes their own prosperity in hers, it can be strengthened by the sense of freedom and necessity, accompanied by the absence of any grounds for an exclusive interest, since no subordination or division of power between the two powers will be allowed.

The biggest states after Austria and Prussia must be big so that they can rise above all suspicion and all fear of their immediate neighbours, can add their weight to the defence of the independence of the whole, and, free from problems of their own, are concerned only with removing their common problems. Only Bavaria and Hanover find themselves in such a position, the middle states, such as Hesse, Württemberg, Darmstadt etc., would for their part have to be kept within their old bounds. Their small size does not allow them to presume to hold views over every minor one-sided issue, which would give a foreign power a great interest in binding any one of these to itself . . .

In any case, the defence against a foreign power would (insofar as one may presume Unity among the Few) benefit from the division of Germany into four or five large states. Only Germany has, more than any other *Reich*, openly assumed a dual position in Europe. Not equally important as a political power, she has acquired very beneficial influence through her language, literature, customs and way of thinking; this last advantage must now not be sacrificed, but linked to the former, although a few more problems have to be surmounted. At the moment, however, this advantage is wholly due to the great variety of education, which arose as a result of our great dismemberment and which would be mostly lost, were this to end. The German is only aware that he is a German, in that he feels himself to be an inhabitant of a particular *Land* within a Fatherland shared in common, and that his strength and striving would be impaired if he were to sacrifice his provincial autonomy and be subordinated into a foreign and incompatible whole. Patriotism is also influenced by this and even the security of each state, which is best guaranteed by their citizens' spirit, would benefit most from the principle of leaving to each one its old subjects. Nations, like individuals, tend to go their own way and are not to be swayed by any government. Germany's tendency is to be a Union of States, and consequently it has not merged together into a single mass, like France and Spain, nor has it, like Italy, arisen out of disparate individual states. This is, however, how the whole business would inevitably disintegrate, were one to allow only four or five big states to persist. A Union of States requires a greater number and the choice lies only between unity, which is in any case impossible (and, in my opinion, wholly undesirable), and this majority. It does indeed seem strange that precisely the principalities of the Rhine Confederation should be retained, and that Justice should proceed by confirming the work of Injustice and Coercion. It is only piecemeal changes which can always be achieved, and, in any case, in politics once something has happened and has gone on for years it accrues claims that cannot be denied – which is one of the most important reasons for steadfastly opposing injustices right from the start.

Whether the frontiers with France should be established by great states seems to be more of a military question. Germany's security rests solely on the strength of Austria and Prussia, as increased by the other German princes, and these can protect her more freely, when they, being further away and secured by their own firm frontiers, have between themselves and the enemy a region subject to their supervision and influence.

Article from the *Deutsche Blätter*, 10 November 1814.

The weekly newspaper *Deutsche Blätter*, published by Friedrich Arnold Brockhaus in Altenburg between 1813 and 1816, combined contributions from very different political perspectives. Since the middle of 1814 the volume of warning and pessimistic voices concerning the German question had increased. The anonymous article reproduced here anticipates the collapse of nationalist hopes in the face of the Austro-Prussian confrontation and urges the Prussian government to preserve the Liberal lead over the other German states which it achieved through its reforms, so that in the future it may remain the guarantor of a truly German nation state. This is one of the first public voices to demand a Liberal constitution in conjunction with a united nation-state.

Source: *Deutsche Blätter*, published by F.A. Brockhaus, vol. 5 (Altenburg 1814), pp. 510f. (excerpt).

It is clear from the premises outlined above that Germany has not even weathered the first epoch of a European state. She is not a country, not a nation, but a mixture of lesser peoples with one language, and in this respect she is at the same stage that France and Spain were at in the fifteenth century. She has not yet survived the first hour of birth, yet here and there, in places where the French Revolution has provided a little political education, she apparently already wants to labour at the second hour of birth. Neither in Nature, however, nor in Politics, is it possible to jump. Individuals, like peoples, must first have mounted that educational step, which for the middling sort to climb is one higher still, before they can hope to reach the last one. The question therefore arises, whether the moment for the epoch of Germany's unification into a great whole has come. The true politician, who does not flatter the nation but wants to deal honestly, must unfortunately answer this question in the negative. The moment seems favourable, but it only seems so. Since the genius of Frederick the Great created a second leading power in Germany, the puzzle (which was previously easier to solve) has become more insoluble than ever before. Even before she joined the *Grande Alliance*, Austria, as anyone familiar with more secret circumstances is aware, had been negotiating on good terms with the southern German courts lest they, in the event of her joining, should return to the earlier conditions against Austria. And although later on this power, equally weary, appeared to lead the Protectorate of Germany (now taken for granted by her) only by sacrificing her own forces, to direct her intentions more towards the Protectorate of Italy and, where German matters were concerned, to want only to obstruct them. And all this simply in order to prevent any other state from achieving supremacy over Germany, an attempt which seems primarily disposed to put off Germany's first epoch of unification into a great Whole.

What has been said about the Imperial dignity which alternates between Austria and Prussia, belongs among the foolish brainchildren of idle bookworms who, with no knowledge of people or the world, with no diplomatic connections, want to instruct the good-natured but politically still naive German public and to reform the world . . .

The moment now seems to have come, when the Nation may expect in return for so much loyalty and sacrifice an appropriate recognition of its worth in a proclaimed constitution, whose main basis is an independent Representation established according to rational principles . . . Prussia has gone too far for her to go backwards without danger. It is not just in this moment of power crisis that she must maintain this revolutionary position. She must complete this tendency, and with it the basis of her moral and political power. All Liberal dispositions in Germany are directing their gaze on this Northern Star. What do you expect? What indeed do all non-Slav and non-slave peoples now expect of their rulers? Recognition of the lofty principle that the will of the nation, as expressed by an equal and independent representation, is the basis of every constitution.

6 From a speech by the student Arminius Riemann given at the Wartburg Festival on 18 October 1817

Riemann, a *Burschenschaftler* from Jena, gave his speech at the beginning of the Wartburg Festival. It reveals how vehement and at the same time how vague were the nationalist hopes of those students who had participated in the War of Liberation. Reading between the lines of his rhetoric, which, in the fashion of the age, is rich in metaphor, one may glimpse the great gathering tide of frustration which was to sweep a whole academic generation into an as yet programmatically vague National Liberal opposition against Metternich's 'system'. The only Prince of Germany to have honoured his given word is Archduke Charles Augustus of Saxe-Weimar, who had already granted a constitution in 1816, based on the French *Charte constitutionelle* of 1814: the south German *Länder* only followed with their own constitutions from 1818 onwards.

Source: Paul Wentzke, *Geschichte der Deutschen Burschenschaft*, vol. 1 (Heidelberg 1919), pp. 213–15 (excerpt).

Four long years have flowed by since that Battle (of Leipzig); the German people had built up lovely hopes, THEY have ALL BEEN FRUSTRATED. Everything has turned out differently from what we expected. Much that is great and splendid, that could and should have happened, has not taken place; many holy and noble feelings have been treated with mockery and derision. Of all the Princes of Germany, only one has honoured his given word, that one in whose free *Land* we are celebrating this Festival of the Battle. Many doughty men have grown faint-hearted over this outcome, thinking that the much-vaunted splendour of the German people does not amount to anything, and withdrawing from public life (which promised to blossom so beautifully) and seeking compensation for this in the quiet pursuit of knowledge. Others even prefer to seek a new Fatherland in distant parts of the world, where new life is stirring. Now, I ask you, gathered here together in the bloom of youth with all the enthusiasm which fresh young vitality can muster; you, who will one day be the people's teachers, advocates and judges, on whom the hopes of the Fatherland are set, you, who have fought for the salvation of the Fatherland, part of you with weapons in your hands, and all of you in spirit and with your will; I ask you, whether you share this mentality? No! Not now and never! In times of need we have recognised the will of God and have followed it. Now, however, we want to adhere to what we have acknowledged, for as long as a single drop of blood flows in our veins; the spirit which has led us here together, the spirit of Truth and Justice, should guide us throughout our lives, so that we, all the Brothers, all the Sons of one and the same Fatherland, may build a wall of bronze against every external and internal enemy of the Fatherland, that the roar of death in open battle may not frighten us from enduring the fiercest fighting, when the Conqueror threatens; that the brilliance of the ruler's throne may not blind us and prevent us from speaking the strong free word, when Truth and Justice are at stake; that the striving for knowledge of Truth may never be extinguished in us, the striving for every human and patriotic virtue. With such principles, we want some day to return to civic life, with our eyes fixed firmly on our aim of the common good, and our hearts full of deep and ineradicable love for one single German Fatherland. You man of God (Luther), you firm rock of Christ's Church, for which you fought with iron courage against the darkness, for which you in this castle subdued the Devil, accept our vow, if your spirit is still in fellowship with us! You, the spirits of our fallen heroes, Schill and Scharnhorst, Körner and Friesen, Braunschweig-Oels and all the rest of you, who have poured out your heart's blood for the splendour and freedom of our German country, who now hover over us in eternal brightness and freedom and see clearly into the future, we call on you to witness our vow. The thought of you shall give us strength for the fight, and make us capable of any sacrifice. Just as you will remain in your people's memory and their blessing has also followed you to your graves, so may we also bless all those who are glowing for the good of the Fatherland, for Justice and Freedom, for which they live and work in word and deed. The destruction and hate of good people for all those who forget the common good in debased and dirty selfishness, who prefer a slavish life to a grave in free soil, who would rather creep in the dust than raise their voices freely and boldly against every injustice, who, in order to conceal their piteous inadequacy, mock our holiest feelings, and dismiss our enthusiasm and patriotic disposition and manners as empty foolishness, as the extravagant notions of an impaired intellect. You are already many; may the time soon come, when we no longer need to name you!

7 Friedrich von Gentz, French critic of the 1819 Federal Decrees

Gentz, as advisor to Prince Metternich, Chancellor to the Austrian Imperial Household, Court and State, was one of the decisive figures of the restoration epoch. He defended the Carlsbad Decrees of 20 September 1819 suppressing the nationalist and Liberal movement. This was a reaction against, among others, the academic opposition, which had become visible for the first time at the Wartburg Festival. Behind all this lay the archetypal horror of Revolution which dominated the Courts of Europe in the nineteenth century, as well as a well-founded anxiety about the collapse of the European Balance of Power, which had only just been established at the Congress of Vienna, and which rested decisively on the partition of Central Europe.

Source: Friedrich von Gentz, *Schriften*, Edited by Gustav Schlesier, vol. 2 (Mannheim 1838), pp. 198–201 (excerpt).

It is already clear from the facts (which have until now been revealed only piecemeal and are surely not yet exhausted) about the whole sequence of disturbances, that an unexpectedly large number of unruly heads, part seducers and part seduced, have participated in the extravagant plans for a radical transformation of Germany, according to first one then another idiotic model. This would certainly not have been the case if the last few years had not witnessed the prevalence of the opinion that Germany, viewed as an integral state and in her federal condition, basically only exists in name, has no real means of supporting herself, is liable any day to disintegrate and, in a word, is a blank slate on which anyone can write and sketch anything that the genius of caprice (which is called Freedom) might suggest. It is above all through the latest Federal Decrees, but especially through the establishment of this Commission, that this madness, although not quite eradicated, has yet been visibly shattered. It has now been shown that the life principle of that integral body was far stronger than even the Best of the Nation had thought, that it did not stint the Confederation of the means and powers of establishing its existence and its laws, and – by far the most important – that when extraordinary circumstances demanded great common measures, all the German princes without exception were able to recognise and promote the good of the whole . . . Given that the unification of all the German tribes into an undivided state is a dream which has been refuted and finally rejected by the experience of a thousand years, a dream whose fulfilment no human combination has managed to achieve, and which the bloodiest revolution has not obtained through duress, and which only madmen can still pursue, then maybe we will sooner or later achieve through perseverance that which, in its present form and along the road selected by Fate, even honest and intelligent men have on a few occasions in history accepted for the sake of this dream, insofar as it can be realised and is compatible with the true good of Germany . . .

There is indeed one aspect, according to which the Frankfurt Decrees are not extraneous to the other states either, but which cannot possibly be used to reproach the German sovereigns with. The Spirit which has unmistakably directed these decrees – a spirit of preservation, of fortification, of discipline and order, of a well-understood love of the people, and of a well-understood civil freedom – is in any case inseparable not only from the prosperity of Germany, but from the security and continuation of various states; and, if this spirit does not hold the upper hand everywhere in Europe, a wilderness full of bloody ruins will be the only inheritance awaiting our successors.

8 Johann Georg August Wirth. The Political Reform of Germany, 1832

> Fifteen years after the Wartburg Festival the front-lines in the
> National Question had been very clearly drawn. The Bavarian
> publicist Wirth, a co-founder of the left-wing Liberal Press and
> Fatherland Union and the main speaker at the Hambach Festival,
> wrote this pamphlet, extracts of which are reproduced below, in
> prison at Zweibrücken, because he had advocated creating a
> 'Confederation of Patriots' and had thus infringed the Bavarian
> prohibition of assembly. His argument was attractively simple: Unity
> and Freedom for Germans are two sides of the same medal; once the
> Princes, who deny the *Volk* free self-determination, have been
> divested of power, this will naturally result in the Germans
> combining to form a nation.
>
> Source: *Restauration und Frühliberalismus 1814–1840*, edited by
> Hartwig Brandt (Darmstadt 1979), p. 321ff.

More than for Freedom and for the material prosperity of the separate provinces, . . . the resolute patriots of Germany long for the political unity of their Fatherland. And in fact they are right: for this is the only means to Freedom and Prosperity for the separate provinces; without it there can be no guarantee that true Freedom will survive and flourish, without it no prospect for the lasting organisation of this part of the world and no salvation for Europe! The enemies of Freedom and of the German Volk accuse the resolute patriots of attaching no clear concept to the 'Unity of Germany', and of advocating an idiotic organisation of the country. We ask these gentlemen to convince themselves of the opposite from the following scheme of things. Not by forcible centralisation, that is not by arbitrarily making all the German provinces, without considering their particular interests, bow to the sceptre of one single government, shall the political Unity of Germany emerge, but far more by binding the various German tribes with a natural and indissoluble bond, while retaining their sovereign administration of their particular concerns, in order to obtain a cast-iron guarantee for the Freedom, Integrity and Autonomy of every individual province against the others and for the Freedom, Integrity and Sovereignty of the whole Fatherland against the outside world. Such an indissoluble bond, however, lies not in empty state agreements, dictated by the interests of princely families, but in the power of

126

sympathy by binding it to the interests of the races. Nature has already provided a fervent bond for the German races, the strong bond of language; History has strengthened this by giving one name to all the individual races and the memory of our forefathers' great deeds; Learning has finally dedicated this bond and ennobled it through the splendid bloom of Literature, which thanks to our common language has been cultivated to the common benefit of all our races and fills all our hearts with the same pride. The only bond to be even stronger than the bond of a common Language, of our Name and our Literature is that of our Interests. Much as these bonds impel us towards the indissoluble unification of the different German races, they would still be powerless, once the spiritual or material interests of the individual *Länder* were at variance with one another. In a state of Freedom such variance would indeed be impossible, because both the intellectual and the material interests of all the German races are intimately connected, partly through the geographical situation of their *Länder* and partly through the common bond of their language, name and literature. In this connection, a quarrel would only be possible if the ruling authorities of the individual brother-races divided their interests from those of their *Volk* and were to wrest sovereignty by such an unnatural system, destructive of the whole people as by forcibly suppressing the *Volk*'s public life. Now, other races may, by intolerably mishandling their interests, including the intellectual ones (among which are to be counted Freedom), wholly forget the bond and voice of Nature and desire Unification with a foreign *Volk*, if their spiritual or material position is thereby to be improved. Now, once the system of government in those *Länder*, through which the interests of all the brother-races and thereby of the whole fatherland are harmed, encounters no powerful opposition and even some support from public opinion in those *Länder*, then the whole country will be further afflicted by the curse of inner discord. For between the injudicious adherents of an anti-national system and the loyal friends of the whole Fatherland there can never be peace. Who is not aware that our precious Fatherland has been reduced to this terrible position? Who does not know that it was cast into this dreadful pit by the policy of the Cabinets at Vienna and Berlin, that worthless policy which, through the ravages of customs lines and the grievous suppression of public life, has destroyed Commerce and Freedom and has, in particular, wounded the highest interests of the South German races unto death? As a result of this disloyal and treacherous policy the loveliest provinces of Germany have been cast into the desperate position of having to choose between their nationality and their interests, on account of external political storms. Since the bond of interests, given man's rational nature, is stronger than that of nationality, so Germany's strength has been broken outwardly and the integrity of the country has been exposed to very great peril in every storm. This danger can only be averted by reconciling our interests. Once the quarrel over the latter has lifted, the natural compulsion towards nationality will come of its own accord into its rights again and will then be mighty enough to maintain the Dignity of the Nation and the Integrity of the Region against any external enemy. Since, as was pointed out above, the interests of all the German races are necessarily equal, in conformity with the natural order, and can only be set at variance by the self-interested or ambitious aims of princely families, so too the political unity of Germany depends firstly on the princely families being deprived of their uncircumscribed dictatorship in all public affairs affecting not just one single German *Land*, but also the interests of the rest of our brother races, and secondly, on the leadership in every matter of common concern, as much internal as external, being naturally transferred to the organs of public opinion of all our brother races.

On the eve of the 1848 revolution, this Bavarian feudal lord, who was attacked by the conservative side because of his Liberal views, diagnosed the motives behind the German Nationalist Movement, which he defended against the German governments. The Unification movement was provided with a powerful impetus reaching beyond German Liberalism by the sense of 'nullity', of Germany's inferiority as a whole in comparison with the other European states. The extent to which the black, red and gold colours were automatically viewed as the German national flag is remarkable.

Source: *Denkwürdigkeiten des Fürsten Chlodwig zu Hohenlohe-Schillingsfürst*, ed. Friedrich Curtius, vol. 1 (Stuttgart, Leipzig, 1907), pp. 40f.

Wherever we look, we see the emergence of an unprecedented participation by the Volk in public affairs. But the governments misunderstand this movement. They see or wish to find in this movement only the work of a radical propagandistic clique and they are filled with suspicion. One reason for the dissatisfaction is generally prevalent in Germany, and every thinking German man feels it profoundly and painfully. Do not tell us that Austria and Prussia, as great powers, represent the power of Germany abroad. For one, Austria does very little representing abroad, because she lacks the inner strength, and for the other, Prussia's position among the great powers is, to speak bluntly, only tolerated and if her internal political movement continues as it has begun she will not hold this position much longer. However, that still leaves us with just Prussia and Austria, and the rest of Germany still playing a minor role as tub-thumping bystanders. No one will deny that it is a sad fate for a thinking and competent man not to be able to say when abroad: I am a German, or look proudly at the German flag on his ship; to find no German consul when in trouble, but to have to say: I am a Kur-Hessian, a Darmstädter, and Bückeburger, my fatherland was once a great and mighty country, but is now split into thirty-eight patches. And when we look at the map and see how the Baltic, the North Sea and the Mediterranean lap against our shores and how no German ship, no German flag on the sea flies the usual greetings at the proud English and French, do we not have to feel the colour of shame, all that is left of our black, red and gold band, mounting in our cheeks? And will the miserable talk about the Unity of Germany and the German Nation not have to remain depressingly ridiculous until the word is no empty echo, no longer a phantasm of our good-natured optimism, and we really do have a great and united Germany? The present extension of trade is no longer adequate for industry, which has grown enormously through the Customs Union, and the wealthy commercial class seeks external markets and overseas outlets. Complaints about the inadequate German fleet will multiply and the question of the unity of Germany, a unity that really is politically acceptable, will be handled with renewed energy by the now free press.

10 From the Debates in the German National Assembly – Little Germany or Greater Germany? – 1848–9

The following extracts from the debates in the Paulskirche Assembly are intended to illustrate the change in mood from the initially widespread anti-Prussian, pro-Habsburg attitude of the majority of the delegates to their final decision to offer the German Imperial Crown to the Prussian King. We start off with their decision on the provisional central authority. A proposal was put to the National Assembly about setting up an Austro-Prussian-Bavarian Directorate of Three; it is revealing that the Prussian delegate Braun's proposal, that the central authority be conveyed to Friedrich Wilhelm, was drowned by laughter. Instead, the Austrian Archduke Johann was proclaimed Imperial Administrator (*Reichsverweser*). The decisive debates about the *Reich*'s frontiers and the role to be played by Austria and Prussia took place only in the autumn of that year. The constitution committee's draft required Austria to bring about a personal union between her German and non-German *Länder*, so that her German part could be included in the German state. This was unacceptable to the Austrian government and to the majority of the Austrian delegates to the Paulskirche; the Habsburg monarchy having just regained its unity in a series of bloody battles, no responsible Viennese statesman would have dared surrender or attenuate this actual unity in favour of an ideal German unity. In the Kremsier programme the Austrian government, at the end of November 1848, announced its rejection of the National Assembly's demands. Heinrich von Gagern now replaced the Austrian Anton von Schmerling at the head of the *Reichs*-ministry, and on 18 December 1848, he demanded Austria's exclusion from the future German Federal State as the only realistic chance for German unity. Von Gagern prevailed with a narrow majority after protracted and bitter debates. When the Austrian government proclaimed a General Constitution on 4 March 1848, thus finally abandoning the possibility of Austria's entering the German Nation State, it was one of the leaders of the great-German faction, the liberal Theodor Welker from Baden, who put forward the motion of electing the Prussian king as hereditary German Emperor. The election took place on 28 March, with 290 votes in favour of Welker's motion, and 248 delegates refraining from voting.

Source: *Deutsche Nationalversammlung. Stenographische Berichte*, vol. 1, pp. 443–6; vol. 6, pp. 4233–4, 4236, 4626–9; vol. 8, pp. 5666–9.

20 July 1848
Braun (for Coeslin)

The amendment runs:
'Until the definitive foundation of a supreme government authority for Germany the exercise of the same in all common affairs will be transferred to the Prussian Crown . . .' (Hilarious laughter in the assembly)
President: Gentlemen! Do let everyone speak his mind.
A voice (from the floor): The Speaker on the rostrum himself is also laughing.
Braun: . . . with such conditions and provisos as have been cited in the report for the proposed Federal Directorate.'

Concerning the grounds for this amendment, most of which grounds have already been found in every speech made by those who spoke before me, I will permit myself to add only a few words. Gentlemen! That the Fatherland is in danger, has often been said here. Whether we turn our glances inwards or cast them outwards, it lies clearly before our eyes. Inwardly all is tumult and bloody riots. Confidence in the survival of the social order has been shattered. Hence the poverty of our manufactures and our commerce, hence the poverty of our masses. Outwardly, there is war and the threat of war . . . Whether we form a three-headed or thirty-three-headed *Bundestag* is a matter of some indifference. (Finish! Finish!) I am still at it, I haven't finished yet. In peaceful and pleasant times it might work; now, however, when the danger is great and urgent, a powerful hand must grasp the reins of government, and, fortified by respect, moral strength and the energy of the Assembly, must put an end to the revolution at home, and, defend the Independence and Honour of Germany abroad through the might of a great and single Volk. Your commission, Gentlemen, appears in any case to have recognised this, but it has proceeded cautiously. In these days of peril, Gentlemen, all caution lies outside the bounds of Patriotism. The princes' and the peoples' love of the Fatherland must have the courage to suppress this caution and these jealousies. It is a time of iron, and this time of iron requires an iron-clad fist. Who at this moment can offer the Fatherland this fist – other than Prussia? (*A voice:* Prussia will offer us her fist, we need her hand.) It is not just the fifteen million Germans who support this view. It is her geographical position. It is in particular the Prussian Army, on which Germany can rely.

The German's habitual inclination is directed towards his old Imperial House. Yea, if Austria could free herself from all non-German parts and merge completely in Germany, like Prussia, than one might risk it. Gentlemen! There is no one more cognisant of the claims of habit and tradition than myself. But at this moment I do not believe that Austria is in a position to undertake this mission. I ask you, which other *Land* could there be in Germany which could undertake the Directorate as vigorously as Prussia? I do not know of any. Gentlemen! I do not speak of the Princes, neither unkindly nor flatteringly. The princes' persons are transient, but their people remain. For the moment, indeed, we are talking only about a provisional arrangement, but even if we were dealing with the future, I would, for myself, call on the *Bundestag* in the words of the great poet: "Enrich one from among all and your Olympus will surely vanish." '

President: The wish has been expressed, that we put the question of whether such an amendment is supported straightaway so that this matter need not be enlarged on any further.

A voice (from the left): That's something we really don't have to fear.

President: 'The Amendment runs: "Until the definitive foundation of a supreme governmental authority for Germany the exercise of the same in all common affairs will be transferred to the Prussian Crown with such conditions and provisos as have been cited in the report for the proposed Federal Directorate." I put the question to you: Does this proposal have any support? (From all sides: No!) The proposal thus has no support and so is dropped. At least twenty members should have supported the proposal if it were to be discussed further. My question can result in no more than the request, that proposals which do not find sufficient support, should not be further enlarged on.'

Reh from Darmstadt: 'Gentlemen! I do not want to reply to anything in the Delegate from Hinterpommern's speech . . .'

18 December 1848
Reichs minister von Gagern

' . . . the position which Austria has assumed respecting the German National Assembly and the provisional central authority for Germany, imposes on the *Reichs*-ministry the duty of putting these subjects for discussion to the National Assembly, whose attention has already been claimed by these important questions.

The Austrian ministry's programme of 27 November declares:

(1)   that all Austrian lands should remain allied in an united state;

(2)   that Austria's relations with Germany could only be organised as a state when both state complexes have achieved new and firm forms, that is, when their internal organisation has been carried out.

This interpretation of Austria's position regarding Germany has won the applause not only of the Austrian *Reichstag* at Kremsier, but also appears to accord with the wishes and views of the great majority of the inhabitants of the German-Austrian lands. On the Austrian side, the answer has hereby been given to the question put to Austria in the National Assembly's resolution about the draft constitution: 'Chapter about the *Reich* and the *Reichs* authority', contained namely in paragraphs 1–3. The *Reichs*-ministry considers, having assessed the central authority's position with regard to Austria, that they must start from the following principles:

(1)   Given the nature of Austria's ties with our German *Länder*, the

duty of the *Reichs*-authority is generally restricted for the moment and for the duration of the provisional government, to maintaining Austria's existing Federal relationship with Prussia. However, Austria's peculiar relationship must be acknowledged, whereby she reserves the right not to join the German Federal State about to be formed under conditions which alter the ties of state between her German and the non-German Austrian lands. (Agitation)

(2)   Austria will thus, consequent upon the passage of the decree pending in the National Assembly whereby the nature of the Federal State is determined, not be regarded as a fully participant member of the proposed German Federal State.

(3)   The ordering of Austria's relationship of Union with Germany by means of a special act of Union, whereby all the kindred, intellectual, political and material requirements which have bound Germany to Austria for ages and could bind them ever more tightly, are to be satisfied as far as possible, is to be reserved for the immediate future. (Agitation; disapproving noises from the Left.)

(4)   Since Austria stands in indissoluble confederation with Germany, as represented by the provisional central authority, but does not enter within the Federal State, then the agreement about all mutual federal duties and rights, both those already existing and those in the future, is to be introduced and discussed through diplomatic channels.

(5)   The suppression of the German Federal state, whose speedy termination lies in the interests of both sides, can however not be the subject of discussion with Austria . . .

Venedy (for Cologne):

' . . . I hereby propose that this proposition be rejected by us directly, immediately and without discussion. (Bravo from the Left.) We have come here, Gentlemen, to constitute Germany's Unity, and we are met with the proposal that we throw a part of Germany out of Germany. (Stormy cheers and claps from the Left.) On that day when we only discuss this proposition, we will be discussing the division of Germany. The German nation, Gentlemen, has already suffered enough, but she has finally prevailed and has sent us here to constitute Germany, and they want us to sell off a part of Germany. I have come here to the Paulskirche with the firm decision to stand or to fall with the Paulskirche. But I do not want to sit here a moment longer if Austria is not here too. (Stormy cheering from the Left side of the house).

Reitter (for Prague):

' . . . I even believe that it is in the interest of the mover himself, that this project be submitted to the Austrian committee for approval. This committee should then approve whether Germany is to become a second Poland. (Cheers from the Left.) When you hand a part of Germany over to Austria, you have handed it over to Russia.' (Stormy cheers from the Left.)

Hartmann (for Leitmeritz):
' . . . I consider it criminal to reply to the new prime minister's proposal in only three words. We have not come here to form treaties with others; our task here is to decide among ourselves about the fate of Germany; we have no ambassadors to send. We Austrians have not come here as prodigal sons to beg for admission to our father's house. We are at home here and are entitled to sit here, like all other Germans. (Cheers from the Left.) We will not let ourselves be driven out, neither subtly, nor roughly, nor by intrigue, nor by force. I hereby submit that we put this proposal onto the agenda at once and without it being called for as it, in my opinion, deserves. (Cheers from the Left.)

Moritz Mohl (for Stuttgart):
' . . . We are 40 million Germans; we do not need to fear these scattered little nations. There are perhaps five million Czechs: there are not five million Magyars, still fewer Croatians and even fewer Wallachians etc . . . All these nations can do no disadvantage to German nationality; it is however of the very greatest importance that they combine with Germany, and that with Germany they form a *Reich* of seventy million persons. Gentlemen! I ask you, when these seventy million people are represented in a German parliament, when this parliament through its influence nominates the ministers of this great *Reich*, and when nothing occurs to the disadvantage of this great *Reich* of seventy million people; I ask you, which power in Europe, even Russia with her sixty-six millions, or France with her thirty-six millions, which power in Europe will be powerful enough to challenge this great *Reich*? I ask, whether this German *Reich* is then not in a condition to dictate war and peace to the whole world; I ask you, to consider this. It is, I think, one of the greatest thoughts of our century, which has already been expressed by various Austrians, and has in fact been elucidated by Herr von Möring in extraordinarily interesting writings. Gentlemen! This thought about the entry of the whole of Austria within the German Federal State; I beg you to fix your eyes on this thought, telling yourselves that it removes every difficulty in this matter . . .

13 January 1849
Beseler (for Greifswald):
' . . . Austria wants her whole monarchy, that is what we wanted to know and that is enough for us. But if she wants her whole monarchy, then she cannot leave the German provinces out of the whole monarchy and align them with the German Federal States. No one can serve two masters. If there

is a sovereign authority here and another there, then one cannot be subject to both at the same time. Neither can Germany allow German policy to be divided, with Austria ruling here and Germany there. Either, or! One must either give up the former or not want the other . . . I consider it possible to establish a really indissoluble relationship between Austria and Germany, one which does not just run along the lines of the usual alliance in international law. I consider this possible, because we have a Federal Act, on the basis of which we can negotiate. There is no formal obstacle to this. I want, however, to name three more guarantees, which will chain us together indissolubly. The first is German freedom . . . the second guarantee is German learning. Let the turnpikes be thrown down, let the breath of free learning enter within Austria, and you will find that this, more than any outward power, will join the peoples of Austria to Germany. And, finally, the community of material interests . . . On the basis of the Federal Act, under these guarantees, in the sense of our common nationality with the dominant part in the whole Austrian state, with the honest desire on the part of German men, that they really want what is good, what is best for both parts; I now maintain that something worthy of our time and bringing equal advantage to all ought to be established. Truly, gentlemen, although it is no absolute division, no absolute separation, it is nevertheless a relief that we cannot admit Austria's German inhabitants within the same close alliance within which the rest of the German people is now ready to enter. It will be acknowledged not without pain by everyone with any feeling for not only the Unity of the German nationality, but also for the splendid German races, which stand beneath the Austrian Imperial sceptre . . . We will not weep as women do, but, (laughter from the Left) should we see our Austrian friends depart, we would take our leave with an honest manly handshake and retain an upright, manly love for Austrians . . .'

12 March 1849
Urgent Motion proposed by Delegate Welcker
'The constituent German National Assembly, recognising the urgency of the Fatherland's situation, determines:

(1)   In view of the repeated public news reports about foreign protests against the constitution about to be determined by the German nation, to express both its indignation at such attacks by externals against the holiest original right of free peoples, and its profound revulsion towards every German, be he Prince or burgher, who might treacherously incite such attacks, and at the same time its firm expectation, that the German Nation will defend its honour to a man and prevent all harm to it . . .

(3)   The hereditary Imperial Dignity established in the Constitution will be conveyed to His Majesty the King of Prussia (Great sensation).

(4)   The various German Princes will be invited to agree generously and patriotically to this condition, and to promote its realisation according to their ability . . .

(6)   His Majesty the Emperor of Austria, as Prince of the German-Austrian lands, and the various brother races in these lands, are invited and encouraged both individually and unitedly to join the German Federal State and its Constitution now and for all time.

(7)   The German National Assembly pronounces for all time a solemn refutal of any right claimed whether by the government of the German-Austrian lands, or by these lands themselves, to withdraw from the German Fatherland and from its constitution as established by common consent.

(8)   It is, however, prepared to maintain the existing national fraternal conditions for as long as difficulties remain to obstruct a definitive realisation of the German-Austrian lands' complete entry into the constitution of the German *Reich*, albeit without harming the autonomy of the German Constitution. (Big sensation. Several voices: 'von Welker?')

President: The motion is proposed by Herr Welker of Frankfurt (Big, prolonged sensation and agitation in the Assembly.)

Welker to establish the urgency of the motion:

' . . . My reservations about the hereditary Imperial title derive neither from a dislike of Prussia nor from a preference for Austria. I had nothing else in mind but that which we all want, the Unity of our great Fatherland. I did not want to see this prejudiced by any regulation which might endanger this Unity. When I thought that we might not yet decide on the Prussian hereditary imperial title, I did not allow myself be influenced by any brilliant expectations of Austrian cabinet policy . . . My view was simply this: Our duty prescribes keeping the whole fatherland together, and taking no step which might possibly rip it apart, even temporarily, before every means of binding the whole Fatherland has been exhausted . . . I wanted to know that every means had been exhausted, I wanted finally to be firmly convinced that the furthest limit had been reached, before such a great, momentous step should occur. I now believe, Gentlemen, that the means have been exhausted, I now believe, that it has long been clearly demonstrated by the work of the ministers' own hands, by their Babylonian constitution, that we cannot expect Austria's union with the Federal State from them. The latest events are known to you. I now believe that the times require the rest of Germany to unite all the more firmly, strongly and fervently. (Lively cheering from the Right and Centre.) When I look around at my old friends here, I may perhaps encounter a little triumph in their hearts, if not in their faces, that they had viewed matters correctly weeks and months ago, and I only so tardily. Be proud of it, if you want, but forgive me if I too am proud – albeit sad in heart – that I strove as much as possible with all my strength to postpone the separation. (Cheers.) We have won much thereby, and even you, the most zealous adherents of the Prussian Imperial Crown must thank me; for, Gentlemen, consider, if a slur could have adhered to this crown, a reproach, the semblance of guilt, that it had torn Germany apart; if the thought could have arisen that Austria had been driven out by hasty or selfish resolutions, Oh! then this crown would not have been worth as much, nor been as benevolently protective. We wanted to maintain our Austrian brothers in a fraternal alliance with us, and we have tried to achieve this. We wanted to make them aware that here, in all Germany, German hearts are beating for them, ready at any time to stretch out a fraternal hand when they return to us. (Lively cheering.)

Gentlemen! I tell you, the Fatherland is in danger; do not let matters go any further, act now, swiftly and determinedly! However, I ascribe a further special importance to my motion, since only if it is accepted will there remain a single possibility that the Austrian cabinet will quickly settle with what we are firmly convinced is right. WE, however, can no longer negotiate with it, nor allow it a delay of months and years. It will then be the King of Prussia's task, to demand a decision by ultimatum, and a decision there will be in, perhaps, a few days or weeks. (Applause from the Right and Centre.) It is possible that Austria will join us, in which case nothing will have been lost. Should this not be possible, then we want to be armed against the dangers which this break will entail; for, rest assured, so long as this break between Austria and Germany exists, our enemies lurking in the East and West are ready to nip this young Germany's Unity in the bud. I have nothing more to say than: Germany is in danger: rescue our Fatherland!

11 Friedrich Wilhelm IV to Count Christian Karl Josias of Bunsen, the Prussian Ambassador in Berne, 13 December 1848

Friedrich Wilhelm IV's rejection of the Imperial Crown on 3 April 1849 was accompanied by expressions of deep respect towards the National Assembly. That the king nevertheless envisaged allowing the constitutional and imperial solution formulated at Frankfurt to be adopted to some extent by the German princes, seems to indicate a whiff of democratic support. This plan was in any case to collapse in Olmütz in the teeth of Austrian opposition a year later. However, Friedrich Wilhelm IV's actual thoughts about the legitimacy of the parliamentary imperial election were quite different, as his letter to his friend Bunsen demonstrates. Bunsen tried to persuade the king to accept a popular imperial title as envisaged by Heinrich von Gagern, the prime minister of the provisional *Reichs*-government.

Source: Leopold von Ranke, *Aus dem Briefwechsel Friedrich Wilhelms IV. mit Bunsen* (1873). In: *Leopold von Rankes sämtliche Werke*, vol. 50 (Leipzig 1887), pp. 493ff (extract).

My very dear Bunsen! Your last letters have confirmed what I noticed already in Brühl and whenever possible have fought against, that we in Germania do not understand one another, or, much rather, that you cannot understand me. This is a harsh thing to say, and I feel it; but friends must put up with one another. I understand you and your reasonings, but you don't understand mine, or you would not have been able to write thus, that is, you would not then have given (which you have done) the absolute impediments which stand between me and THE !!! Imperial Crown an easy and easily dismissed name. You say (literally as Herr von Gagern said to me on 26 and 27 of last month): 'You want the consent of the Princes; well and good, you shall have it.'

But, my dearest friend, therein lies the rub: I want neither the Princes' consent to THE election, nor THE throne. Do you understand the words I have marked?

I will cast light over them for you as briefly and brightly as possible. THE crown is actually no crown. The crown, which a Hohenzollern could accept, IF the circumstances COULD make this possible, is not one which an Assembly, which, although constituted by princely consent is riddled with the seeds of revolution, MAKES (*dans le genre de la couronne des paves de Louis*

139

Philippe), but one which bears God's mark, which makes HIM, on whom it is set after being anointed with holy Chrism, 'by the Grace of God', because and how it made more than thirty-four princes into Kings of the Germans by the Grace of God and always keeps company with the last ones of that ancient line. The crown, which the Ottonians, the Hohenstaufens and the Habsburgs have worn, a Hohenstaufen can of course wear; it honours him superabundantly with the glitter of a thousand years. THE one, however, which you unfortunately mean, dishonours superabundantly with its carrion reek of the 1848 revolution, the absurdest, the stupidest and the worst, if not, God be praised, also the most evil thing of this century.

Should a legitimate King by the Grace of God allow himself to be given an imaginary circlet, welded out of dirt and tatters, let alone the King of Prussia, who has THE blessing of wearing if not the oldest, then the noblest crown, which has not been stolen from anyone?

Search your heart, dear Bunsen; what would you, a former member of the Prussian diplomatic corps and my truly Privy Councillor, and invested with the rank of the high nobility, say and do, if you were, for instance, retired and living in Corbach, were to be elevated to an Excellency by the Waldeckian sovereign *Landes* Assembly? There you have a faithful picture of my position *vis à vis* Gagern and his *Traction*. You would write very politely to the sovereign Waldeck: 'That which you want to give me is not yours to give, but I have one of the standard weight and alloy.' And precisely so will I too reply . . .

I tell you roundly: Should the thousand-year-old crown of the German Nation, which has rested for 42 years, be given away again, then I am HE and my EQUALS, WHO WILL GIVE IT AWAY. Woe to him, who usurps that to which he has no right.

12 Declaration by an Enlightened Friend of the Fatherland, 19 July 1859

The 'Hanoverian Declaration', as it was known, constituted the first step towards founding the German National Society. It carried 25 signatures, 20 of which were of members of the Hanoverian Second Chamber. Among the signatories were Rudolf von Bennigsen and Johannes Miquel. Unlike the statue of the National Society of 16 September 1859, which referred expressly to the Hanoverian Declaration but avoided making any precise statement about political goals, the Prussian and 'Little Germany' orientation is here clearly expressed. Unlike the debates which were still running in the Paulskirche, the necessity for a strong central authority is now given priority over that for a Parliament; the National Society expects the Prussian government to provide the initiative for forming the German Nation State, which the popular nationalist movement will only support.

Source: *Der Weg zur Reichsgründung, 1850–1870*, ed. by Hans Fenske (Darmstadt 1977), pp. 172–5 (abbreviated).

The war between Austria and France has ended. However, this has not resulted in a more secure legal situation in Europe. The conflicts in Italy, which initially led to the outbreak of war, have not been solved and have, according to all appearances, even increased. France's threatening military superiority is further heightened by the war. Everywhere in Europe we find the same discontented situation, with new complications and wars, even wars of aggression against Germany, already appearing possible in the near future.

In order to be able to counter such dangers safely, a powerful revival of Germany's nationalist spirit and a rapid development of her political forces are urgently required. It is however clear that the present forms of the Federal Constitution constitute obstacles to any such revival. This constitution had already been shown to be wholly untenable prior to the year 1848, and even more so during the movements of 1848. After 1848 it was summoned back to life as an emergency measure on the part of the Governments and showed even more clearly that the nation's interests could not be met by it and that firm legal conditions could not be established in the individual German states. The war which has just ended has unfortunately convinced us that the

Confederation's military constitution presents no warrant for swift and unanimous action against external dangers.

Consequently, the demand for a more uniform constitution for Germany, involving the participation of representatives of the German people in charge of its own destiny, must grow even greater. Only greater concentration of the military and political powers, allied with a German parliament, will be able to satisfy the political spirit in Germany, to develop richly its inner strengths, and establish a powerful representation and defence of its interests against external powers.

So long as the German people does not yet despair of a reform of its constitution and does not seek to be rescued from inner and outer dangers solely by means of a revolutionary rising, the most natural way is for one of the two great German governments to undertake to bring the reform of our Federal Constitution into being.

Austria is not capable of this. Her interests are not purely German, nor could they ever become such. Besides, the reform of Austria's internal conditions, which even her government has recently acknowledged to be necessary, will require her full attention for many years. She will have to deploy all her forces to instill order in her bankrupt finances, to improve the conditions of private law and of the church, and by altering the regions' constitutions to counter the outbreaks of discontent which are accumulating in almost every part of her Empire; in Italy, Hungary and many Slav provinces. All this leaves Austria with such extensive and difficult tasks in hand that diverting and dismembering her forces for more remote German aims, initially suggested as the solution to her inner turmoil, would appear to be well-nigh impossible.

Our hopes are thus directed towards Prussia's government, which has demonstrated to its people and to all Germany by changing its system of its own volition during the previous year, that it has accepted that it is its duty to bring its interests and those of its country into agreement. For such a purpose, it does not shrink from sacrificing its discretionary powers or from treading new and difficult roads. The aims of Prussian policy are basically compatible with those of Germany. We may hope that the Prussian government will grow ever more aware that separating Prussia from Germany and pursuing solely those goals which pertain to Prussia as a great power, can only lead to Prussia's ruin. The German people in most parts of our Fatherland has over the last few weeks unanimously demonstrated that, in times of danger and war, the management of our interests and the leadership of our military powers can confidently be placed in Prussia's hands, once clear aims, a firm leadership and decisive dealing are all that are to be expected of Prussia.

Recent months have shown yet again that it is not advisable, with regard to the military states with their monolithic powers which surround us to the West and East, to wait upon the hour of peril, so that only when battle is about to break will we find out whether we can expect the German governments to take common decisions about swift and energetic measures. We need a federal constitution which can offer the prior protection of rapid and unanimous action.

The greater part of Germany – and us with it – consequently expects that, in this time of peace and preparation which has maybe been granted us for but a little while, Prussia will grasp the initiative for the quickest possible introduction of a uniform and free federal constitution. It will thereby undertake a great and difficult task. Neither, however, will it forget that by strengthening Germany, it also protects itself. It will also hold firmly to the hope that a loyal and strong policy will finally enable it to overcome the opposition and difficulties which stand in its way.

The German federal governments will indeed have to make sacrifices for the Whole, if a more centralist constitution is to be introduced in Germany. In view of the looming crises, however, it will scarcely take long to convince them that a more uniform power in Germany is a necessity not only for the Fatherland's interests, but for their own as well. Surrounded by autocratically ruled and strongly centralised military states only the more tightly organised peoples and states in Central Europe will be able permanently to safeguard their independence and existence. After all, it is better to transfer part of one's powers of government to a German Federal authority, than to lose the lot to France or Russia.

For Europe and Germany the peril is great. Only swift decisions can help. May Prussia not hesitate much longer, may it turn openly to the governments' sense of patriotism and to the peoples' nationalist spirit, and take immediate steps to summon a German parliament and to introduce a more uniform organisation of Germany's military and political forces, before new struggles break out in Europe and threaten an unprepared and splintered Germany with awful dangers.

The German people's patriotic feelings will support the Prussian government on this road. Political opinions and party politics will be subordinated to the practical requirements of the moment and to the good of the whole. The governments too, we hope, will not withdraw from the nationalist movement, which is directed towards a peaceful reform and which finds that the German people is ready to make the greatest sacrifice in order finally to achieve a constitution for the whole Fatherland, one guaranteeing the right and free development of the individual within, and the nation's autonomy and independence abroad.

13 The National Liberal Party's founding programme, 12 June 1867

The foundation of the National Liberal Party brought about the simultaneous end of the German nationalist movement: its founding programme also stressed that it was not possible 'to fight with the same weapons at all times for the same tasks'. For National Liberalism, which basically included all the forces of the former Nationalist Society, the German question was solved with the foundation of the North German Confederation as the preliminary step towards the eventual foundation of the German *Reich*. 'Little Germany' took precedence over 'Great Germany', Unity over Freedom, although the Liberal and 'Greater Germany' elements of the nationalist movement persisted as secondary goals. The alliance between the National Liberals and Bismarck sealed the unity of the revolution from above and from below, and nationalism, from being a 'leftist' phenomenon, turned 'rightist' inasmuch as it became a force supporting the state, although it retained its anti-establishment character which was to become an increasingly influential element of German policy by means of nationalist and imperialist mass organisations, by the colonialist 'rush to the sun' (*Drang zur Sonne*) and the construction of a fleet directed against England, and was to prepare the political and ideological way to World War I.

Source: Wilhelm Mommsen (editor), *Deutsche Parteiprogramme* (Munich 1960), pp. 147–51 (extract).

When the previous Alliance broke up last year and the Prussian government declared its earnest desire to maintain the national bond and to establish German Unity on firmer foundations, we had not the slightest doubt that the Liberal forces of the Nation had to work together if Unification was to be achieved and at the same time the people's need for freedom was to be satisfied. For this purpose we were prepared to work together; this would only become possible when the government stopped infringing the constitutional law, recognised the principles which are so emphatically defended by the Liberal Party, and sought for and obtained an indemnity. The groupings within the party determined by the constitutional quarrel were not enough to ensure cooperation. The new requirement was met by the formation of the National Liberal Party, with the purpose of establishing Germany's unity, and ensuring power and liberty, on the aforesaid foundations.

We never lost sight of the difficulties of the task, of promoting Liberal progress with imperfect constitutional weapons and in cooperation with a government, which had maintained the constitutional conflict for years and had run the country without a budgetary law. But we undertook this task with the firm desire of overcoming the problems by pursuing our earnest task and confident that the greatness of our goal will strengthen the people's capacity to act. For we are animated and united by the thought that national Unity cannot be attained without fully satisfying and permanently maintaining the people's Liberal demands, and the people's sense of freedom cannot be satisfied without the energetic and driving power of National Unity. For this reason our election slogan is: The German State and German Freedom must be won at the same time by the same means. It would be a ruinous mistake to think that the people, its promoters and its representatives need only defend the interests of Freedom and that Unity will anyway be established, irrespective of us, by the government in the course of its cabinet policy.

The Unification of Germany under one and the same Constitution is for us the highest task of the present time.

The difficult task of bringing a monarchical Federal State into unison with the terms of constitutional law is one which has not previously been achieved. The constitution of the North German Confederation has neither solved it to a complete extent nor in a finally satisfactory manner. But we view this new task as the first indispensable step on the road to the German state, buttressed by Freedom and Power. The inclusion of South Germany, which the constitution allows for, must be urgently promoted with all our strength, but under no circumstances may it put the uniform central authority in question or weaken it.

A constitution proceeding from the settlement of practical needs has never been effected without some shortcomings, which increase with the number of conflicting interests. Nevertheless, it was always a sign of healthy vitality that the improving hand immediately began to take effect. We have not avoided the fate of human imperfection, but the problems have not discouraged us and the tares have not blinded us to the good wheat. As our Party was concerned right from the start with improving itself, so already by the next *Reichstag* it will labour unceasingly at developing the Constitution as it now stands.

In Parliament we saw the unification of the living and effective forces of the Nation. Universal, equal, direct, and secret suffrage has, with our cooperation, been made the basis of public life. We do not close our eyes to the dangers which it entails so long as the freedom of the press, of assembly and of forming unions are repressed by the police, so long as our schools are crippled by regulations, as elections are subjected to bureaucratic influence, and that the Diets' failure to act restricts eligibility. But since these guarantees were not to be achieved, the dangers have not scared us off. It is now up to the people to demand fair elections; the people's energetic struggle will enable their voice to be heard clearly, and then universal suffrage itself will become the firmest bulwark of freedom, will clear away the rubble of the feudal system which has persisted into the new age and will at last make equality before the law a reality . . .

Recalling the Party's heavy responsibility and faithful to the principles set out earlier, the Party has, in these days of peril and of decision, established inner peace on the foundations of constitutional law, granted adequate supplies and authorised the defence measures which should safeguard the free operation of Prussia's function. For the honour and predominance of our Fatherland we will continue to deal in the same sense. The burdens of chronic mobilisation spur us on, however, quickly to strengthen the new conditions in Germany so as to achieve soon, or at any rate not later than the end of the provisional government, the very necessary economy of a real state of military peace. In the mean time the clause limiting military service to the end of the thirty-second year of life ensured by the *Reichs*-constitution, must be brought in quickly, and wherever possible other reductions be effected.

We do not entertain the hope of being able to meet our many needs all at once, but we will not lose sight of any of them and will put one or other to the fore, depending on the circumstances. But we consider a constitution in accordance with the laws, which unviolably respects the law and freedom both of individual state bodies and of the whole, to be at all times the indispensible condition for beneficial cooperation between government and popular representation and for preventing new conflicts. Any regression to another practice of the past must be whole-heartedly opposed whatever the danger. We can walk hand in hand only with a government that keeps to the laws. With such a one we are ready to seek the right paths.

One pressing experience has taught us that one cannot fight with the same weapons at all times for the same tasks. Where such meaningful and weighty goals are to be struggled for at the same time, as at present in Germany and Prussia, it is not enough, simply to hold firm to traditional tenets and, by favouring a simple and easy tradition, to allow the new and manifold needs to go unheeded. Hard and circumspect work is needed to do justice to the various requirements, to supervise the progress of events and to grasp the momentary advantage. The final goals of Liberalism are unchanging, but its demands and methods are not cut off from life and do not exhaust themselves in rigid formulas. Its innermost being consists of observing the signs of the times and meeting their requirements. The present says clearly that in our Fatherland every step towards constitutional freedom is also an advance into, or carries within itself the impulse towards, the region of freedom.

We are not minded to meet other factions of the Liberal Party with hostility, for we feel at one with them in the service of freedom. With regard to the great factions of the present, however, we are striving and hoping, aware as we are of how much depends on the right choice of means, to apply the principles developed above within the Party.

Notes

Part I Three weeks in March

1 Wilhelm Angerstein, *Die Berliner März-Ereignisse im Jahre 1848*, Leipzig 1865, p. 6.
2 Ibid., p. 13.
3 In: Rudolf Haym, *Reden und Redner des Ersten Preussischen Vereinigten Landtages*, Berlin 1847, p. 458.
4 Jacob Grimm to Gervinus, 20.4.1847. In: Tim Klein (editor), *1848. Der Vorkampf deutscher Einheit und Freiheit*, Munich, Leipzig 1914, p. 92.
5 Adolf Wolff, *Berliner Revolutions-Chronik. Darstellung der Berliner Bewegungen im Jahre 1848 nach politischen, socialen und literarischen Beziehungen.* Vol. 1, Berlin 1851, p. 7.
6 Angerstein, *Berliner März-Ereignisse*, p. 15 f.
7 Ref. *Berliner Revolutions-Chronik*, vol. 1, p. 30.
8 Report in the *Zeitungshalle* of 12.3.1848, taken from: *Berliner Revolutions-Chronik*, vol. 1, p. 41.
9 Ref. Veit Valentin, *Geschichte der deutschen Revolution von 1848–49*, vol. 1, Berlin 1939, p. 418.
10 The Police President to the Berlin Government, 13. 3. 1848, reproduced in: Klein, *1848*, p. 146 f.
11 Karl Frenzel, *Die Berliner Märztage*, Leipzig, undated, p. 43.
12 Ibid.
13 Angerstein, *Berliner März-Ereignisse*, p. 23.
14 Prince Kraft zu Hohenlohe-Ingelfingen, *Aufzeichnungen aus meinem Leben.* Vol. 1, Berlin 1897, p. 20.
15 Minister of the Interior von Bodelschwingh writing in the *Neue Preussische Zeitung*, no. 15 on 19.1.1849, see Sources.
16 Report by Police President to Berlin Government, 15.3.1848, reproduced in Klein, *1848*, p. 150.
17 Ernst Kaeber, *Berlin 1848*, Berlin 1948, p. 47.
18 Otto Hoetzsch, Peter von Heyendorff, *Politischer und privater Briefwechsel.* Vol. 2., Berlin 1923, p. 47, letter of 17.3.1848.
19 Leopold von Gerlach, *Denkwürdigkeiten.* Vol. 1, Berlin 1891, p. 130.
20 Ref. Klein, 1848, p. 149 f.
21 Major-General von Schaeffer-Bernstein to the Hesse State ministry, 18. 3.1848; reproduced in Valentin, *Geschichte der deutschen Revolution*, vol. 1, p. 424.
22 *Berliner Revolutions-Chronik*, vol. 1, p. 97.
23 Kaeber, *Berlin 1848*, p. 55.

24 *Berliner Revolutions-Chronik*, vol. 1, p. 125.

25 Valentin, *Geschichte der deutschen Revolution*, vol. 1, p. 428 f.; the official investigation report: Lieutenant-General von Mayernick, *Die Tätigkeit der Truppen während der Berliner Märztage 1848*, published in: *Beiheft zum Militär-Wochenblatt*, 1891, p. 99 ff.

26 Max Weber, *Objektive Möglichkeit und adäquate Verursachung in der historischen Kausalbetrachtung*, in: *Gesammelte Aufsätze zur Wissenschaftslehre*, edited by J. Winckelmann, Tübingen 1973, 4th ed., p. 266 ff.

27 Theodor Fontane, *Von Zwanzig bis Dreissig*, Berlin 1982, p. 348.

28 *Berliner Revolutions-Chronik*, vol. 1, p. 159.

29 Heinrich von Sybel, *Die Begründung des Deutschen Reiches durch Wilhelm I.* Vol. I, Munich, Leipzig 1889, p. 139.

30 Angerstein, *Berliner März-Ereignisse*, p. 50.

31 Hohenlohe-Ingelfingen, *Aus meinem Leben*, vol. 1, p. 27.

32 Ibid., p. 34.

33 Ref. Kaeber, *Berlin 1848*, p. 70.

34 Quoted in: Klein, *1848*, p. 178 f.

35 Adolf von Menzel to Carl Heinrich Arnold, 23.3.1848. Quoted in: Else Cassirer (editor), *Künstlerbriefe aus dem neunzehnten Jahrhundert*, Berlin 1919, p. 23.

36 *Denkwürdigkeiten aus dem Leben des General-Feldmarschalls Kriegsministers Grafen von Roon*, edited by Waldemar Graf von Roon, vol. 1, Breslau 1892, p. 143.

37 Werner von Siemens, *Lebenserinnerungen*, Berlin 1901, p. 48 f.

38 Ref. *Berliner Revolutions-Chronik*, vol. 1, p. 251 f.

39 Angerstein, *Berliner März-Ereignisse*, p. 65.

40 Fontane, *Von Zwanzig bis Dreissig*, p. 370.

41 *Dokumente zur deutschen Verfassungsgeschichte*, publ. by Ernst Rudolf Huber, vol. 1, Stuttgart, 3rd edition, 1978, p. 448 f.

Part II The German nationalist movement's road to the creation of the Reich

1 Friedrich Carl Moser, *Von dem Deutschen Nationalgeist*, Leipzig 1766, p. 5f.

2 Justus Moser, *Der Autor am Hofe, In: Sämtliche Werke*, part 2. Compiled by Ludwig Schirmeyer, vol. 6, Berlin 1943, p. 12.

3 *Friedrich Gottlieb Klopstocks Oden.* Edited by Franz Munker, vol. 1, Stuttgart 1889, p. 222.

4 Germaine de Staël, *De l'Allemagne* (1813). German edition, Stuttgart 1962, p. 68.

5 Adolph Freiherr von Knigge, *Joseph von Wurmbrand* (1792). Edited by Georg Steiner, Frankfurt am Main. 1968, p. 11.

6 Ernst Moritz Arndt, *Geist der Zeit*, Part 3, Altona, London, Berlin, 1814, p. 430.

7 Hardenberg to Altenstein, 26.3.1808. In: Heinrich Scheel, *Das Reformministerium Stein. Akten zur Verfassungs- und Verwaltungsgeschichte aus dem Jahre 1807/8.* Berlin 1966, p. 468.

8 From the 'Federal Constitution', according to a statement by one of its members before a board of inquiry in connection with the 1821 'persecution of Demagogues'. Ref: Percy Stulz, *Fremdherrschaft und Befreiungskampf*, Berlin (East) 1960, p. 124f.

9 Ibid., p. 128.

10 Gneisenau to the King, 20.8.1811. In: Karl Griewank (Editor), *Gneisenau. Ein Leben in Briefen*, Leipzig 1939, p. 175.

11 Quoted in: Michael Hodann, Wilhelm Koch, *Die Urburschenschaft als Jugendbewegung*. Jena 1917, p. 15f.

12 Paul Achatius Pfizer, *Gedanken über die Aufgaben und das Ziel des Deutschen Liberalismus* (1832). New edition by G. Kuntzel. Berlin 1911, p. 341.

13 Paul Wentzke, Der Deutschen Mai 1832. Voraussetzungen, Verlauf und Folgen des Hambacher Festes. In: *Aus Politik und Zeitgeschichte*, 15.5.1955, p. 296f.

14 Sir Stratford Canning to Lord Palmerston, 3.4.1848. Extract from the original in Michael Stürmer, Die Geburt eines Dilemmas. Nationalstaat und Massendemokratie im Mächtesystem 1848. In: *Merkur 35* (1981) 1, p. 5 (translated from the German).

15 Memorandum of June 1829. In: *Vorgeschichte und Begründung des Deutschen Zollvereins 1815–1834*. Hermann Oncken, Friedrich Saemisch, Eds. Vol. 3, Berlin 1934, p. 534.

16 Report to Francis I, June 1833. In: *Metternichs nachgelassene Papiere*. Edited by Fürst Richard von Metternich-Winneburg, Vol. 5, Vienna 1885, p. 504ff.

17 N.T. Gross, Die industrielle Revolution im Habsburgerreich 1750–1914. In: *Europäische Wirtschaftsgeschichte*, C.M. Cipolla, K. Borchardt Eds., vol. 4, Stuttgart, New York 1977, p. 219.

18 Ferdinand Lasalle, *Der italienische Krieg und die Aufgabe Preussens. Eine Stimme aus der Demokratie*, Berlin 1859, p. 52.

19 The full text was first published in: *Deutsche Allgemeine Zeitung* 4.3.1937, supplement.

20 Hermann Schulze-Delizsch, *Flugblätter des Deutschen Nationalvereins*, Vol. 1, Coburg 1860, p. 16. Words emphasised in the original.

21 Otto von Bismarck, *Die gesammelten Werke*, Friedrichsrüher Edition, vol. 10, Berlin 1926, p. 139.

22 Johann Caspar Blüntschli to Heinrich von Sybel, early February 1863. In: Johann Heyerdorff, Paul Wentzke Eds., *Deutscher Liberalismus im Zeitalter Bismarcks*. Vol. 1, Bonn 1921, p. 131.

23 Hermann Baumgarten to Heinrich von Sybel, 22.5.1863. In: Heyerdorff, Wentzke, vol. 1, p. 151.

24 A.Pf., Die neue heilige Allianz, *Wochenschrift des Nationalvereins*, no. 156 dated 24.4.1863.

25 Rudolf von Ihering to Julius Glaser, 1.5.1866. In: Karl-Georg Faber, *Realpolitik als Ideologie*, In HZ 203 (1966), p. 15.

26 Rudolf von Ihering to Bernhard Windscheid, 19.8.1866, Ibid., p. 16.

27 Hermann Baumgarten, *Der deutsche Liberalismus. Eine Selbstkritik* (1866). Edited by Adolf M. Birke, Frankfurt am Main, Berlin, Vienna 1974, p. 146.

28 Bismarck to Graf von der Goltz, 9.7.1866. In Bismarck, *Gesammelte Werke*, vol. 16, p. 233.

29 Otto Fürst von Bismarck, *Gedanken und Erinnerungen*, Vol. 1. Stuttgart 1899, p. 293.

Bibliography and source material

I. General bibliography

There is no such thing as a modern bibliography of German history of the 18th and 19th centuries capable of satisfying the requirements of historical research. Although we do have Dahlmann-Waitz's monumental work, his information is, going by the latest edition, already thoroughly out of date.[1] Nor, for that matter, are the *Handbücher zur deutschen Geschichte* based on the latest state of research, although it is advisable to have recourse to them if one wants to assemble a coherent picture of German history. Gebhardt's work is dry, brief and precise, and serves as a preliminary overview, whereas the work by Bradt, Meyer and Just is colourfully written, although much more limited in scope.[2] Some of the serial publications about German history, which have appeared since the end of the 1970s, are very useful. Although the series called *Oldenbourg Grundriss der Geschichte* offers only terse factual descriptions, its bibliographies are all the more extensively commentated and reflect the latest state of research and historical controversy. The series called *Deutsche Geschichte der neuesten Zeit* is also primarily aimed at schools, students and historians; the volume included below may serve to illustrate how the series is structured and how it can be used. On the other hand, anyone looking for a comprehensive and well-written account of German history, based on the latest research, should reach for the volumes in the series Die Deutschen und ihre Nation.[3]

II General bibliography about the history of nationalism

Friedrich Meinecke's work, *Weltbürgertum und Nationalstaat*, came out in 1908 in an attempt to describe what was special about the road to the '*Kleindeutsch*' Reich using the tools of the history of ideas, and based on historical events.[4] This work is still worth reading nowadays on account of its clear language, pregnant judgement and the way the details are set within a comprehensive and closed scheme. It is, however, only useful in a historical sense, being methodologically obsolete; although drawn up according to guidelines provided by a few great thinkers' and politicians' ideas, its geographical range is limited to Prussia and its judgement is inevitably tied to the viewpoint of a National Liberal university teacher of the later Wilhelmine Empire.

Since then a number of works touching Meinecke's great theme have appeared, but these are either merely articles, subordinate parts of general descriptions, or they are limited to questions of detail. There has until now been no comprehensive research into the German road to the nation-state, which describes and explains the process of German nationalisation from the 18th century to the creation of the Reich, using the tools of modern social, *'mentalités'* and political history; this applies surprisingly enough not only to Germany, but also to France and Italy, to name but two other notable desiderata, whereas a splendid work dealing with the development of national identity in Great Britain has recently appeared.[5]

The phenomenon of nationalism has been researched and analysed in many ways, mostly on a theoretical plane. Eugen Lemberg and Peter Alter have presented very exciting comparative research, allowing them to formulate general statements about nationalism, with Lemberg tackling the broader historical horizon and Alter keeping to the firmer basis of concrete historical findings.[6] Helmut Plessner's classic work about the *Verspätete Nation* (delayed nation) of Germany is also fundamentally a theoretical statement, presenting nationalism as the destructive surrogate ideology of a German bourgeoisie alienated from its roots; a contribution to the theory of a special German path (*Sonderweg*).[7]

Recent discussion has taken place mainly in the sphere of modernisation theorems; within the framework of research by the American Research Council's Committee on Comparative Politics one series of significant works has emerged which is especially important for our inquiry, since it attempts to make accessible research of a categorising and analytical nature into every aspect of nation building.[8]

Impressive and overlapping analyses from the viewpoints of Karl Marx's and Max Weber's theories have also appeared, which aim at developing theoretical and comparative ideas.[9] But all these works remain unsatisfactory in that they all build on faulty empirical foundations. Here, as so often, the town has already been roofed over before strong foundations have been built with the help of historical data based on documents.

III German nationalism

In the post war era, the question about the development of the German Nation State was neglected by historical studies for decades. A remarkable omission, given that it is obvious that answering this question constitutes the basic precondition for understanding the German catastrophe of the 20th century. Since the beginning of the 1980s, however, historical interest in these problems has altered enormously – reacting, as is generally the case, to an altered political climate. A period of economic prosperity, of full security in the Western Alliance and of general confidence in the future and in progress was followed by economic depression and a loosening of the federal system, allied with a crisis of confidence in the resilience of democratic institutions, all of which were felt more keenly in the German Federal Republic than in other Western countries. In such times the collective need for traditional reserves and for safeguarding one's national identity grows, giving rise in Germany to a flood of hugely popular historical exhibitions, to the founding of a *Deutsches Historisches Museum* in Berlin and to what is called the '*Historikerstreit*' (Battle of the historians), which split German historiography down the middle over the interpretation of National Socialism and its role in German history.[10] So German historical studies also turned to the analysis and description of the German question, of the problem of the Nation in the heart of Europe.

The fruits of these efforts include in the first place simply collections of articles and conference papers,[11] which the interested reader must sift through to find the pearls; the Anglo-Saxon reader should find an edition by this author, which sheds light on the social, economic, ideological and political aspects of the German question within an European perspective, and also contains an introductory bibliography to the whole theme.[12] There is, in any case, also a comprehensive and exceptionally well commentated bibliography to the History of German nationalism.[13]

A few articles outlining the whole problem deserve to be picked out. Robert A. Berdahl has made an interesting attempt (though not entirely satisfactory on account of its one-dimensional approach) to describe the development of the German nationalist movement as a function of economic modernisation.[14] James J. Sheehan has pointed out in a notable article that, viewed from the perspective of the German nation-state of 1871, the preceeding history has been presented in much too streamlined a fashion as an uniform and teleologically-bound history of the German nation, although it emerged from many points of view, many of which were not based in the slightest on nationalism.[15] Finally, Otto Dann's article about nationalism and social change in Germany 1806–50 must be pin-pointed as rich in facts and thoughts and one of the very few attempts to trace the German Nationalist Movement back to its social foundations.[16]

With regard to the German nationalist movement, there are two recent works which look at this phenomenon as a whole. George L. Mosse places the connection between social organisation and ritualisation at the centre of his reflections and thus interprets the Nationalist Movement entirely within the framework of its conventional presentation as a special German way (*Sonderweg*), unbroken in continuity from the War of Liberation to National Socialism, Christoph Priegnitz on the other hand restricts himself to a rather dull recital of its developmental history up to the revolution of 1884, forgoing any comprehensive interpretation of its whole political, social and economic historical background.[17]

IV   The early phase of the nationalist movement until 1815

There are as yet no works which reflect the beginning of the Nationalist Movement in connection with the educated middle-classes' trend towards self-organisation in the 18th century. One essential aspect, that of the middle-class trend towards forming associations, has nevertheless already been extremely well researched for this period;[18] there exists an extensive literature about the development of public literary life prior to the Napoleonic era, covering the reading public, publishing and the reading societies mainly in the Germanic field,[19] while the politico-social context has been outlined by Helmut Berding and Hans Peter Ullmann.[20]

The process of nationalisation in the Napoleonic era has mostly still to be researched; Meinecke's *Weltbürgertum und nationalstaat* is still generally relied on for method and assessment. This also applies to recent studies, which judge the development of collective national themes critically within the framework of the *Sonderweg* theory.[21] A few detailed studies make it easier to approach the theme; for the North-German area there are a few works which investigate the political debate of that time.[22]

It is only in the German Democratic Republic that historians have been more intensively concerned with the nationalisation process before 1815, which they assess mostly in a positive manner, in accordance with Friedrich Engels' statement that the struggle against Napoleon enabled the masses to achieve political awareness for the first time since the Peasants' Wars; in spite of the Marxist-Leninist bias, very notable works have been produced, both in the methodological sense and in relation to their source material, which also do justice to the ambivalence of the early Nationalist Movement.[23] The same applies to the War of Liberation as the instigator of a nationalist frame of mind among the masses; on account of the legitimising role which the Prussian military reformers are supposed to have played for the German Democratic Republic's National People's Army, but also on account of the Prussian-Russian alliance at that time, the historiography of the German Democratic Republic has lovingly adopted the years 1813–15, whereas history writing in the German Federal Republic is scarcely aware of the theme. As frequently happens with our theme, it is worth taking a look beyond the subject's limits. The connection between national sensibility and belligerent lyrical production, an important indicator of collective emotions, is the object of Germanic analysis.[24]

V   Pre-March and Revolution 1815–1850

The pre-March period, on the other hand, is among the favourite subjects of recent academic research, especially where the political and social organis-ations and movements are concerned. Previous literature about gymnastic and singing clubs has been rendered obsolete by Dieter Düding's *Habilitat-ionsschrift* which has recently appeared. Düding's special merit consists of having demonstrated, contrary to earlier research, that prior to the revolution of 1848 most of these clubs were distributed not in the north, but in south-western and south Germany – an important pointer for further regional studies.[25] Liberalism, the political sector of the nationalist movement, has been looked at in this connection in a new work by James J. Sheehan, with reference to all the previous research, although Sheehan does not reveal clearly the connection between Liberalism and nationalism, vital though this is for German history. There is still no history of the *Burschenschaften* capable of meeting the requirements of modern historical study, nor does a closer investigation into the Riflemen's Associations (*Schützenvereine*) exist, which played such an important role in Catholic Germany as transmitters of nationalist ideology.[26] Much remains to be done to illuminate the background to and conditions for the development of a National movement – we know far too little about its underlying social strata and, indeed, about how the history of communications fits in.[27] It would be delightful to re-write the history of the Wartburg Festival, perhaps in connection with the other great and small national festivals which took place around it, this time as a special contribution to the history of nationalistic rites, liturgies and symbols; previous works on the subject are scarcely aware of these dimensions.[28]

The Revolution of 1830 has subsequently been put in the shade by the attention paid the 1848 revolution, and has still not been adequately researched, especially where regional and social history are concerned, whereas the circle of the Hambacher Festival in 1832 appears to have been better illuminated. The new nationalist wave of the 1840s has until now been described much too one-sidedly from the point of view of political repression, social deterioration and the onset of protest with reference to the revolution which came after. The Nationalist Movement's ambivalence, which included hope that progress could be made concerning the National Question, the mood-swing of the Rhine Crisis and the National Monument Movement in the early forties, still need to be illuminated. In spite of Irmline Veit-Brause's excellent Dissertation on the Rhine Crisis of 1840, much of it is still unclear; which social classes and which regions were gripped by the wave of nationalist enthusiasm? There is plenty of scope for more research into the history of regions and *mentalités* here.[29]

It is precisely the history of research into the 1848 revolution which shows clearly how much the questions asked in the course of research depend on the political mood and interests of the day; nationalist and political components had lain in the foreground up to the end of World War I, but during the Weimar Republic the Liberal and democratic aspect came much more to the fore, and after 1933 it gave way once more to the 'Struggle for Unity and Freedom' (Paul Wentzke). In the historiography of the German Democratic Republic the 'revolutionary traditions of German history' stand in the foreground, with particular emphasis on the 'revolutionary working class' as the sole legitimate heir to 1848, whereas in the Federal Republic the democratic tradition has won particular respect; among the central themes of West-German research also belong (in connection with the change in peoples' interests since 1968) the separation of Liberal and constitutional streams from democratic and radical streams, as well as a special tendency since the last few years to investigate the politicisation and mobilisation of the population, mostly in connection with local and regional studies. This last research interest is exceptionally valuable for our inquiry into the national components of the Revolution, for whereas attitudes and disputes on the level of political institutions and elites have been extensively explained, latterly by Günter Wollstein's work *Grossdeutschland in der Paulskirche*, nationalisation from below – the emergeance in the population of a supra-regional German national consciousness – can at the moment be followed up only superficially.[31]

VI   Between the Revolution and the foundation of the Reich 1840–71

The economic components of the German Unification Movement require further elucidation as well; one of the problems here lies in the German tendency to separate historical research into general history and economic history, so that both lines of research often run parallel without ever joining up. After all, the influence of the economic situation on the emergence of a German nation is to a great extent obvious; the economic-Liberal tendency towards larger economic regions synchronised with the nationalist-Liberal tendency towards establishing a nation-state, and the economic fluctuations matched the peaks in nationalist enthusiasm, as in the case of the dates of the bigger and smaller economic depressions of 1817, 1830, 1847 and 1859 which also featured simultaneous outbreaks of collective nationalist feeling. A special case is the economic success story of the Customs Union, since this was also one of the preconditions for the head start which the 'little Germany' solution to the German question had acquired since the 1850s at the latest over all alternative solutions.[32]

The Italian Crisis of 1859 caused the nationalist movement to step once again into the political arena; here too much is still unknown. On the one hand scarcely any research has been done into the revival of nationalist feeling as an attitude of collective expectancy; the Schiller celebrations in particular merit comparative investigation. The associations movement of the outgoing fifties and the sixties is as good as unresearched, apart from work on the history of political parties, which concentrates in the first instance on Prussian Liberalism during the constitutional conflict and on the emergeant phase of social democracy. While Willy Real has provided a full and detailed picture of the Reform Society, more recent works about the Nationalist Society are at present only being prepared. In any case, much would have been gained here too, if the prevailing general studies had been conducted in association with specific regional inquiries, which would have drawn a picture of the Nationalist Movement 'from below', of its representative classes and its various networks. Generally speaking, it can be said of the period between the revolution of 1848 and the creation of the Reich of 1866–71 that there still exists a considerable preponderance of traditional political history, with research into parliamentary, diplomatic and governmental levels, to the disadvantage of work on social history, and the history of associations and of *mentalités*. What the creation of the Reich actually meant to Germans 'below' the top journalistic and political circles we simply do not know.[33]

It should be generally considered that the history of the Liberal and national German unification movement as a social and political force, working 'from below', ended with Koniggrätz and the founding of the North German Confederation, and that German nationalism began its movement from the 'left' to the 'right' of the political spectrum with the establishment of National Liberalism as a prop of Bismarck's policy. However, this is not the case with the overall interpretation of the German road to the nation-state; does the term 'revolution from above' describe the process adequately? Was it not much more a case of complicated interaction between the governmental forces 'from above' and the middle-class Liberal Unification Movement 'from below', which finally led to the 'little German' and 'great Prussian' Reich, and thereby had some effect on the final alliance between national Liberalism and constitutional authority? It would be easier to interpret this relationship if we were better informed about the currents within the social sphere of German history in the 19th century. There is still much to be done here for regional history, for the history of associations, and for the history of collective mentalities and how they changed.[34]

VII   The source material

Anyone wanting to use German archival material to research the history of the German nationalist movement will come up against a whole series of problems. Firstly, there are the many scattered German archives themselves; for as long as the German *Länder* were autonomous, that is until 1871, every state and every imperial town had its own archive, and since even after the *Reichs*-unification the *Länder* have to this day retained their supremacy in cultural matters, the archives have remained a regional concern. This has resulted in only the records of the few central institutions of the German Confederation and of the top government offices in the German Reich and the Federal Republic, being kept in a central archive similar to the British Public Record Office or the U.S. National Archives. This is the Federal Archive in Coblenz; the records of the German Confederation are to be found in a branch of the Federal Archive in Frankfurt. Apart from this last depot, however, only the regional archives are necessary for the purposes of our investigation. One needs to have a good knowledge of the history of German administration and government to know where to look; a few handbooks do have useful advice to offer.[35] A few more peculiarities of the German archives should be mentioned. Nowadays very many sources are no longer to be found, having been destroyed during the wars, especially World War II. As well as this, much archival material has been split up and distributed, without any recognisable system, between archives in the Federal Republic of

Germany and in the German Democratic Republic – depending on which towns and forced stops the allied armies had reached by May 1945.

A final feature of our theme is that the sources are not always easily found. A historical subject like the German nationalist movement, which is so extremely heterogeneous both regionally and socially, is very difficult to grasp and involves extraordinarily disparate and difficult sources. The expression 'nationalist movement' is simply an umbrella term for a confusing multitude of persons, groupings, societies, parties and publicistic organs, which never combined to form a common organisation; as a result, the usual way of researching the organisational and administrative structural connections through their archives is closed to us. This even applies to the larger alliances of a later date, the National and Reform Societies. Although fragmentary archives survive in both cases (for the former in the *Staatsarchiv* in Coburg, for the latter in the Frankfurt branch of the *Bundesarchiv*), because the complete files and records have never been in an archive they are only fragments, and have to be supplemented mainly by inventories and correspondence bequeathed by leading society members, in individual cases also by official records, but above all by the public outpourings of society activists.

It is already clear from this comparatively simple example that the source base for any work about the German Nationalist Movement must comprise a colourful patchwork of archival and publicity material, possibly of other sources as well. Where the relevant archives are concerned, one should in the first instance search the state records for correspondence and situation reports by internal government, police and security officials. Depending on the regional limitations of the research material, this will involve not only government record offices (nowadays to be found in the state and *Land* archives of the *Bundesländer*, which have taken on the legacy of the states of the old Reich, of the Rhine Confederation and of the German Confederation), but also material pertaining to the lower ranks of the administration, to towns, administrations and districts; this applies particularly to the Austrian archives and to the *Land* and State archives of the German Democratic Republic. As well as this, the relevant literary legacies in the archives must be gone through, since in some circumstances they include the files and various remaining records of societies and other organisations; Wolfgang A. Mommsen and Ludwig Deneke have provided a very incomplete survey of the material in question.[36] The disciplinary records of older university archives are also worth inspecting, as are the archives of the gymnastic and singing societies.

The next level of investigation is that of 'grey literature', the broadsheets, proclamations, programmes, essays and speeches as well as the societies' *Festschriften*, the *Jubiläum* publications, and the chronicles of clubs and associations. This comprises a tricky and not easily accessible group of sources, yet evaluating them is equally indispensable when dealing with the history of societies, with slogans and collective moods. I would recommend as a preliminary move looking through the collections of printed papers and broadsheets in the archives and libraries, most of which constitute cemeteries of unclassifiable material, but which sometimes allow surprising discoveries to be made. Given the key function of the press in the political debate of the 18th and 19th centuries, practically every study of the nationalist movement will include an analysis of contemporary journalism. Helpful publications include a list giving the locations of the older products of the German press, and a few voluminous critical bibliographies which review the most important journalistic productions of a period by means of summaries. Among these, Paul Czygan's history of ephemeral publications during the War of Liberation, Hans Rosenberg's survey of national political journalism between 1859 and 1866 as well as Karl-Georg Faber's follow-on book about the years 1866 to 1871, are worth mentioning.[37] It is, however, the case that only comparatively highbrow sources are to be found in this way; anyone who wants to undertake the difficult but particularly necessary and fruitful business of regional, local or club history must delve into the area of 'grey literature'.

When it is a question of sources dealing with a phenomenon involving social and cultural history and the history of *mentalités*, then it is not enough to draw on the written testimony of the past. Such a vague, unstructured and unorganised historical manifestation as the German nationalist movement needed a lot of symbols and distinctive signs, which enabled it to reveal its identity and acquire a sense of community. This means looking at the products of art, architecture and the material culture, often an unfamiliar activity for historians tied to the traditional sources of German history writing, which leads them into the fields of cultural history, *Germanistik* and cultural anthropology. Symbols and slogans can be spotted on contemporary buildings, monuments and tombstones; mottoes and quotations on postcards, beer-mugs and crochet samplers can together be more revealing than many a long programmatical text, whose pictorial presentation of politics and history requires interpretation. Schoolbooks, songbooks and lyrical antholo- gies can constitute first-class sources; here as in the other cases mentioned above it is not the individual statement which is generally emphasised, but the serial evaluation: a large number of similar sources has to be assembled in order to assess the distribution and greatest extent of key terms, of symbols or catchwords, and thus be able to make a statement about collective mental phenomena. Research into this aspect is still in its infancy.

Where publicity sources are concerned, we enter the broad field of editions of records, of document collections, and of publications of sources and personal documents. Given the scope of this material, it would be senseless to try to survey it here; instead the reader is referred to the relevent volumes of the *Quellenkunde zur deutschen Geschichte der Neuzeit*.[38] A few important publications of sources should also be mentioned. These include the series

Quellen zum politischen Denken der Deutschen im 19. und 20. Jahrhundert by the Freiherr-vom-Stein Gedächtnisausgabe, which presents a great number of excellently edited programmatic texts, correspondence, broadsheets and other published but often not easily accessible sources about the development of political publicity in the 19th century.[39] A very useful collection of extracts about the history of the 19th century is provided by the fourth volume of the series *Geschichte in Quellen*; relevent material about the German Nationalist Movement between the Congress of Vienna and the revolution of 1884 is published by Karl Obermann, and in spite of his somewhat dated criteria for selection and assessment, Paul Wentzke's great compilation about the *Burschenschaft* and Unification Movement is indispensable.[40]

A few words about our final class of important primary source material: that of personal testimonies: memoirs, diaries and collections of letters. Where the leading politicians, diplomats, military men and officials are concerned, they have been given fairly reliable bibliographies and characteristics in the *Quellenkunde zur deutschen Geschichte der Neuzeit* mentioned above. However, this provides only a fragment of the material in question; never before in history had the members of the educated class, the natural backbone of the German nationalist movement, been so keen on writing and communicating as in the period between the era of the French Revolution and the creation of the Reich. There is no complete bibliography of German-language personal testimonies, and one is urgently needed. The search involves not only catalogues and bibliographies published as books, but also newspapers; local and regional newspapers can be very rewarding. For similar reasons, publications of letters and diaries are preferable to memoirs, in which judgements after the event and faulty recollections may be set down in an unverifiable manner. This type of source-material can be evaluated not only in a traditional qualitative, but also in a very rewarding quantitative manner: which themes, which terms appeared most frequently in particular periods; at what was the collective interest aimed; were there differences and agreements in the nationalist discussions between north and south, between the different confessions, between middle class and nobility, between the generations, between women and men?

It is clear from all this that only a fragment of the available sources dealing with our theme has been exploited, and that by looking at even well known sources in a new methodological manner, one can discover new answers. Research into the German nationalist movement has only just begun.

Notes to bibliography

1 Dahlmann-Waitz. *Quellenkunde zur deutschen Geschichte. Bibliographie der Quellen und der Literatur zur deutschen Geschichte*, edited by H. Heimpel und H. Geuss, 10th Edn., 5 vols., Stuttgart 1969– (not all volumes have yet appeared); period covered: up to 1960.

2 Gebhardt. *Handbuch der Deutschen Geschichte*, 9th Ed., vol. 3: *Von der Französischen Revolution bis zum Ersten Weltkrieg*, Stuttgart 1970; *Handbuch der Deutschen Geschichte*, founded by O. Brandt, continued by O. Meyer, new edition by L. Just, vol. 3, 3 parts; *Deutsche Geschichte im 19. Jahrhundert seit 1789*, Wiesbaden 1968–1980; complemented by: H. Aubin und W. Zorn (Eds.): *Handbuch der deutschen Wirtschafts- und Sozialgeschichte*, 2 vols., Stuttgart 1971.

3 *Oldenbourg Grundriß des Geschichte*, vol. 12: E. Fehrenbach: *Vom Ancien Régime zum Wiener Kongreß*, München und Wien 1981; vol. 13: D. Langewiesche: *Europa zwischen Restauration und Revolution 1815–1849*, München und Wien 1985; vol. 14: L. Gall; *Europa auf dem Weg in die Moderne 1850–1890*, München und Wien 1984; *Deutsche Geschichte der neuesten Zeit*: vol. 1: P. Burg: *Der Wiener Kongreß*, München 1984; vol. 2: W. Hardtwig: *Vormärz*, München 1985; vol. 3: H. Schulze: *Der Weg zum Nationalstaat*, München 1985; vol. 4: M. Stürmer: *Die Reichsgründung*, München 1984; *Die Deutschen und ihre Nation*: H. Möller: *Fürstenstaat oder Bürgernation. Deutschland 1763–1815*, Berlin 1988; H. Lutz: *Zwischen Habsburg und Preußen. Deutschland 1815–1866*, Berlin 1985; M. Stürmer: *Das ruhelose Reich. Deutschland 1866–1918*, Berlin 1983.

4 F. Meinecke, *Weltbürgertum und Nationalstaat*, München 1908 (Engl. translation: *Cosmopolitism and the National State*, transl. by R.B. Comber, with a preface by F. Gilbert, Princeton 1970).

5 H.A. Winkler, Th. Schnabel (Ed.), *Bibliographie zum Nationalismus*, Göttingen 1979; G. Newman, *The Rise of English Nationalism. A Cultural History, 1740–1830*, London 1987.

6 E. Lemberg, *Nationalismus*, 2 vols., Reinbeck 1964; P. Alter, *Nationalismus*, Frankfurt 1985.

7 H. Plessner, *Die verspätete Nation*, Stuttgart 1959; re: 'deutscher Sonderweg' see: H.-D. Loock, H. Schulze (Eds.), *Parlamentarismus und Demokratie im Europa des 19. Jahrhundert*, München 1982; H. Grebing, *Der 'deutsche Sonderweg' in Europa 1806–1945. Eine Kritik*, Stuttgart 1986; G. Eley, D. Blackbourn, *The Peculiarities of German History*, Oxford 1985; D. Calleo, *The German Problem Reconsidered*, Cambridge 1978.

8 Especially important are: K.W. Deutsch/W.J. Foltz (Eds.), *Nation-Building*, N.Y.

1963; R.L. Merrit/St. Rokkan (Eds.), *Comparing Nations*, New Haven/London 1968; Ch. Tilly (Ed.), *The Formation of Nation-States in Western Europe*, Princeton 1975.

9 B. Moore, *Social Origins of Dictatorship and Democracy*, Boston 1966; following after Moore is the more recent: E. Gellner, *Nations and Nationalism*, Oxford 1983; especially rich and comprehensive in the thematic and philosophical context: R. Bendix, *Kings or People. Power and the Mandate to Rule*, Berkeley, Los Angeles, London 1978.

10 'Historikerstreit': *Die Dokumentation der Kontroverse über die-Einzigartigkeit der nazional-sozialistischen Vernichtung der Jüden*, München 1987.

11 O. Büsch/J.J. Sheehan (Eds.), *Die Rolle der Nation in der deutschen Geschichte und Gegenwart*, Berlin 1985; K. Weigelt (Ed.), *Heimat und Nation. Zur Geschichte und Identität der Deutschen*, Mainz 1984; J. Becker/A. Hillgruber (Eds.), *Die deutsche Frage im 19. und 20. Jahrhundert*, München 1983; H. Lutz/H. Rumpler (Eds.), *Österreich und die deutsche Frage im 19. und 20. Jahrhundert*, München 1982; Otto Dann (Ed.), *Nationalismus und sozialer Wandel*, Hamburg 1978; Heinrich A. Winkler (Ed.), *Nationalismus* (= Neue Wissenschaftliche Bibliothek, vol. 100), Königstein/Ts. 1978.

12 H. Schulze (Ed.): *Nation-Building in Central Europe* (= German Historical Perspectives 3), Leamington Spa, Hamburg, New York 1987.

13 D.K. Buse, J.C. Doerr, *German Nationalism. A Bibliographic Approach*, New York, London 1985.

14 R.A. Berdahl, Der deutsche Nationalismus in neuer Sicht, in Winkler, National- ismus in Neuer Sicht, in Winkler, *Nationalismus*, pp. 138–54.

15 J.J. Sheehan, What is German History? Reflections on the role of the Nation in German History and Historiography, in *The Journal of Modern History* 53 (1981), pp. 1–31.

16 O. Dann, Nationalismus und sozialer Wandel in Deutschland 1806–1850, in Dann, *Nationalismus*, pp. 77–128.

17 G.L. Mosse, *The Nationalization of the Masses*, New York 1975; Chr. Priegnitz, *Vaterlandsliebe und Freiheit*, Wiesbaden 1981.

18 O. Dann, Die Anfänge politischer Vereinsbildung in Deutschland, in U. Engelhardt i.a. (Eds.), *Soziale Bewegung und politische Verfassung*, Stuttgart 1976, pp. 197–232; H.H. Gerth, *Bürgerliche Intelligenz um 1800. Zur Soziologie des deutschen Frühliberalismus*, Göttingen 1976; F. Kopitzsch (Ed.), *Aufklärung, Absolutismus und Bürgertum in Deutschland*, München 1976; P. Chr. Ludz (Ed.), *Geheime Gesellschaften*, Heidelberg 1979.

19 Summarising the latest state of research: H.A. Glaser (Ed.), *Deutsche Literatur. Eine Sozialgeschichte*, vols. 4 und 5, Reinbek 1980.

20 H. Berding, H.-P. Ullmann (Eds.), *Deutschland zwischen Revolution und Restauration*, Düsseldorf 1981.

21 H. Kohn, *Prelude to Nation-States. The French and German Experience 1789–1815*, Princeton 1967; A. Kemiläinen, *Auffassungen über die Sendung des deutschen Volkes um die Wende des 18. und 19. Jahrhunderts*, Helsinki, Wiesbaden 1956.

22 R. Ibbeken, *Preußen 1807–1813. Staat und Volk als Idee und in der Wirklichkeit*, Köln, Berlin 1970; W. v. Groote, *Die Entstehung des Nationalbewußtseins in Nordwestdeutschland 1790–1830*, Göttingen 1955.

23 H. König, *Zur Geschichte der bürgerlichen Nationalerziehung in Deutschland zwischen 1807 und 1815*, Berlin (East) 1973; P. Stulz, *Fremdherrschaft und Befreiungskampf. Die preußische Kabinettspolitik und die Rolle der Volksmassen in den Jahren 1811 bis 1813*, Berlin (East) 1960; H. Scheel (Ed.), *Das Jahr 1813. Studien zur Geschichte und Wirkung der Befreiungskriege*, Berlin (East) 1963.

24 E. Lämmert, Preuß*ische Politik und nationale Poesie, in: Berlin zwischen 1789 und 1848*, publ. by the Akademie der Künste, Berlin 1981, pp. 43–51.

25 D. Düding, *Organisierter gesellschaftlicher Nationalismus in Deutschland (1808–1847)*, München 1984; see too, by the same author; The Nineteenth-Century German Nationalist Movement as a Movement of Societies, in H. Schulze (op. cit.), pp. 19–50. Re. north Germany see: H.-G. Husung, *Protest und Repression im Vormärz. Norddeutschland zwischen Restauration und Revolution*, Göttingen 1983.

26 J.J. Sheehan, *German Liberalism in the Nineteenth Century*, Chicago 1987; see too: W. Schieder (Ed.), *Liberalismus in der Geschichte des deutschen Vormärz*, Göttingen 1983. A valuable study in depth is provided by L.E. Lee, *The Politics of Harmony. Civil Service, Liberalism and Social Reform in Baden, 1800–1850*, Newark 1980.

27 Available are only: W. Conze (Ed.), *Staat und Gesellschaft im Vormärz 1815–1848*, 2nd Ed. Stuttgart 1970; P. Aycoberry, Der Strukturwandel im Kölner Mittelstand 1820–1850, in: *Geschichte und Gesellschaft* 1 (1975), pp. 78–95; J. Bergmann, *Das Berliner Handwerk in den Frühphasen der Industrialisierung*, Berlin 1973; R. Engelsing, *Analphabetentum und Lektüre*, Stuttgart 1973; H.A. Glaser (Ed.), *Deutsche Literatur. Eine Sozialgeschichte*, vol. 6: Vormärz 1815–1848, Reinbek 1980.

28 H. Kühn, *Das Wartburgfest am 18. Oktober 1817*, Weimar 1913; G. Steiger, *Aufbruch, Urburschenschaft und Wartburgfest*, Leipzig 1967; About the state's reaction see: E. Büssem, *Die Karlsbader Beschlüsse von 1819*, Hildesheim 1974.

29 K. Hoffmann, *Preußen und die Juli-Monarchie 1830–1834*, Berlin 1936; V. Eichstädt, *Die Deutsche Publizistik von 1830. Ein Beitrag zur Entwicklung der konstitutionellen und nationalen Tendenzen*, Berlin 1933; In connection with the national, social and constitutional movement of 1830 see: E.R.H., *Deutsche Verfassungsgeschichte seit 1789*, vol. 2, Stuttgart 1975, pp. 30–183; Re. Hambacher Festival in its social and organisational context: K. Baumann (Ed.), *Das Hambacher Fest. 27. Mai 1832*, Speyer 1957; P. Wende, *Radikalismus im Vormärz. Untersuchungen zur politischen Theorie der frühen deutschen Demokratie*, Wiesbaden 1975; H. Hirsch, *Freiheitsliebende Rheinländer. Neue Beiträge zur deutschen Sozialgeschichte*, Düsseldorf/Wien 1977; C. Förster, *Der Preß- und Vaterlandsverein von 1832/33*, Trier 1982.

30 H.-G. Husung, *Protest und Repression im Vormärz*, Göttingen 1983; I. Veit-Brause, *Die deutsch-französische Krise von 1840. Studien zur deutschen Einheitsbewegung*, Phil. Diss. Köln 1967; F. Keinemann, *Preußen auf dem Wege zur Revolution*, Hamm 1975; J. Kocka, Preußischer Staat und Modernisierung im Vormärz, in: H.-V. Wehler (Ed.), *Sozialgeschichte heute*, Göttingen 1974; L. Kerssen, *Das Interesse am Mittelalter im deutschen Nationaldenkmal*, Berlin/New York 1975; Th. Nipperdey, Nationalidee und Nationaldenkmal in Deutschland im 19. Jahrhundert, in: *Historische Zeitschrift* 206 (1968), pp. 529–585.

31 V. Valentin, *Geschichte der deutschen Revolution von 1848–1849*, 2 vols., Berlin
1930/31, Cologne 1970; P.N. Stearns, *The Revolutions of 1848*, London 1974; for
the present state of research: D. Langewiesche, Die deutsche Revolution von
1848/49 und die vorrevolutionäre Gesellschaft. Forschungsstand und For-
schungsperspektiven, in: *Archiv für Sozialgeschichte* 21 (1981), pp. 458–98: G.
Wollstein, 1848 – Streit um das Erbe, in: *Neue Politische Literatur* 1975, pp.
491–507, 1976, pp. 89–106: Collections of articles giving an idea of the breadth of
the theme and of the present state of research, which also contain extensive
bibliographies: H. Stuke, W. Forstmann (Eds.), *Die europäischen Revolutionen
von 1848* (= Neue Wissenschaftliche Bibliothek, vol. 103), Königstein/Ts. 1979;
D. Langewiesche (Ed.) *Die deutsche Revolution von 1848/49*, Darmstadt 1983;
three important new publications about the 'national question' during the
Revolution: M. Stürmer, Die Geburt eines Dilemmas. Nationalstaat und
Massendemokratie im Mächtesystem 1848, in: *Merkur* 36 (1982), pp. 1–12; G.
Wollstein, *Das "Großdeutschland" der Paulskirche. Nationale Ziele in der
bürgerlichen Revolution 1848/49*, Düsseldorf 1977; H.-H. Brandt, The Revolution of 1848 and the Problem of Central European Nationalities, in: H. Schulze
(op. cit.), pp. 107–35.

32 W. O. Henderson, *The Zollverein*, London 1939, 3rd ed. 1968; H.W. Hahn,
Wirtschaftliche Integration im 19. Jahrhundert, Göttingen 1982; F. Zunkel, *Das
rheinisch-westfälische Unternehmertum*, Köln/Opladen 1962; J. Bergmann,
ökonomische Voraussetzungen der Revolution von 1848, in: *Geschichte und
Gesellschaft*, Sonderheft 2, Göttingen 1976, pp. 258–73; W.G. Hoffmann, The
Take-Off in Germany, in: W.W. Rostow (Ed.), *The Economics of Take-Off into
Sustained Growth*, London/Basingstoke 1969, pp. 95–147; H. Böhme, *Deutsch-
lands Weg zur Großmacht. Studien zum Verhältnis von Wirtschaft und Staat
während der Reichsgründungszeit 1848–1881*, Köln 1966; H. Kiesewetter,
Economic Preconditions for Germany's Nation-Building in the Nineteenth
Century, in: H. Schulze (op. cit.), pp. 81–106.

33. A. Mittelstädt, *Der Krieg von 1859*, Stuttgart 1904; W. Andreas, *Die Wandlungen
des großdeutschen Gedankens*, Berlin 1924; H. v. Möller, *Großdeutsch und
Kleindeutsch*, Berlin 1937; G. Ritter, *Großdeutsch und Kleindeutsch im 19.
Jahrhundert. Festschrift für S. A. Kähler*, Düsseldorf 1950; R. Le Mang, *Der
Deutsche Nationalverein*, Berlin 1909; L. O'Boyle, The German Nationalverein,
in: *Journal of Central European Affairs*, 16 (1957), pp. 23–45; W. Real, *Der
Deutsche Reformverein. Großdeutsche Stimmen und Kräfte zwischen Vil-
lafranca und Königgrätz*, Lübeck/Hamburg 1966.

34 The expression 'Revolution from above' used to describe Bismarck's Unification
of the Reich appears to have been coined by Bismarck himself, as is proven by his
circular of 27.5.1866 to the Prussian Missions (*Gesammelte Werke*. vol. 5. no.
359), and it was used that very year both by Bismarck's supporters and by his
opponents. In history books this expression is generally employed to designate a
special German development which occurred in the nineteenth century instead of
the 'proper' revolution, which did not take place: see e.g.: Engelberg, Über die
Revolution von oben. Wirklichkeit und Begriff, in: Ibid., *Theorie, Empirie und
Methode in der Geschichtswissenschaft*, Berlin (East) 1980, pp. 339–84; compare
the critical approach by B. Vogel, 'Revolution von oben' – Der 'deutsche Weg' in
die bürgerliche Gesellschaft?, in: *Sozialwissenschaftliche Informationen für*

Unterricht und Studium, 8 (1979), pp. 67–74. About the change from Liberalism and nationalist movement in 1866: F. Sell, *Die Tragödie des deutschen Liberalismus*, Stuttgart 1953; K.G. Faber, Realpolitik als Ideologie. Die Bedeutung des Jahres 1866 für das politische Denken in Deutschland, in *Historische Zeitschrift 203* (1966), pp. 1–32; H.A. Winkler, Bürgerliche Emanzipation und Nationale Einigung, in; H. Böhme (Ed.), *Probleme der Reichsgründungszeit 1848–1871*, Köln/Berlin 1968, pp. 227–41.

35 Minerva-Handbücher, Archive. *Archive im deutschsprachigen Raum*, 2 vols., München, Wien 1974; C. Haase, *Record Repositories in Germany. A short survey of the most important archives, libraries and other institutions with the facilities that they offer for research in German History*, New Jersey 1974; A further useful survey of German archives in: E.G. Franz, *Einführung in die Archivkunde*, Darmstadt 1977.

36 *Verzeichnis der schriftlichen Nachlässe in deutschen Bibliotheken*, vol. 1: *Die Nachlässe in den deutschen Archiven*, edited by W.A. Mommsen, 2 part vols., Boppard 1971/83; vol. 2: *Die Nachlässe in den Bibliotheken der Bundesrepublik Deutschland*, edited by L. Deneke/ T. Brandis, 2. ed., Boppard 1981.

37 P. Czygan, *Zur Geschichte der Tagesliteratur während der Freiheitskriege*, 2 vols., 2nd ed., Leipzig 1909/11; H. Rosenberg, *Die nationalpolitische Publizistik Deutschlands vom Eintritt der Neuen Ära in Preußen bis zum Ausbruch des Deutschen Krieges*, 2 vols., Berlin 1935; K.-G. Faber, *Die nationalpolitische Publizistik Deutschlands von 1866 bis 1871*, 2 vols., Düsseldorf 1963, G. Hagelweide, *Deutsche Zeitungsbestände in Bibliotheken und Archiven*, Düsseldorf 1974.

38 *Quellenkunde zur deutschen Geschichte der Neuzeit von 1500 bis zur Gegenwart*, Gen. Ed. W. Baumgart: vol. 3: *Absolutismus und Zeitalter der Französischen Revolution (1715–1815)*, edited by K. Müller, Darmstadt 1982; vol. 4: *Restauration, Liberalismus und nationale Bewegung (1815–1870)*, edited by W. Siemann, Darmstadt 1982.

39 *Quellen zum politischen Denken der Deutschen im 19. und 20. Jahrhundert*, founded by R. Buchner, continued by W. Baumgart, vol. 1: *Deutschland und die Französische Revolution 1789–1806*, edited by T. Stammen/F. Eberle, Darmstadt (in preparation); vol. 2: *Die Erhebung gegen Napoleon 1806–1814/15*, edited by H.-B. Spies, Darmstadt 1981; vol. 3: *Restauration und Frühliberalismus 1814–1840*, edited by H. Brandt, Darmstadt 1979; vol. 4: *Vormärz und Revolution 1840–1849*, edited by H. Fenske, Darmstadt 1976; vol. 5: *Der Weg zur Reichgründung 1850–1870*, edited by H. Fenske, Darmstadt 1977.

40 *Geschichte in Quellen*, Gen Eds. W. Lautemann/M. Schlenke, vol. 4: *Das bürgerliche Zeitalter 1815–1914*, edited by G. Schönbrunn, München 1980; *Einheit und Freiheit. Die deutsche Geschichte von 1815 bis 1849 in zeitgenössischen Dokumenten* compiled and introduced by K. Obermann, Berlin (East) 1950; *Quellen und Darstellungen zur Geschichte der Burschenschaft und der deutschen Einheitsbewegung*, edited by H. Haupt (vols. 1–13)/P. Wentzke, 17 vols., Heidelberg 1910–1940; *Darstellungen und Quellen der Deutschen Einheitsbewegung im 19. und 20. Jahrhundert*, edited by P. Wentzke et al., vols. 1–11 have already appeared, Heidelberg 1957–.

A critical bibliography of works in English

By T.C.W. Blanning

Bibliographies
Useful recent bibliographies are John C. Fout, *German History and Civilisation 1806–1914. A Bibliography of Scholarly Periodical Literature* (Metuchen, New Jersey, 1974); F.R. Bridge, *The Habsburg Monarchy 1804–1918: Books and Pamphlets Published in the United Kingdom Between 1918 and 1967; a Critical Bibliography* (London, 1967) and especially Dieter K. Buse and Jürgen C. Doerr, *German Nationalisms. A Bibliographic Approach* (New York and London, 1985).

Historiography
The distinctive German approach to the study of history is discussed in George G. Iggers, *The German Conception of History: the National Tradition of Historical Thought from Herder to the Present* (Middletown, 1968). There is a good deal on German historiography in G.P. Gooch, *History and Historians in the Nineteenth Century* (2nd ed., London, 1952). For the most uncompromising statement of the *kleindeutsch* interpretation, there is a good translation of Heinrich von Treitschke's *History of Germany in the Ninteenth Century* available (7 vols, London, 1915–19). An example of a more recent trend towards elevating the importance of economic factors is Helmut Böhme's *An Introduction to the Social and Economic History of Germany. Politics and Economic Change in the Nineteenth and Twentieth Centuries* (Oxford, 1978). A thoughtful essay is James J. Sheehan, 'What is German history? Reflections on the role of the *Nation* in German history and historiography', *Journal of Modern History*, 53 1 (1981). The centrepiece of a protracted debate about the nature of German developments in the nineteenth and twentieth centuries has been David Blackbourn and Geoff Eley's *The Peculiarities of German History. Bourgeois Society and Politics in Nineteenth Century Germany* (Oxford, 1984). On this theme, see also David Calleo, *The German Problem Reconsidered. Germany and the World Order, 1870 to the Present* (Cambridge, 1978). A brilliant and profound recent interpretive study of German history in the nineteenth and twentieth centuries is Harold James' *A German Identity 1770–1990* (London, 1989).

General histories of Germany
The most substantial is Hajo Holborn's *A History of Modern Germany*, vols. 2–3 (London, 1965, 1969). More lively is Golo Mann's *The History of Germany Since 1789* (London, 1968). Perverse but stimulating and still worth reading is A.J.P. Taylor's *The Course of German History: a Survey of the Development of Germany Since 1815* (London, 1945). A good recent general account is Michael Hughes' *Nationalism and*

Society: Germany 1800–1945 (London, 1988). On the Austrian dimension of German history, C.A. Macartney's *The Habsburg Empire 1790–1918* (London, 1968) is thorough but rather dry. More lively but less reliable is A.J.P. Taylor's *The Habsburg Monarchy 1809–1918. A History of the Austrian Empire and Austria-Hungary* (London, 1948). In a more reflective vein is Werner Conze's *The Shaping of the German Nation. A Historical Analysis* (London, 1979). On the German intellectual tradition there is Hans Kohn, *The Mind of Germany: the Education of a Nation* (New York, 1960) and the more profound but less lucid study of Leonard Krieger, *The German Idea of Freedom: History of a Political Tradition* (Boston, 1957).

General studies of nationalism

A good recent introduction is Peter Alter's *Nationalism* (London, 1989). Also useful, especially in its discussion of theories of nationalism, is John Breuilly's *Nationalism and the State* (Manchester, 1982). Not an easy read, but penetrating and powerful is Elie Kedourie's *Nationalism* (3rd ed., London, 1966). More accessible is Kenneth Minogue's *Nationalism* (London, 1967) and J.P.T. Bury's 'Nationalities and nationalism', in J.P.T. Bury (ed.), *The New Cambridge Modern History*, vol. 10 (Cambridge, 1960). A wide-ranging survey is Louis L. Snyder's *German Nationalism: the Tragedy of a People. Extremism Contra Liberalism in Modern German History* (Harrisburg, Pa., 1952). Two short but highly original studies are Benedict Anderson's *Imagined Communities: Reflections on the Origin and Spread of Nationalism* (London, 1983) and Ernest Gellner's *Nations and Nationalism* (Oxford, 1983). A very important recent collection of articles by various authors is Hagen Schulze (ed.), *Nation-building in Central Europe* (Leamington Spa, 1987).

The eighteenth century

The best modern introduction to the German cultural revival is Victor Lange's *The Classical Age of German Literature 1740–1815* (London, 1982). Still useful is W.H. Bruford's *Germany in the Eighteenth Century. The Social Background of the Literary Revival* (2nd ed., Cambridge, 1965), as is the same author's *Theatre, Drama and Audience in Goethe's Germany* (London, 1950). See also Alan Menhennet, *Order and Freedom. Literature and Society in Germany from 1720 to 1805* (London, 1973). Two helpful volumes in the 'Literary History of Germany' series are Friedhelm Radandt, *From Baroque to Storm and Stress* (London, 1977) and T.J. Reed, *The Classical Centre: Goethe and Weimar 1775–1832* (London, 1980). The best book in English on the 'Storm and Stress' movement is still Roy Pascal's *The German Sturm und Drang* (Manchester, 1953). In a class by itself is Friedrich Meinecke's *Historism: the Rise of a New Historical Outlook* (London, 1972). Specifically on the relationship between cultural developments and nationalism are two articles by Robert R. Ergang, 'Möser and the rise of national thought in Germany', *Journal of Modern History*, 5, 2 (1933) and 'National sentiment in Klopstock's odes and *Bardiete*', in Edward Mead Earle (ed.), *Nationalism and Internationalism. Essays Inscribed to Carlton J.H. Hayes* (New York, 1950). An important aspect is discussed in Koppel S. Pinson's *Pietism as a Factor in the Rise of German Nationalism* (New York, 1934). On the music of the period, with much of importance on the development of national styles, the best book is Giorgio Pestelli, *The Age of Mozart and Beethoven* (Cambridge, 1984).

There is an extensive literature on Herder in English. F.M. Barnard has edited an excellent anthology of his work – *Herder on Social and Political Culture* (Cambridge,

1969) – and has also written an important interpretive study – *Herder's Social and Political Thought. From Enlightenment to Nationalism* (Oxford, 1965). Two brilliant pieces by Sir Isaiah Berlin are *Vico and Herder. Two Studies in the History of Ideas* (London, 1976) and 'The counter-enlightenment', published in his collected essays *Against the Current: Essays in the History of Ideas* (London, 1979). Self-explanatory is Carlton J.H. Hayes' article 'Contributions of Herder to the doctrine of nationalism', *American Historical Review*, 32, 4 (1927).

The French Revolution and Napoleon

Hans Kohn, *Prelude to Nation-states: the French and German Experience, 1789–1815* (Princeton, 1967) is limited in depth but covers a lot of ground. It can be supplemented by his article 'The eve of German nationalism, 1789–1812', *Journal of the History of Ideas*, 12, 2 (1951). There is a good chapter on intellectual developments in Germany in R.R. Palmer's *The Age of the Democratic Revolution*, vol. 2 (Princeton, 1964). Still useful is G.P. Gooch, *Germany and the French Revolution* (London, 1920; reprinted, 1965). Of more general importance than the title suggests is Klaus Epstein's *The Genesis of German Conservatism* (Princeton, 1966). Reactions to the French occupation are analysed in T.C.W. Blanning, *The French Revolution in Germany. Occupation and Resistance in the Rhineland 1792–1802* (Oxford, 1983). The Napoleonic period is covered in William O. Shanahan, 'A neglected source of German nationalism: the Confederation of the Rhine 1806–1813', in Michael Palumbo and William O. Shanahan (eds.), *Nationalism: Essays in Honour of Louis L. Snyder* (Westport and London, 1981).

Little of value has been written on the Habsburg Monarchy during the revolutionary–Napoleonic period. Walter C. Langsam's promisingly titled *The Napoleonic Wars and German Nationalism in Austria* (New York, 1930) is disappointing. More satisfactory is his article 'Count Stadion and Archduke Charles', *Journal of Central European Affairs*, 6, 2 (1946). Better still is James Allen Vann's 'Habsburg policy and the war of 1809', *Central European History*, 7, 4 (1974).

A great deal is available in English on the Prussian reform movement, although most of it has been overtaken by recent German work, as yet untranslated. There is a good translation available of Friedrich Meinecke's classic *The Age of German Liberation, 1795–1815*, ed. Peter Paret (Berkeley, 1977). Still worth reading are G.S. Ford, *Stein and the Era of Reform in Prussia, 1807–1815* (Princeton, 1922) and W.M. Simon, *The Failure of the Prussian Reform Movement, 1807–1819* (Ithaca, 1955). More specifically addressed to the problem of German nationalism is E.N. Anderson's *Nationalism and the Cultural Crisis in Prussia 1806–1815* (New York, 1939; reprinted, 1966). A good introduction to Stein is Klaus Epstein's 'Stein in German historiography', *History and Theory*, 5 (1966), which can be supplemented by Walther Hubatsch, 'Stein and constitutional reform in nineteenth-century Germany: preconditions, plans and results', published in his collected essays *Studies in Medieval and Modern German History* (London, 1984). Particularly illuminating is a review article on an important German work by Jonathan Sperber, 'State and Civil Society in Prussia: Thoughts on a New Edition of Reinhart Koselleck's *Preussen zwischen Reform und Revolution*', *Journal of Modern History*, 57, 2 (1985).

A great deal has been written in English about the cultural nationalism of the period. Outstanding, of course, is Friedrich Meinecke's *Cosmopolitanism and the National State* (Princeton, 1970), which covers a wider period. Good introductions to the literature, political thought and visual arts respectively are Alan Menhennet, *The Romantic Movement* (London, 1981), W.D. Robson-Scott, *The Literary Background of the Gothic Revival in Germany: a Chapter in the History of Taste* (Oxford, 1965), H.S. Reiss (ed.), *The Political Thought of the German Romantics* (Oxford, 1955), Reinhold Aris, *History of Political Thought in Germany from 1789 to 1815* and William Vaughan, *German Romantic Painting* (New Haven, 1980). A very useful anthology of translated excerpts is Hermann Glaser's *The German Mind of the Nineteenth Century: a Literary and Historical Anthology* (New York, 1981). Three important articles are E.N. Anderson, 'German romanticism as an ideology of cultural crisis', *Journal of the History of Ideas*, 2, 3 (1941); Gordon Craig, 'German intellectuals and politics: the case of Heinrich von Kleist', *Central European History*, 2, 1 (1969); and Shlomo Avineri, 'Hegel and nationalism', *Review of Politics*, 24 (1962).

There are several articles on nationalism in this period by Hans Kohn: 'The Eve of German Nationalism (1789–1812)', *Journal of the History of Ideas*, 12, 2 (1951); 'Romanticism and the Rise of German Nationalism', *The Review of Politics*, 12 (1950); 'The Paradox of Fichte's Nationalism', *Journal of the History of Ideas*, 10, 3 (1949); 'Father Jahn's Nationalism', *The Review of Politics*, 11 (1949); 'Napoleon and the Age of Nationalism', *Journal of Modern History*, 22, 1 (1950); 'Arndt and the Character of German Nationalism', *American Historical Review*, 54, 4 (1949). Other articles on the same theme are W.M. Simon, 'Variations in Nationalism in the Great Reform Period in Prussia', *American Historical Review*, 59, 1 (1953–4) and George L. Mosse, 'Friendship and Nationhood: About the Promise and Failure of German Nationalism', *Journal of Contemporary History*, 17, 2 (1982). Robert M. Berdahl's important article, 'New Thoughts on German Nationalism', *American Historical Review*, 77, 1 (1972), is critical of Meinecke's treatment and argues that more attention should be paid to economic developments.

Restoration and revolution 1815–1849

The relationship between nationalism and liberalism has been discussed by James J. Sheehan in several important books and articles, notably *German Liberalism in the Nineteenth Century* (Chicago, 1978) and 'Liberalism and Society in Germany, 1815–1848', *Journal of Modern History*, 45, 4 (1973). Also helpful on the development of opposition movements after 1815 are F. Eyck, 'The political theories and activities of German academic youth between 1815 and 1819', *Journal of Modern History*, 27, 1 (1955); Rolland Ray Lutz, 'The German Revolutionary Student Movement 1819–1833', *Central European History*, 4, 3 (1971); and Gary D. Stark, 'The Ideology of the German *Burschenschaft* Generation', *European Studies Review*, 8, 3 (1978).

Of the numerous good studies of German economic and social history of the period, particularly helpful are Clive Trebilcock, *The Industrialisation of the Continental Powers 1780–1914* (London, 1981) and W.O. Henderson, *The Rise of German Industrial Power, 1834–1914* (London, 1975). Other important studies by W.O. Henderson are *The Zollverein* (2nd ed., London, 1959) and *Friedrich List, Economist and Visionary, 1789–1845* (London, 1983). Good on the relationship between economics and politics are Theodore S. Hamerow, *Restoration, Revolution, Reaction: Economics and Politics, 1815–1871* (Princeton, 1958) and Martin Kitchen, *The Political Economy of Germany 1815–1914* (London, 1978). Also important is Frank B. Tipton, 'The National Consensus in German Economic History', *Central European History*, 7, 3 (1974).

On the origins of the revolution of 1848 in Germany, see K.H. Jarausch, 'The Sources of German Unrest 1815–1848', in Lawrence Stone (ed.), *The University in Society*, vol. 2 (Princeton, 1974); Lenore O'Boyle, 'The Problem of an Excess of Educated Men in Western Europe, 1800–1850', *Journal of Modern History*, 42, 4 (1970); and Frederick D. Marquardt, '*Pauperismus* in Germany During the *Vormärz*', *Central European History*, 2, 1 (1969). Of the large number of works on the events in Germany in 1848, still valuable is Veit Valentin's *1848: Chapters of German History* (London, 1940). It should be supplemented by Rudolf Stadelmann, '*Social and Political History of the German 1848 Revolution* (Athens, Ohio, 1975). Frank Eyck's *The Frankfurt Parliament* (London, 1968) conveys a good deal of relevant information. Although very much a product of its time, Sir Lewis Namier's expanded lecture *1848: the Revolution of the Intellectuals* (London, 1944) is still indispensable. Karl Marx and Friedrich Engels' participation in and comments on 1848 can be found in David Fernbach's edition of Karl Marx, *The Revolutions of 1848* (Harmondsworth, 1973). A particularly illuminating review article is John Breuilly's 'The Failure of Revolution in 1848', *European Studies Review*, 11, 1 (1981).

The period of unification

Both stimulating and useful historiographical essays are Geoffrey Barraclough, 'German Unification. An Essay in Revision', *Historical Studies*, 4 (1963); Michael Stürmer, 'Bismarck in Perspective', *Central European History*, 4, 4 (1971); David Blackbourn, 'Bismarck: the Sorcerer's Apprentice', published in his collected essays *Populists and Patricians. Essays in Modern German History* (London, 1987); Andreas Dorpalen, 'The Unification of Germany in East German Perpective', *American Historical Review*, 73, 4 (1967–8); and Otto Pflanze, 'Another crisis among German historians? Helmut Böhms's *Deutschlands Weg zur Grossmacht: a Review Article*', *Journal of Modern History*, 40, 1 (1968). Böhm's book has not been translated into English but his views can be found expressed in the introduction to his collection of documents *The Foundation of the German Empire* (Oxford, 1971) and in his article 'Big-business Pressure Groups and Bismarck's turn to protection 1873–9', *The Historical Journal*, 10, 2 (1967). Hans-Ulrich Wehler's controversial interpretation of the period can be found in his *The German Empire, 1871–1918* (Leamington Spa, 1985) and 'Bismarck's Imperialism, 1862–90', *Past and Present*, 48 (1970).

On the political history of the period, admirably sensible and lucid is the first part of Gordon Craig's *Germany 1866–1945* (Oxford, 1978). Two important articles on nationalism in the period by Otto Pflanze are 'Characteristics of Nationalism in Europe, 1848–1871', *Review of Politics*, 28 (1966) and 'Bismarck and German Nationalism', *American Historical Review*, 60, 3 (1955). On the same subject, see Lenore O'Boyle, 'The German *Nationalverein*', *Journal of Central European Affairs*, 16, 4 (1957). Self-explanatory is Theodore S. Hamerow's *The Social Foundations of German Unification 1858–1871* (2 vols, Princeton, 1969).

On Bismarck the best biography is Lothar Gall's *Bismarck: the White Revolutionary*, 2 vols (London, 1986), but also distinguished – and more readable – is Otto Pflanze's *Bismarck and the Development of Germany. The Period of Unification, 1815–1871* (Princeton, 1963). See also his articles 'Towards a Psychoanalytic Interpretation of Bismarck', *American Historical Review*, 77, 2 (1972) and 'Bismarck's "Realpolitik"', *Review of Politics*, 20 (1958). Still worth reading for its odd insights is A.J.P. Taylor's *Bismarck: the Man and Statesman* (London, 1955).

Index

national character, German, 107–8
National Liberal Party, 95
  founding programme, 144–6
National Society, *see* German National
  Society
Naunyn (mayor of Berlin), 27–8
Nauwerk (Berlin town councillor), 10
Nicolai, Friedrich, 47
North German Confederation, 95, 144, 145,
  156

Obermann, Karl, 159
Ode to the Fatherland (Klopstock), 46

Palm, Johann Philipp, 49
Parliament
  demand for German national, 70
  Frankfurt, 16, 73
  Prussian, 6, 8, 15–16, 19, 21
Paulskirche Assembly (1848–9), 75–6, 85,
  131–8
peasants
  landless, 68
  and Prussian nationalism, 53–4
Peucker, General Eduard von, 71–2
Pfizer, Paul Achatius, 61
Pfuel, General Ernst von, 15, 18, 21, 22
Plessner, Helmut, 151
poems, nationalist, 52
Poland
  and German unification, 74
  partition of, 48
  Revolution (1781), 40
  Revolution (1830), 40, 60
  uprising (1863), 93
Polignac, Prince de, 60
population
  Berlin (1848), 5
  Germany, 106
  growth in Europe, 35–6, 37, 41
  growth in Germany, 68
Potato War (1847), 6, 9, 13, 14
poverty
  in Berlin (1848), 10–12
  in Germany, 80
Priegnitz, Christoph, 152
Prittwitz, General Karl-Ludwig von, 6, 15,
  22, 26–7, 28–9
Prohaska, Eleonore, 54
Protestant Germany
  and German nationalism, 98
  and Prussia, 86
Prussia (*see also* Berlin)
  1848 Berlin revolution, 5–31
  and Austria, 116, 117–18, 119
  Bismarck as Prime Minister, 92–6
  censorship abolished in, 19, 52
  Customs Union, 77, 78, 79, 80, 81

and the German Confederation, 89
German National Assembly debates
  (1848–9), 131, 137–8
and German national culture, 44–5
and the Hanoverian declaration, 142, 143
legal code, 43–4
Napoleonic occupation, 49–51
and Schleswig-Holstein, 94
Volunteer Units, 53–4, 56
Prutz, Robert, 66
public opinion
  and the 1848 revolution, 7
  and German nationalism, 64–5
  and reform of the German
    Confederation, 100
  and Schleswig-Holstein, 73

Radowitz, Ambassador Joseph Maiuer, 16
railways, 37
  Austrian, 80
  German, 78–9
Ranke, Leopold von, 86
Raumer, Friedrich von, 59
Real, Willy, 155
Reform Society, 87, 88, 98, 100, 157
Reinhart (Württemberg ambassador), 12
religion
  decline of, 38–9
  in the Holy Roman Empire, 43
Revolution of 1830, 60–1, 62, 154
Revolution of 1848, 40, 69, 70–2, 90, 98,
  154
  in Berlin, 5–31
Rhine Confederation, 55, 91, 101, 109–10,
  118, 157
  Charter, 48–9
Rhine crisis (1840), 64–6, 84, 99, 154
Rhine song movement, 65–6, 83
Riemann, Heinrich Arminius, 122–3
Riesbeck, Johann Kaspar, 105–8
Rochau, August Ludwig von, 66, 77
Roon, Albrecht von, 28
Rosenberg, Hans, 158
Rössler, Constantin, 83
Rotteck, Karl von, 62
Ruge, Arnold, 83
Russia
  partition of Poland, 48

Sand, Karl Ludwig, 57
Schenckenburgher, Max
  Wacht am Rhein, 65–6
Schenkendorf, Max von, 55, 58–9, 92
Schiller festivals, 84
Schleswig-Holstein, 72–3, 88, 93–4
Schmerling, Anton von, 131
Schulz, Wilhelm, 61
Schulze-Delitzsch, Hermann, 85, 86

Printed in the United Kingdom
by Lightning Source UK Ltd.
122673UK00002B/253/A